THE CALEDONIAN RAILWAY

By the same Author:

Special Express leaving Glasgow for the South, near Eglinton Street. The train is composed of "Grampian" type 8-wheeled stock and hauled by rebuilt Copper 0-4-0 No. 46 and a "Dunolastair III" No. 80. III Web.

THE CALEDONIAN RAILWAY

By

O. S. NOCK

B.Sc., M.I.C.E., M.I.Mech.E., M.I.Loco.E.

LONDON:

Ian Allan Ltd

Made and printed in England by
STAPLES PRINTERS LIMITED
at their Rochester, Kent, establishment

Contents

Preface

IF ever there was a railway among the old companies existing prior to the Grouping of 1923 that possessed 'character', an assemblage of attributes, of traits, of historical background, and a few idiosyncrasies as well, that line was the Caledonian. It had all the solidarity, the dignity, the massive imperturbability of its great English ally, the London & North Western; but whereas the North Western was all the time driven by a quest for ruthless efficiency, the Caledonian, little less efficient, had the additional qualities of charm and colour, and that romance that is invariably associated with the Western Highlands and with navigation on the Firth of Clyde. As to history, it was Sir James Thompson, General Manager at the turn of the century, who once said that the most exciting part of the Caledonian Railway history was before the line was built at all.

A railway is no greater than the men who own and run it, and one has only to recall the names of some of the great men who have been associated with the Caledonian to realize that it would have been strange if the 'Caley' had *not* been full of character, atmosphere and colour: Hope-Johnstone, Locke, Brassey, Coddrington, James Baird, Robert Sinclair, Allan, George Graham, Kempt, Dugald Drummond, McIntosh, Matheson, Guy Calthrop, Robert Killin, John Barr. To these must be added Sir James Thompson, one of the really great General Managers, and that tremendous character Captain James Williamson, the Marine Superintendent, who was a steamship owner in his own right before he joined the Caledonian just prior to the time when the Steam Packet Company was formed. It would be equally surprising if such a railway had not been a favourite with the travelling public and a favourite with the corps of railway *littérateurs*. Rous-Marten, singing to heaven the praises of the 'Dunalastair' locomotives drew, by his unbridled enthusiasm, the fire of his more critical and cynical readers in the correspondence columns of *The Engineer*; others have clearly been mesmerized by the sight and memory of the blue engines, while those whose sentiments lie elsewhere have determined that the 'Caley' shall go down in history as nothing if not a ruthless and resolute opponent! By some younger enthusiasts to whom the Caledonian is only a name I have heard the

7

friendly abbreviation pronounced to rhyme with 'daily'; it is, of course, no more than an abbreviation of the full word Caledonian, and rhymes with 'rally'.

In the preparation of this book I have had help from many friends, and among present-day officers of Scottish Region I must mention particularly Mr H. C. Orchard, Chief Civil Engineer, who very kindly had looked out for me the magnificent photographic record of the enlargement of Glasgow Central Station, and numerous drawings associated with that work, while Mr Colin Neil Mackay, the Public Relations & Publicity Officer arranged many facilities for me. In Edinburgh Mr Robert M. Hogg, Custodian of Historical Records, British Transport Commission, and his staff turned up numerous records for me. Among railway enthusiasts I must mention especially Mr A. J. S. Paterson, and Mr W. D. M. Stephen, while Mr Graham E. Langmuir has given me the benefit of his encyclopaedic knowledge of the Clyde steamers. The contribution of Mr R. D. Stephen will be apparent to all who study the beautiful photographs of locomotives taken by him in the years 1920 and 1921. To Mr G. J. Aston I am indebted for loan of the train running log books compiled by the late R. E. Charlewood, which contain a mass of interesting data, and many an amusing side-light on the travelling conditions of the day, in the dry, laconic notes pencilled by the side of the logs themselves.

My handwriting does not seem to improve as the years go by, even if the speed of execution shows some increase. Nevertheless, Olivia, my wife, has shown her usual skill in deciphering it, and filling in those words that were there in spirit rather than in the letter! To her, as always, my very best thanks are due.

O. S. NOCK.

20 Sion Hill,
Bath.
September 1961.

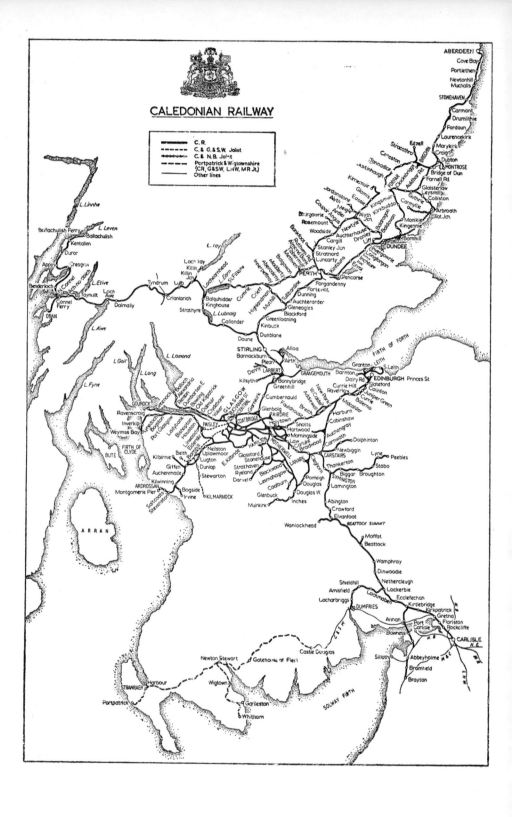

CALEDONIAN RAILWAY

Legend:
- C.R.
- C. & G.&S.W. Joint
- C. & N.B. Joint
- Portpatrick & Wigtownshire (CR, G&SW, LNW, MR Jt.)
- Other lines

I

Pre-Railway Rivalries

LONG before any trains began to run, before even any constructional work had started, the Caledonian Railway was beset by rivals on all sides. The enmity of the Glasgow & South Western towards it lasted for the entire life of both railways. It was a feud so deep-seated, and so sustained, as to be hard for many an Englishman to understand. The rivalry with the North British was rather more subtle. For much of their history the two Scottish companies were parties to traffic agreements entered into in partnership with their respective English allies, and however much the Caledonian and the North British might feel urged to a resumption of the 'cat and dog' relations of old, all was at peace between the East Coast and West Coast routes in England, and this consideration did perhaps lead to some restraint.

The rivalry with the North British grew up after the railway was built, though to be sure two concerns that eventually became vested in the rival companies had a battle royal of their own for the traffic between Edinburgh and Glasgow. These two concerns, strange though it may seem, were the Forth & Clyde Canal and the Edinburgh & Glasgow Railway. This was a case of intense competition over a small field for a limited objective – albeit an important one; on the other hand the rivalry with the Glasgow & South Western arose over a matter of major strategy, that eventually came to affect the internal transport system of Great Britain as a whole. The broad conception of a trunk route continuing northward from Lancashire and onwards to Glasgow came from the Board of the Grand Junction Railway, and the mere fact that the idea *did* originate in England was probably the root cause of much of the trouble that eventually developed in Scotland.

A year before the Grand Junction Railway itself was open for traffic, in 1836, that company sent Joseph Locke to make some preliminary surveys. There were rival projects to be considered in making a way between Lancaster and Carlisle, and these were eventually resolved without leaving too much acrimony in their wake. In pressing on into Scotland Locke's terms of reference from his Board were to report on the possibility of a route to Edinburgh

and Glasgow – not merely to Glasgow. He journeyed north from
Gretna by the Edinburgh coach route via Beattock, and all was well
until he reached a point about three miles south of what is now so well
known, by road as well as rail, as Beattock Summit. Then there came
so steep and sustained an ascent, through so rough and bleak a
countryside, that Locke turned back, and began a survey of Nithsdale. Though the really difficult ground in the approach to Beattock
Summit is confined to no more than three miles, the roughest preliminary surveys show that the incline would have to commence as
far back as Beattock village if the gradient was not to exceed that
which Locke had in mind for crossing the Shap Fells. Even so the
bank would be nearly twice as long.

In those early days Locke was virtually a free-lance so far as
Scottish business interests were concerned; but when he turned from
his probing investigations in Annandale, and began to work northward from Dumfries it was another matter. This latter course was
precisely in harmony with the ideas of the Glasgow merchants, who
had already promoted two railways of a local character – the
Glasgow, Paisley & Greenock, and the Glasgow, Ayr & Kilmarnock.
If a new line was promoted from Carlisle, passing through Dumfries
and up through Nithsdale, with the massive backing of the Grand
Junction, the local railways running west and southwest of Glasgow
would naturally have been ready enough to join forces. And when
Locke went back to England and recommended the Nithsdale route
they were naturally delighted. At that time Glasgow was the im-
mediate objective. One presumes that the intention was to reach
Edinburgh by way of Glasgow.

At that early period in railway history circuitous routes were not
unusual. Brunel incorporated plenty of them into the broad gauge
network of the Great Western, and the South Eastern route to
Dover, as first opened, could scarcely have been less direct. How
individual members of the Grand Junction Board reacted to Locke's
report we are not to know, but two gentlemen in the Lowlands of
Scotland fairly pounced upon it! It was J. J. Hope-Johnstone, M.P.
for Dumfries-shire, who first queried its wisdom, and he received
the utmost support for his opposition from Charles Stewart, factor
for the Annandale estates. So far as Hope-Johnstone was concerned
it might have been thought that he would have had an open mind,
since the line would have passed through his constituency whether it
was taken up Annandale, or Nithsdale; Stewart, one could appreciate, would have more reason for his strong partisanship. But both
men were thinking far more in terms of the commission given to

Locke by the Grand Junction Board than of purely local interests.

Stewart got to work with the utmost energy. He wrote to the Secretary of the Grand Junction Railway, the celebrated Henry Booth, stressing the immense advantages to be derived from taking the line over Beattock Summit into upper Clydesdale, where the spear from the south could become a trident, with the three prongs directed leftwards to Glasgow, rightwards to Edinburgh and ahead for a direct route to Stirling, Perth and the far north. No such facility could possibly be extracted from a line passing up Nithsdale and becoming enmeshed in the tangle of lines already springing up in the rising industrial districts immediately west of Glasgow. Stewart wrote to Locke as well, and in the following year, when his labours further south were consummated by the opening of the Grand Junction Railway, Locke went north again, and made a rather more detailed survey of the Annandale route. This time he did concede that a line over Beattock Summit was practicable. Having gained this point Charles Stewart lost no time in fostering interest and enthusiasm for the railway.

In studying the lives and works of the early railway engineers Joseph Locke stands out among all his contemporaries as one of the most practical, businesslike and far-seeing of them all. It did not fall to his lot to build any spectacular works, in Great Britain at any rate; but he was a master of organization, as witness the speed with which his railways were built, and in his second report on the Carlisle–Glasgow project he touches on a point of great operational importance. Concerning the Beattock Bank he was not so much worried about the difficulties in getting up it: 'In the descent', he wrote, 'there is more danger, and this is a question of importance.' At a time when the energies of engineers were concentrated upon the job of getting more tractive power in locomotives it is remarkable to find Locke so far in advance of his times as to be worried about brake power. It was not until thirty years later that the inadequacy of brake power began to be realized, and serious consideration came to be given to it.

From the time of Locke's second report the fat was fairly in the fire. The Annandale scheme took the proposed railway through a lonely, depopulated countryside. Even after Clydesdale was reached it did not pass through the only town of any size, Lanark. Consequently the support for the line was at first very slight, compared with the solid and ever-increasing enthusiasm for the Nithsdale route, which would serve a number of thriving townships *en route*, quite apart from providing a direct link between two such important centres as Dumfries and Kilmarnock. In the view of the Nithsdale partisans the fact that the Annandale route saved 20 miles on the run from Carlisle to Glasgow cut no ice; it was the intermediate interests that outweighed any such overall advantage. The Annandale people stressed also the very great saving of 70 miles on the run from Carlisle to Edinburgh, but about this the Nithsdale supporters, in modern parlance, could not have cared less!

In the meantime interested parties in Glasgow itself were beginning to take a broader and more impartial view, though the suggestion of a joint survey by two engineers, one English and one Scottish, ended in deadlock. The two engineers appointed were Locke and John Miller, and their 'joint' report was in fact two reports expressing diametrically opposite opinions. Locke had indeed renounced all his earlier preferences for the Nithsdale route, and was now whole-heartedly in favour of going over Beattock Summit. It was at this stage that the Government of the day intervened. In Westminster the question was not so much the question of the Nithsdale or the Annandale route from Carlisle to Glasgow, but as to which would be *the* route from England into Scotland. I have emphasized the word 'the'. The situation in Parliament was recalled by Mr Gladstone in a speech in the House of Commons in May, 1888.

'It is almost ludicrous', he said 'to look back upon the infant state of the whole question at that period, when compared with the enormous development it has now attained. The unusual course was adopted by the Government of Sir Robert Peel of appointing a commission or a scientific agency to examine the whole question of what ought to be the line of railway into Scotland. The motive was, that as it was known, or firmly believed, to be absolutely impossible that there should ever be more than one railway into Scotland, it was considered of the highest importance that the best scientific power of the country should be brought to bear on the choice of the line.'

So, in the year 1839 two Government Commissioners, Lt.-Col. Sir Frederic Smith and Professor Barlow, were appointed to investigate. By the terms of their commission they were not confined to a choice between Annandale and Nithsdale; there were two schemes that had their southern ends starting in Newcastle. One of these latter was the present East Coast main line through Berwick and Dunbar to Edinburgh, and the second, that was never built on the precise location originally planned, ran via Hexham, Jedburgh and Galashiels to Edinburgh. Both the Newcastle schemes had the same disadvantage as the Nithsdale route in that they served one of the Scottish cities to the detriment of the other. If there was to be only one railway from England into Scotland the Annandale route stood out pre-eminently as providing an equally good route to both Edinburgh and Glasgow.

The Commissioners cannot be criticized for taking their task lightly, or sketchily. They took two years over the job, and then issued two reports. In the time that had elapsed since the time of their appointment ideas had evidently changed a little as to the probable volume of traffic to be carried between England and Scotland. One senses that before they had finished they realized their original terms of reference were unrealistic, and that it was not much good recommending one route if all the signs pointed to the need for two routes, or even more within a very few years. Consequently they recommended that if there was to be only one route it should be Annandale, but if they had been called upon to recommend two routes they would have suggested the Annandale route to Glasgow, and the East Coast route, via Berwick, to Edinburgh.

These recommendations were a great triumph for Hope-Johnstone. Stewart, and their friends, as their proposals were vindicated either way. The Commissioners did, however, qualify their findings by one very important point. At that time no positive steps had been taken to provide for the line connecting the Grand Junction and its northern associates with Carlisle. There had been a railway in Carlisle since 1836, when the first section of the Newcastle & Carlisle had been opened, but although that line was completed in 1838 it was evidently considered not good enough to reach Carlisle from London by way of Newcastle. Had any such proposal been made in actual fact it would cut clean across the long-term strategy of the Grand Junction, whose management was alive enough to the need for constructing the link to Carlisle. The Annandale scheme was only part of the grand strategy. The fact that it came into such prominence *before* the Lancaster & Carlisle Railway was projected is largely due to the intense opposition it encountered in Scotland.

The Commissioners' reports were issued in March, 1841, and immediately the Annandale Committee got into touch with the Grand Junction and the Lancaster & Preston Railway with a view to concerted action. The first meeting of the Lancaster & Carlisle Railway was held in October, 1841, and with that project definitely launched the Annandale people felt that they were in a position to press on. It is not altogether surprising, however, that interest north of Beattock Summit remained cool and indifferent. The recommendations of the Government Commissioners seem to have succeeded merely in stiffening the opposition in Glasgow, so Stewart very wisely and tactfully avoided a frontal attack at this enemy bastion, but concentrated instead upon Lanark. This important burgh would have gained nothing from the Nithsdale route, and although it lay some miles to the west of the proposed line through Beattock, connection would be easy and convenient. At the same time Stewart was feeling his way in Edinburgh, which it was intended would be served by the eastward branch from Carstairs.

So far as Upper Clydesdale was concerned Stewart did not mince his words. In the autumn of 1841 he wrote thus to the Town Clerk of Lanark: 'Now we think that you Lanarkshire people, landed proprietors, and burghers along the Vale of Clyde have shown a strange coolness and indifference in not supporting us in what is of great importance to you.' The boundless energy of Stewart and the Dumfries-shire party was at last beginning to bear fruit. After lengthy deliberations, and much heated debate the Glasgow Chamber of Commerce decided to support the recommendation of Barlow and Sir Frederic Smith. A committee of merchants and manufacturers was formed, and with the holding of a large and representative meeting in Lanark, just before Christmas 1841, the project was at last beginning to get under way. This latter meeting was attended by a strong and enthusiastic deputation from Dumfries-shire, who seem to have done much to change the Lanarkshire attitude from apathy to one of considerable interest, if not outright enthusiasm.

Progress still remained slow and difficult. A tremendous amount of spade work had yet to be done before things had reached the stage of presenting a Bill to Parliament, but one very important event marked the year 1844, for it was in that year that the name 'Caledonian Railway' was first used. There is no doubt that a good deal of the half-heartedness in support shown to the enthusiasts of Annandale was due to the strength of their English associations; more than half the financial support proposed was from England, and the choice of the resounding title 'The Caledonian Railway' did something to disguise these origins, at any rate so far as the ordinary public was concerned. Hope-Johnstone and his friends, men of vision as they were, looked forward to the time when their railway would be the only one of any consequence in Scotland, and in that original title one feels that the accent was intended to be on the one word 'the'!

Despite the findings of the Royal Commission, the Nithsdale party determined to present their Bill to Parliament, and the result was a long and severe contest. The Caledonian Railway Bill, however, passed through all the Committee stages between May 20th and

The Promoters of the Caledonian Railway.
[*Courtesy B.T.C. Historical Relics*

Above: Carstairs old station in course of demolition.

Below: Moncrieff Tunnel, near Perth: single line working during re-lining.

[*British Railways*

July 5th, 1845, and the Royal Assent was given on July 31st. The legislation proved extremely expensive and eventually amounted to the huge sum, for those days, of £75,000. The total mileage at first authorized was 122, made up as follows:

Carlisle to Garriongill Junction	$84\frac{3}{4}$
Cumbernauld to Castlecary	10
Carstairs to Edinburgh	$27\frac{1}{4}$

The above looks a rather odd collection of bits and pieces, but in the approach to Glasgow advantage was taken of the existence of two largely mineral lines, the Garnkirk & Glasgow, and the Wishaw & Coltness. Before the approach of the Caledonian Railway the former was extended at its eastern end, and changed its name to the Glasgow, Garnkirk & Coatbridge. At the latter point it linked up with the Wishaw & Coltness which ran southwards through Motherwell and was joined by the Caledonian near the site of the present Law Junction. It is interesting to recall that both these local railways were originally laid to a gauge of 4 ft 6 in., but were changed to standard gauge at the time of their linking up with the Caledonian.

Once the Bill was passed no time was lost in getting to grips with the constructional work, and with the famous combination of Locke as Engineer and Thomas Brassey as Contractor the works were organized on a gigantic scale. By August, 1847, no fewer than 20,000 men were engaged on the job. It was not as though the Caledonian was the only railway then being built. The whole chain of railways linking up Carlisle with Aberdeen had been sanctioned at the same time, together with the Clydesdale Junction Railway, and the effect upon the country of the invasion of the enormous army of navvies can be better imagined than described. There is perhaps no better description than that by Thomas Carlyle, in writing to a friend in August, 1846. The main line ran through the place of his birth, Ecclefechan.

'The country is greatly in a state of *dérangement*,' he wrote. 'The harvest, with its black potato fields, no great things, and all roads and lanes overrun with drunken *navvies*; for our great Caledonian Railway passes in this direction, and all the world here, as everywhere, calculates on getting to Heaven by steam! I have not in my travels seen anything uglier than that disorganic mass of labourers, sunk three-fold deeper in brutality by the three-fold wages they are getting. The Yorkshire and Lancashire men, I hear, are reckoned the worst; and not without glad surprise, I find the Irish are the best in point of

Caledonian Railway.

Act Passed, 31st July, 1845.

Authorized Capital, £2,800,000.

Miles authorized, 122¼.

Ceremony of cutting first sod by LADY JANE JOHNSTONE DOUGLAS, Saturday, 11th October, 1845.

NOTE.—At this date there was a length of 102½ miles of railway opened and since acquired by the Company.

Opened, Carlisle to Beattock, 10th September, 1847.

Do.   Edinburgh and Glasgow, 15th February, 1848.

FIRST BOARD OF DIRECTORS.

JOHN JAMES HOPE JOHNSTONE, of Annandale, M.P., *Chairman.*

Lieut.-Col. WILLIAM GRAHAM, of Mossknow.

WILLIAM LOCKHART, of Milton Lockhart, M.P.

ROBERT JOHNSTONE DOUGLAS, of Lockerbie.

ROBERT MONTEITH, of Carstairs.

DAVID DICKSON, of Hartree.

JAMES SETON WIGHTMAN, of Courance.

CHARLES STEWART, of Hillside.

JOHN MASTERMAN, Jun., London.

RICHARD PATERSON, Blackheath.

ALEXANDER HASTIE, Glasgow.

JOHN ANDERSON, Glasgow.

JOHN HOULDSWORTH, Cranstonhill, Glasgow.

WILLIAM MacDONALD, of Powderhall.

CHARLES MURRAY BARSTOW, Edinburgh.

JOSEPH LOCKE, C.E., F.R.S., } *Engineers.*
J. E. ERRINGTON,

DAVID RANKINE, *Secretary.*

behaviour. The postmaster tells me several of the poor Irish do regularly apply to him for money drafts, and send their earnings home. The English who eat twice as much beef, consume the residue in whisky, and', as Carlyle drily concludes, 'do not trouble the postmaster.'

The Caledonian Railway itself was one of the largest works authorized up to that time in a single Bill; but it is remarkable to contemplate the whole chain of railways authorized at the same time, all of which were vested in the Caledonian within the ensuing 21 years. The Scottish Central took the line forward from Castlecary to Perth, but it was north of the Tay that some of the most interesting projects were involved. In Angus five railways were in operation before the Caledonian received its Act of Incorporation, and not one of them was laid to the standard gauge. They were not all alike either! The Dundee & Arbroath and the Arbroath & Forfar were 5 ft 6 in. gauge, while the Dundee & Newtyle was 4 ft 6 in. Newtyle was quite a centre of railway prospecting in those days, for in addition to the line to Dundee there were lines running north to Glamis and southward to Coupar Angus. The Scottish Midland Junction tied up the loose ends, so far as the through route was concerned, filling in the gaps and joining the various pieces to make a continuous line from Perth to Forfar.

When the chain of railways was complete a through journey from Carlisle to Aberdeen would then have been made over the metals of the following companies:

Carlisle to Garriongill Junction . . .	Caledonian
Garriongill to Coatbridge . . .	Wishaw & Coltness
Coatbridge (Gartsherrie) to Garnqueen	
	Monkland & Kirkintilloch
Garnqueen to Castlecary	Caledonian
Castlecary to Perth	Scottish Central
Perth to Coupar Angus . . .	Scottish Midland Junction
Coupar Angus to Newtyle (now Alyth Junction)	
	Newtyle & Coupar Angus
Newtyle to Glamis.	Newtyle & Glamis
Glamis to Forfar	Scottish Midland Junction
Forfar to Guthrie	Arbroath & Forfar
Guthrie to Aberdeen	Aberdeen Railway

The Monkland and Kirkintilloch was eventually incorporated in the North British Railway, *not* the Caledonian.

Although so many individual pieces were involved it was in reality one gigantic piece of co-ordinated railway planning, for all of which Joseph Locke was engineer. Though additions and improvements were made afterwards it can be said that the Caledonian in all its essentials was planned in a single entity. Expansionist visions did not rest with the lines to Edinburgh, Glasgow and Aberdeen. The Glasgow, Paisley & Greenock Railway was already in existence in 1845, and the Clydesdale Junction project provided for a link-up with this, utilizing a piece of another small local line, the Pollok & Govan. The development around Glasgow, from quite early days, was so intense, and on such fiercely competitive lines as to need special reference.

II

Early Days

LONG before the Caledonian Railway itself was promoted there had been a considerable railway development in Scotland centred upon the port of Dundee. As long ago as 1826 the Act of Incorporation had been passed for the Dundee & Newtyle Railway, and although it was some years after completion before steam locomotives were employed, this curious old railway can well claim to be the oldest part of the Caledonian. At this stage in time it is a little difficult to appreciate the reasons that led to the construction of the Dundee & Newtyle Railway. Newtyle lies in the vale of Strathmore, and was no more than one of a number of small centres of rural, farming life. Yet the railway to Dundee was laid out with little or no regard for intermediate gradients, making an almost straight line between the two places. It was worked like some of the mineral lines in Durham, with stationary winding engines for the heavy inclines, and horse traction intermediately.

From all accounts the ropes on the inclines were not merely troublesome, but were a source of positive danger. When the cable actually severs on an incline of 1 in 10 trains can quickly attain a terrifying pace, and this is what happened one day with a passenger train on the bank descending into Dundee. It was indeed a marvel that no one in that one-coach train was killed when it arrived precipitously at the bottom. The experience can best be described by a countrywoman laden with farm produce to sell in the Dundee market. On arrival, passengers, their goods and chattels were all thrown out of the carriage into a heap on the platform. The countrywoman was no more than mildly concerned, and after disentangling herself from her butter, eggs and what-not, drily commented: 'Od, sirs, I liked the ride on the railway, but they hae sic a rough way o'coupin' fouk oot, I dinna think I'll come back by eet!'

There is also a good story of the early days of steam locomotive traction on the line. This was in 1833, and the event caused tremendous interest and curiosity in the district. An old fisherman who lived in one of the villages near Arbroath had been told about the 'steam horse', and being of an inquiring nature he set out to see for himself. With some care he selected a vantage point on the high ground by Dundee Law, just beyond the summit of the cable-worked incline out of the terminus. What he did not appreciate was that there was a short tunnel intervening. Eventually the locomotive came along, and what happened can best be described in the words of the old fisherman:

'It's a humbug, a perfect humbug. It puffed a', it puffed a', it cam, an' it cam, an' when it saw me it ran into a hole i' the hull an' hoded itsel'.'

This locomotive was none other than the *Earl of Airlie*, built by Carmichael's of Dundee, while the third locomotive of the company, built by Stirling & Co. of the Dundee foundry, is of interest in that one of those who helped to build it and who took part in the commissioning trials on the line was none other than Archibald Sturrock. The town of Newtyle was the starting point of two other early Scottish railways, the Newtyle & Coupar Angus, and the Newtyle & Glamis. Both these lines were designed for horse traction, though it seems that the steam locomotives of the Dundee & Newtyle made occasional trips over them at times of heavy traffic.

Although none of the railways concerned were very extensive Dundee was becoming quite a centre of railway activity and loco-motive building even before the eighteen-thirties were out. The Dundee & Arbroath Railway was incorporated in 1836. It is evident that this was an individual effort, quite distinct from anything in the way of a planned railway network. The Dundee & Newtyle had adopted 4 ft 6 in. as the rail gauge, but the Dundee & Arbroath was laid to 5 ft 6 in. There were no half measures about the latter line. It was double-track throughout, and substantially laid to the best standards of the day. If there was no thought of convenience in linking up with other railways at the Dundee end there was still less in Arbroath. The original terminus was near to the harbour, while at the same time the Arbroath & Forfar Railway, also laid to the 5 ft 6 in. gauge, was establishing itself in the centre of the town. The two stations were connected by a railway running through the streets, and passengers were conveyed by a horse-drawn carriage.

The Dundee & Newtyle Railway was a failure financially, and some unsuccessful attempts were made by shareholders and mort-gagees to seize parts of the equipment in lieu of payment. The company was not able to resist all these attempts, and in January, 1845, the whole concern was advertised as 'To be let'. Fortunately for the Dundee & Newtyle it was the time of the concerted projects for a complete railway network between Carlisle and Aberdeen, and it was not long before two of the companies promoting Bills in Parliament were sparring over the well-nigh bankrupt Dundee & Newtyle Railway. A year was to pass however before things were finally settled, and this curious little line was leased in perpetuity to the newly authorized Dundee & Perth Railway.

The promotion of the group of railways connected with the Caledonian and Grand Junction development changed the whole outlook of those connected with railways in Dundee. Instead of existing as two independent, isolated local concerns, the Dundee & Arbroath and the Arbroath & Forfar now saw themselves fitting into the grand strategy of Scottish railway development, and a decision was taken at once to alter the rail gauge to the standard 4 ft 8½ in. It was not a great task to convert two relatively small railways, but it is interesting to recall that during the 5 ft 6 in. period trains ran on the right-hand rather than the left-hand track.

Before tracing out further developments in Angus a more detailed consideration is needed of the lines that existed around Glasgow before the authorization of the Caledonian. So far as the gauge was concerned the Dundee & Newtyle was not by any means an isolated case. Immediately north of the Clyde there was a group of largely mineral lines all laid for the 4 ft 6 in. gauge. The map on page 25 shows the extent of these lines, and the way most of them became incorporated into the Caledonian system. The oldest of them was the Monkland & Kirkintilloch, which connected the Monkland Canal, and the coal districts south-east of Coatbridge with the Forth & Clyde Canal at Kirkintilloch. This was opened in 1826, and changed over from horse to steam traction in 1831.

In the same year of 1831 came the Garnkirk & Glasgow. This latter line was from the outset more extensive than its name suggested. From its first opening it made a junction with the Monkland & Kirkintilloch, at Gartsherrie, and in 1845 it was extended southwards and roughly parallel with the Monkland line for 3 miles to make an end-on junction with the Wishaw & Coltness, at Whifflet. At that time, 1845, the latter line extended through Motherwell and Wishaw to Coltness and Morningside (Chapel Colliery). Thus at the time the Caledonian received its Act of Incorporation there was a continuous line of 4 ft 6 in. gauge railway from Morningside into Glasgow, with two alternative routes alongside each other from Whifflet to Gartgill, half a mile north of Gartsherrie.

In its original approach to Glasgow and its extension to the northward the Caledonian Railway made use of all three of these railways. It joined the Wishaw & Coltness at Garriongill Junction, curiously enough at a point almost exactly half-way between Wishaw and Coltness. Bound for Glasgow, Caledonian trains took the left-hand fork at Whifflet, and using the Garnkirk line passed through Coatbridge. But if bound for the north direct, the Monkland & Kirkintilloch Railway had to be used, since it was from this that the north main line diverged at Garnqueen. This original piece of projecting was eventually to lead to one of the most curious anomalies in railway geography to be found anywhere in Britain. North of Garnqueen the line was pure Caledonian, to Greenhill Lower Junction, where an end-on junction was made with the Scottish Central Railway.

The Monkland & Kirkintilloch was absorbed into the North British system, but despite the rivalry between this latter railway and the Caledonian the north main line from Carlisle to Aberdeen continued to include 52 chains of North British metals, and this continued so after Grouping, through the North British and the Caledonian being absorbed into the L.N.E.R. and the L.M.S.R.

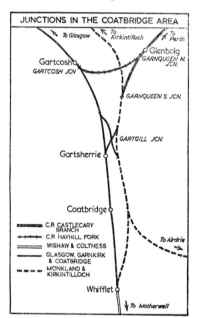

respectively. The junctions at the end of this short link were authorized by the Caledonian Railway Act of 1845, though that at the south end, Gartsherrie, was originally a junction between the Monkland and Kirkintilloch and the Glasgow, Garnkirk and Coatbridge. After the amalgamation of 1865, which brought the Monkland railway into the North British system, an agreement was entered into between the latter company and the Caledonian, in 1868, whereby the North British staffed and maintained the signal boxes at Gartsherrie and Garnqueen Junctions, duly passing on most of the charge to the Caledonian. Eight years later, however, when it was observed that the North British was using the line to no more than a limited extent and running no passenger trains at all over it, it was agreed that in future the Caledonian should appoint, pay and clothe the signalmen concerned. There was another curiosity about this group of junctions that persisted until the end of 1869. From the opening of the Scottish Central Railway trains from the north to

Glasgow, if travelling over the Caledonian line from Castlecary, had
to reverse direction in the Coatbridge area, as will be appreciated
by the accompanying map. It might have been expected that they
would have reversed at Gartsherrie, and proceeded into Buchanan
Street. This was not so. The north trains transferred to the Edinburgh and Glasgow main line of the North British at Greenhill
Junction, and ran to Queen Street.

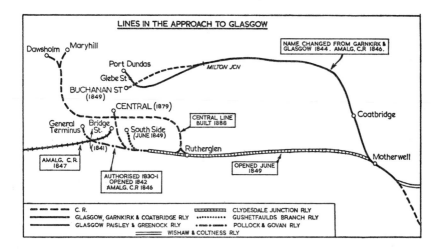

This arrangement continued even after the Caledonian had
absorbed the Scottish Central, in 1865; indeed, Queen Street
station, and its services to the north, were included in the Caledonian
timetables. In the meantime the so-called 'Hayhill Fork' was constructed between Gartcosh and Garnqueen North Junction. This
connecting line was opened for goods traffic in February, 1866, but
for some reason its use for passenger trains was postponed for 4 years.
When it was opened, in January, 1870, the occasion marked the
transference of the Caledonian north service to Buchanan Street.
Since nationalization, however, the convenience of the transfer
connection at Greenhill Junction has permitted the use of Queen
Street as an alternative terminus for Stirling, Perth and Aberdeen
trains by the Caledonian route, and only a few months before
writing this chapter I travelled that way from Glasgow to Perth on a
Sunday. The reverse facility, using Buchanan Street as a starting
point for destinations on the North British system, does not, however,
exist at Greenhill.

The connections were considerably more complicated south of the

Clyde. A map on page 25 shows the railway connections with the various ownerships as they existed originally. The Caledonian entered the area from the east over the Clydesdale Junction line, which was opened in June, 1849. The original point of divergence from the Wishaw & Coltness was at the original Motherwell station, near the present Flemington station; but the Motherwell Deviation line was opened in 1857, leaving the Clydesdale line at Lesmahagow Junction, west of the present Motherwell station. The Clydesdale Junction Railway provides the present main line into Glasgow from the south as far as Rutherglen where the route of the Pollok & Govan line is entered upon, for a short distance, to Gushetfaulds Junction, where the original line swung round to the north to reach the original Caledonian terminus south of the Clyde at 'South Side'.

From the west, the Glasgow, Paisley & Greenock Railway came in through Pollokshields to its terminus at Bridge Street, immediately on the south side of the Clyde. This line, like most of those eventually incorporated in the Caledonian, was built by Joseph Locke, and at one time it had as secretary Captain Mark Huish, who afterwards made such a name for himself as General Manager of the L.N.W.R. The Paisley line was later widened to provide four running lines between Shields Junction and Paisley. Joseph Locke had expressed the view that there would never be the need for more than one railway between Glasgow and Paisley, and so when the Glasgow, Paisley, Kilmarnock & Ayr Railway was projected arrangements were made for the section between Glasgow and Paisley to be joint with the Greenock line, and these two companies originally shared the terminus at Bridge Street.

Both these railways were in being before the Caledonian was incorporated, and this joint association was at times a point of embarrassment in later years. The greatest rival of the Caledonian, both in the years of prospecting and forever afterwards – the Nithsdale route to Carlisle – was planned and built as an extension of the G.P.K. & A., and yet the terminus had to be shared at Bridge Street. Deadly rivals though they might have been the Caledonian and the G. & S.W. were closely interlinked, nay entwined in the southern suburbs of Glasgow, as the map clearly shows. The second piece of major line, namely the Glasgow, Barrhead & Kilmarnock, came about in a rather different way, and was at one time purely Caledonian. It began as an independent company, the Glasgow, Barrhead & Neilston Direct, which was authorized in 1845, opened in 1848, and leased to the Caledonian in 1849. It was fully absorbed in 1851.

The General Terminus line dates from 1849, and the southern fork from the Pollok & Govan Railway to the Barrhead line – Cathcart Road Junction to Langside Junction – was also opened in 1849. It is evident, however, that from the viewpoint of through traffic the Caledonian Railway regarded the South Side terminus as of secondary importance. As soon as the new line from the old Garnkirk route, at Milton Junction, into Buchanan Street was ready the English traffic was transferred at once from South Side. The passenger station at Buchanan Street, which is today little changed from the original terminus of 1849, eventually became quite inadequate for the most important Caledonian passenger traffic; but the adjoining goods station, by successive enlargements and modernizing is now one of the largest and best equipped in Scotland.

By the end of the year 1849 the general pattern of railways serving the city of Glasgow had taken the shape it was to maintain for roughly a quarter of a century. In Glasgow itself no railway had, as yet, bridged the River Clyde, and although traffic was developing rapidly on the south bank it was local, rather than of a long distance character. The use of the terminus named South Side and Gushetfaulds by the Caledonian for the English traffic was short-lived, and the opening of Buchanan Street station enabled through passengers to be brought to a point that was much more convenient for the business and social centres of the city. The fact that a considerable detour was necessary to reach Buchanan Street from the main line from Carlisle was of no account at that stage in Caledonian history. They enjoyed a virtual monopoly of the English traffic, and although the Nithsdale route to Carlisle was opened throughout in 1850 its only outlet to the south was then over the Lancaster & Carlisle line, unless the cross-country route to Newcastle be included.

The seeds of severe competition were there nevertheless. This is no place to follow out the various steps by which the rival railway was built up. It is enough to say that in 1847 the Glasgow & South Western Railway was incorporated, taking in the Glasgow, Paisley, Kilmarnock & Ayr, and its subsequent extension to Cumnock. Not for nothing was it sometimes known as 'The Long Road'. It ran through Paisley, and over the Ayr main line as far as Dalry, then turned south-eastwards to Kilmarnock to follow the present main line to Gretna Junction. The Glasgow terminus was at Bridge Street, which was shared with the Glasgow, Paisley and Greenock section of the Caledonian, and from this station the distance was 125 miles, compared with 100 miles from 'South Side and Gushetfaulds', via Carstairs and the Caledonian Railway. The imposing façade of

Bridge Street terminus still exists, looking like a slightly smaller version of the Doric arch at Euston Station.

The Barrhead line, which was to assume major importance in years to come, was at first no more than a local line. Its terminus, named simply 'South Side', was on the southern extremity of the district known as the Gorbals, and was quite near to the 'South Side and Gushetfaulds' terminus of the Caledonian. At this distance of time it seems a little strange that some arrangement was not made for co-operation at this point, as a southward fork was afterwards put in, as mentioned earlier, between the Pollok & Govan line at Cathcart Road Junction, and the Barrhead line at Langside. Be that as it may, in 1849 there were no fewer than four railway termini on the south bank of the Clyde, with approach lines roughly at right angles to the river. Travelling upstream, as it were, the four in order were, General terminus, Bridge Street, South Side (Barrhead line) and South Side and Gushetfaulds.

If relations and connections with the Glasgow & South Western were necessarily complicated and delicate in Glasgow itself, the Caledonian was in a far stronger and virtually commanding position at the southern end of the line. The history of railways in Carlisle dates back to far beyond the construction of the Lancaster & Carlisle, and of the Caledonian. The opening of the western end of the Newcastle & Carlisle Railway took place in July, 1836, with a passenger station at London Road, and in May, 1843, the Wigton section of the Maryport & Carlisle Railway was opened. Relations between these two companies was close and cordial from the outset, though there was more than a hint of future financial difficulties when the Newcastle company had to lend the Maryport engines and carriages for its official opening!

The accommodation at London Road station was barely sufficient for both the Newcastle and the Maryport companies, so that when the West Coast Route was planned negotiations were opened, in October, 1846, for building a joint station, on land that had been purchased by the Lancaster & Carlisle Railway. Although they had been first in the field at Carlisle, the Newcastle and the Maryport companies realized that once railways of the magnitude and connections of the Caledonian and of the Lancaster & Carlisle were established in the city they would necessarily become the junior partners. They were, however, pleased enough to join in the original discussions, though both afterwards withdrew when it came to participating in the cost of the new station. Thereafter the Caledonian and the Lancaster & Carlisle alone shared the cost, and it became therefore a purely

West Coast station, so far as ownership was concerned. It is interesting to recall its original cost, built by Messrs Brassey and Stephenson, £155,689. Of this sum the Caledonian contributed £51,367.

The Citadel station was opened in 1848, and connecting lines were laid in so that passenger trains of both the Maryport and the Newcastle companies could enter. From the outset the amount of rent that these two companies should pay the owners was a matter of discussion and dispute, but apart from the straightforward question of rent the establishment of the West Coast companies in Carlisle led to one of the earliest skirmishes in the long drawn out rivalry between the East Coast and West Coast groups of railway companies. One of the original aims of the Newcastle & Carlisle Railway had been an extension to Whitehaven, and when the Maryport & Carlisle Railway was projected and built, the Newcastle company made various offers to secure a perpetual lease of the line. In 1848, however, the Caledonian Board was in its most extravagantly ambitious mood and a determined effort was made to secure control of both the smaller companies!

The mere thought of a protégé of the Grand Junction entering Newcastle was enough to touch off a violent explosion in York, where the notorious George Hudson was still a mighty power in the land, and so the Caledonian offer of terms for the absorption of the Newcastle & Carlisle was promptly countered by a more attractive one from the York, Newcastle & Berwick Railway. The Newcastle & Carlisle Railway accepted Hudson's offer, which included the Maryport & Carlisle Railway as well. In this, of course, Hudson was taking a lease of the two railways on behalf of the York, Newcastle & Berwick, but at that time the opposition to the Railway King was gathering momentum, and the Y.N.B. shareholders refused to accept the lease, and for a time the two railways thus became the personal property of George Hudson!

It is perhaps as well that the Caledonian offer was refused, because the latter company got into severe enough financial difficulty as it was, through its numerous associated lines. As it was their energies in Carlisle could henceforth be concentrated upon making things as awkward as they could for the Glasgow & South Western. For running powers over the $8\frac{1}{2}$ miles from Gretna Junction into the Citadel station it was eventually agreed that a sum of £5,000 a year should be paid to the Caledonian, while for the use of the station itself the G. & S.W.R. was required to pay £1,000 per annum from 1851, and a substantial sum each year towards the working expenses. This latter was always a bone of contention, and it was settled only after long arbitration before an independent assessor. In the 'eighties' of last century, for example, the assessor was Henry Oakley, then General Manager of the Great Northern Railway. It was the same with locomotive stabling. From the outset the G. & S.W. evidently found it cheaper to rent some accommodation in the Caledonian shed at West Walls, beside the original Citadel station, than to build a shed of their own. It was not, indeed, until 1894 that the 'Sou'-West' had its own locomotive running shed in Carlisle, and even then it was reached only by running powers over the Maryport & Carlisle Railway!

From south of the Clyde and relations with the Glasgow & South Western Railway to north, one may comment for a moment upon what would appear to be the inevitable rivalry between the terminal stations of Buchanan Street and Queen Street. In the earliest days while the Scottish Central and the lines leading northward to Aberdeen were close associates, the Caledonian trains from the north used the Edinburgh & Glasgow line from Greenhill, rather than take the Caledonian's own line southward to Garnqueen and reverse at Gartsherrie. As yet, however, the associates of the Caledonian provided the only route to Aberdeen, and the rivalry between Buchanan Street and Queen Street was potential, rather than actual, if we except the brief period of cut-throat competition for the Edinburgh and Glasgow traffic to be mentioned in the next chapter.

Both Buchanan Street and Queen Street were awkward stations to operate. The land rises steadily from the north bank of the Clyde so that any railway coming into the heart of Glasgow must inevitably face a steep descending gradient. The Edinburgh & Glasgow Railway maintained their level grading until the last minute, as it were, and then came down very steeply on a cable-operated incline. The Caledonian sited their new passenger terminus, Buchanan Street, farther up the hill from the river, but had nevertheless an incline nearly three times the length of that from Queen Street, extending practically to Robroyston, 3·4 miles out. Against the Queen Street gradient of 1 in 47 however, those out of Buchanan Street are 1 in 79 for 1½ miles, 1 in 98 for the next mile, and 1 in 125 past Milton Junction, where the new line into Buchanan Street diverged from the original route of the Glasgow, Garnkirk & Coatbridge Railway. As from Queen Street the first part of the incline out of Buchanan Street is in tunnels, and the majority of passenger trains were assisted in rear. Unlike the practice at Queen Street when steam had entirely superseded cable haulage, Caledonian trains drew out of Buchanan Street station, stopped, and then the bank engine would run out from a siding and buffer up in rear for the ascent to Robroyston.

The first section of the main line to be opened was that between Carlisle and Beattock, as from September 10th, 1847. The journey forward to Glasgow or Edinburgh was made by coach. Then, the night mail left Euston at 8.45 p.m.; the connection left Carlisle at 10 a.m. next morning, and calling at all stations reached Beattock at 12 noon. The connecting coach arrived in Edinburgh at 6 p.m., but the Glasgow arrival was not until 7.43 p.m. The day express leaving Euston at 10 a.m. was a little faster over the Caledonian line. It omitted the stops at Rockcliffe, Kirkpatrick, Nethercleugh and Wamphray, but even so took 1 hr 50 min to cover the 39·7 miles from Carlisle to Beattock. Then, at the bewitching hour of midnight passengers changed to the coach, and reached Edinburgh at 6 a.m. next morning. The 10 a.m. and 10.10 p.m. down trains from Carlisle carried first and second class passengers only. The service was completed by the 2.30 p.m. 'Parliamentary', which although carrying all three classes was no slower than the 10 a.m. train.

The corresponding up trains leaving Beattock at 6.30 a.m., 1 p.m. and 10.30 p.m. were all timed to make the run to Carlisle in the level 2 hours, even though much of the running was downhill. This timing applied equally to the up night express, which called only at Lockerbie and Ecclefechan. To open the line Robert Sinclair had the little 'Crewe'-type 2-2-2 singles of Alexander Allan's design, with 6 ft diameter driving wheels, 15 in. by 20 in. cylinders, and a boiler pressure of 90 lb per sq in. Even they can scarcely have been exerted in maintaining the original timetable. It is amusing to note from the original time bills that smoking by passengers was not merely prohibited in the carriage but also at the stations. So far as the conveyance of children was concerned, while infants in arms were passed free it was also stipulated that such children should be unable to walk. One can well imagine there were occasions when walking tests were insisted upon by suspicious ticket collectors.

The line had only been open a single day when there was an attempt at sabotage near Gretna. On September 14th, 1847, under the words '£100 Reward', in banner headlines, a poster was issued in Edinburgh reading thus:

'Whereas on the night of Saturday the 11th September, instant, some maliciously disposed Person or Persons did lay a TREE across the rails of the CALEDONIAN RAILWAY on the ESK VIADUCT, by which, had it not been perceived in time, the most frightful consequences to the Ten P.M. Train must have ensued,

'The Directors of the Caledonian Railway hereby offer a RE-
WARD of £100 for such information as will lead to the conviction
of the offender, or offenders within Three Months from this date.

By order,

J. W. Coddrington
Secretary.'

The earliest carriages were four-wheelers with the ribbed sides
that were so popular on the Scottish railways in mid-Victorian times.
The 'thirds' were quite substantial little boxes, with four compartments each seating only eight passengers. The windows were quite
large by contemporary standards, but none of them opened, and
ventilation was by means of three narrow slits above the doors. The
entire coach measured no more than 18 ft long, and it was only 5 ft
6 in. high inside. If the trains happened to be crowded, and there
were standing passengers taller than 5 ft 6 in. the general situation
inside could have well become very uncomfortable. Down to the
time of J. F. McIntosh, however, interior comforts for third class
passengers were not considered on the Caledonian. It was once
suggested to that worthy chief that some new third class coaches
building at St Rollox could be improved by the addition of some
armrests; but all 'J.F.M.' said was: 'Och, come oot! Ye want too
much.'

Above: Dundee West.

PICTURESQUE STATION EXTERIORS

Below: Stirling.
[*British Railways*

Above: Interior, looking south.

ABERDEEN JOINT: THE OLD STATION

Below: Reconstruction work commenced, 1913, with removal of the old roof.
[*British Railways*

III

Serious Difficulties

THE Caledonian Railway had not been in operation for very long before there were many signs that the Board and management were running into serious trouble financially. Glasgow and its immediate environs represented by far the greatest potential source of traffic; but in that city opposition remained strong, and access was obtained only over the metals of a chain of small local railways. It may have been intended as tact in the first place, but it was soon taken as a confession of weakness that the headquarter offices of the Caledonian were established not in Glasgow at all, but in Edinburgh. The use of existing lines may have been a means of avoiding expense in construction in the first place, but the tolls payable in respect of running powers were to prove a steady drain upon Caledonian resources.

The broad outlook of Hope-Johnstone and his associates in interesting themselves in the extension of the lines northward to Stirling, Perth and Aberdeen was unfortunately backed by no appreciable business experience, or ability, and through their clumsy though well-meant operations the Caledonian itself gradually became enmeshed in a frightful tangle of financial commitments. They were obviously perplexed and worried by the situation that was rapidly developing in central Scotland. There, one beheld the ludicrous spectacle of the Edinburgh & Glasgow Railway, with what is still the straightest and most level route to be found anywhere north of the Border, waging a ruinous competition for inter-city passenger traffic with two canals! Instead of developing their one great potential asset, speed, they waged the competition by reducing fares until one could travel third class from Edinburgh to Glasgow for 6d., by either means of conveyance.

Before long the Edinburgh & Glasgow Railway was well on the road to bankruptcy. It was a relatively small concern, and unlike the Caledonian, even in the infancy of the latter company, all its eggs were contained in the one basket of its 47-mile main line. The Caledonian Board watched the progress of this extraordinary competition, and apparently judged the moment to be opportune to amalgamate with the Edinburgh & Glasgow; so, in November, 1849, the first proposals were made. It is difficult to imagine exactly what advantages were foreseen in linking the tottering fortunes of the Caledonian with a railway the traffic policy of which seemed to be going berserk. The usual arguments were advanced that amalgamation would be to the advantage of both companies, and so on; but negotiations had not proceeded far before it was evident that whatever the Edinburgh & Glasgow Railway might lack in traffic operating technique and tactics its management lacked nothing in financial astuteness.

As a major point in settling terms for amalgamation they seized upon the relative frequency of service by the two routes between Edinburgh and Glasgow. However slow and bad their service was, and however unremunerative, because of the fare war with the canal people they immediately had the Caledonian at an overwhelming disadvantage. Although a through line existed by the roundabout route via Carstairs the Caledonian had not seriously attempted a passenger service between the two cities. Yet here was the Edinburgh & Glasgow management claiming that dividends received by the respective shareholders after amalgamation, should be proportional to the frequency of train service on the two routes between Edinburgh and Glasgow. At this distance in time such an argument would seem to be so fallacious as to be dismissed at once, but the early records of the Caledonian Railway show clearly that it was taken in all seriousness.

Although there were signs on every hand of a growing dissatisfaction with their conduct of affairs the Caledonian Board took the Edinburgh & Glasgow proposition at its face value rather than as a point of negotiation, and from December 1st, 1849, they went into full competition for Edinburgh–Glasgow through traffic even though the route was hopelessly roundabout and slow. In later years the Caledonian waged a hot competition for the Glasgow–Edinburgh traffic using the short cut from Midcalder Junction to Holytown, and terminating in Glasgow Central. In 1849, however, the through route, believe it or not, was via Carstairs, Motherwell, Coatbridge, and over the Garnkirk & Glasgow into Buchanan Street – 58·8 miles in all – and for this perambulation of the beauties of central Scotland the through fare, as on the other two competing services, was also 6d! By this extraordinary manoeuvre the Caledonian evidently hoped to negotiate on equality with the Edinburgh & Glasgow.

The company was running into trouble in other directions, all of which were involving financial loss. In June, 1849, the Board had some lengthy deliberations over fires caused by sparks emitted from locomotives. Two claims for heavy damages were received, one from a gentleman who had had a favourite plantation of firs set ablaze, and another from a farmer who claimed he had lost an entire field of oats. Apparently the matter was not considered at its source, for although Robert Sinclair, the locomotive superintendent, was frequently asked to report on other matters no one seems to have given a thought to stopping or checking the emission of sparks. Instead the question was 'remitted to the Secretary to consider whether any effectual means of protection can be devised'. As the job was handed over to the secretary the kind of protection envisaged was evidently legal rather than physical!

Another curious complaint that came to the Board was over 'goods breaksmen'. The Goods Manager complained that these men merely acted as guards of their trains while on the run, and gave no attention to dispatch and delivery of the goods they carried. As a result, he pointed out, goods were frequently mislaid, mis-directed, delayed in transit, and very frequently lost altogether, thus involving much in compensation. The 'breaksmen', as they were then called, were on the pay-roll of the Superintendent of the Line, who, of course, was primarily responsible for running the trains rather than dealing with the commercial aspects of goods handling. It came as somewhat of a surprise that anyone expected the 'breaksmen' to take any responsible interest in the forwarding of goods after they had been conveyed to destination. A proposal was made to transfer the men to the pay-roll of the Goods Manager, though this led to a long and acrimonious wrangle.

The working of the line was evidently in as big a muddle as the finances of the Company, and in November, 1849, it was proposed to ask the London & North Western to take over the responsibility for operating the entire Caledonian Railway. This proposal was received at Euston and turned down flat, whereupon an appeal was made to Thomas Brassey, the civil engineering contractor. The magnificent organizing ability, and immense resources of that great man made him the most likely contractor to take the job on, and before the end of November, 1849, it was reported to the Board that Brassey was endeavouring to form a company for the purpose. Early in December two Caledonian directors, Col. Macdonald and Mr Copling, attended by Robert Sinclair, went to London to discuss details with Brassey; he in turn consulted Joseph Locke, and between them the two men, collaborators in so many great projects, worked out details of equipment and prices to be charged.

Long before this, however, dissatisfaction with the higher management of the Caledonian Railway had begun to take a more serious and definite form. Although the railway was Scottish in its sphere of operating and it was managed from a headquarters in George Square, Edinburgh, a majority of the shareholders was English, and it was the 'London Central Committee of Caledonian Railway shareholders' that became the spearhead of the attack. Debentures for many thousands of pounds were falling far overdue; the banks were pressing for the repayment of loans, and strong objection was raised at one stage to the practice of paying dividends out of capital. As debentures continued to be unredeemed the shareholders began to take things into their own hands, and railway property was seized, by way of compensation.

While individual proprietors took panic measures, which did neither them or the company any credit, the London Central Committee began to press for an interview with the Board. It was significant of the state of tension and 'nerves' that was building up that a wrangle lasting several weeks developed over one particular phrase in the original letter of application from the London Committee. In this letter the *bona fides* of certain directors were called in question, over the spending of Caledonian Railway funds for the purchase of shares in other railway companies. The directors concerned took it as a personal insult and a stiff letter was sent back saying that the Board would receive no deputation while allegations of dishonesty on the part of its members were being made. Both as a body and as individuals the Caledonian Board of those days were unswervingly honest; it was as businessmen that they were patently unable to cope with the situation that was developing around them.

The London Committee appreciated that their first letter had been clumsily worded, and they tried again, taking care this time to state that while they had no doubt that the share transactions had been made with no thought of personal gain to the directors concerned, and with the best interests of the company in mind, they were convinced the procedure was not merely unwise but illegal. Again the Board attempted to stave off, or postpone the meeting that was demanded, but by now the London Committee, very ably and vigorously led by Captain, the Hon. E. Plunkett, R.N., was definitely out to force the issue.

In January, 1850, there was a mild diversion, in that interest was created by publication of the Parliamentary notices regarding three railway amalgamation Bills in which the Caledonian was concerned: with the Glasgow, Paisley & Greenock; with the Wishaw & Coltness; and with the Edinburgh & Glasgow. It is fascinating to speculate as to the subsequent course of Scottish railway history if the last mentioned line had actually been absorbed by the Caledonian, instead of by the North British. With such a stranglehold upon the southern shores of the Firth of Forth it is doubtful if the North British would ever have moved north-westwards from Edinburgh, and the whole of Fife and Angus would have fallen into Caledonian hands. More than that: on the western side of Scotland with the Caledonian in sole possession north of the Clyde, the West Highland project would undoubtedly have come under the same operating control, and the Highland Railway might not have been so violently opposed to the idea of the proposed continuation from Fort William to Inverness, had the company at the southern end been their friend and ally the Caledonian, instead of the North British.

Any interest over the forthcoming amalgamation Bills was soon swept to one side by the dramatic action of the London Committee. Having had no sympathetic response from the Board on January 23rd, 1850, they circulated to every Caledonian shareholder their detailed criticisms of the various transactions to which they took exception. Quite apart from the financial transactions, reference to which had so stiffened the attitude of the Board, there was the proposed working of the line by contract. However honourable their motives the London Committee, or whoever of their number was responsible for approving the draft of letters and notices, do not appear to have been the soul of tact. The circular to the shareholders, while steering clear of the wording that had so incensed the directors referred to the proposed working of the line by Thomas Brassey in such terms as to suggest that he was 'cashing in' on the plight of the Caledonian Railway, and extorting an altogether disproportionate price for the job.

Whether Brassey at once became aware of the circular and of the references to himself contained in it we are not to know; but when an advertisement of the circular, and a summary of its main contents appeared in *The Times* of 2nd February, 1850, he wrote straight off to the Board terminating forthwith the unfinished negotiations for the working of the line. It was indeed unfortunate that the London Committee should have chosen to express themselves so clumsily about Brassey of all men. For he was a deeply religious man, and regarded all his contracts as binding to the most solemn obligation. He was, in fact, proposing to do the job at the slenderest of profit margins, fully aware of the financial risks involved, and there is pain rather than anger in the last sentence of his letter to the Caledonian Board:

'I will only say in conclusion that I believe none of my dealings with the Caledonian, or any other Company will justify the imputation of an attempt at extortion which is so unjustly cast upon me in the circular I now refer to.

> I have the Honor to be,
>> Dear Sir,
>>> Your most Obed. Servt.
>>> (signed) Thomas Brassey.'

In the meantime although the Board might continue to deliberate, and groups of shareholders in London plan to take over control, the railway itself presented a sorry spectacle. It would perhaps be an exaggeration to say that every item of real property to be seen, lamp-posts, station benches, in addition to items of rolling stock bore labels: 'This is the property of ———', giving the name of some unfortunate shareholder. On the Stock Exchange the shares slumped to abysmal depths, and there was every sign of complete lack of confidence in the whole concern. Then came the event which, perhaps even more than the action of Captain Plunkett, resulted in the turning of the corner. The story was told to me many years ago by that great Scottish railway enthusiast of Victorian and Edwardian times, Norman Doran Macdonald. He was an advocate, and he was on the most intimate and friendly terms with every railway personality of the day. I have already told of some of his adventures at the time of the 1895 Race to the North.* Well, some twenty years ago, Macdonald told me that when Caledonian fortunes were at their very lowest ebb, James Baird, the millionaire ironmaster, one day walked into the Edinburgh offices and said to a clerk: 'I'll tak' a wheen "Caledonians" ' – just as if he was buying sweets!

Far from taking a mere 'wheen' – a few – he bought so many, indeed, that the news spread like wildfire, and the fact that a man of his wealth and status had sufficient confidence in the Caledonian to invest heavily in it was good news for the waverers and fainthearts. His action did nothing to bolster up Hope-Johnstone, and his original Board. It was not intended to do so. At a time when complete control of affairs might well have passed to the English section of the proprietors it brought in a large and solid slice of Scottish capital that was to exert great influence in later years. At the next meeting of the Board it became evident that resistance to the demands of the London Committee was useless; many of the directors resigned, and

* In *The Railway Race to the North*.

among those taking their places were Captain Plunkett, and, significantly, James Baird. At a meeting at the London Tavern in February,
1850, presided over with great dignity by Mr Hope-Johnstone, the
change in direction of the Company's affairs was virtually settled.

Captain Plunkett led the attack. Whatever tactless insinuations
had been made in the past about the parts played by individual
directors he was now most careful to represent them as gentlemen
of the highest honour whose every deeds had the best interests of
the Company in view. Unfortunately, as he was forthright in pointing
out, the most honourable intentions can muddle away their own and
other people's money, and this is what the directors of the Caledonian
had done. It was a bitter moment for Hope-Johnstone, the man whose
vision and dogged persistence had secured the adoption of the
Annandale route; who could see his idea of a great, co-ordinated
network of railways in Scotland taking shape, and with the now-
possible inclusion of the Edinburgh & Glasgow becoming more
extensive and far-reaching than he had ever originally foreseen. Now
he had no other course than to resign, and towards the end of
February, 1850, Plunkett took his place.

There was an immediate investigation ordered into the accounts
of the Company, and for what appeared to be the first time a full
statement was prepared for the Board showing all the Company's
financial obligations. One of the most pressing items was the hopelessly unremunerative competition for the through Edinburgh and
Glasgow traffic. As it was by the running of this service that the
Caledonian hoped to secure favourable terms for amalgamation with
the Edinburgh & Glasgow Railway the new Board was immediately
faced with a most difficult decision: either to keep it going at a
grievous loss in the hope that the amalgamation Bill would go
through and all would eventually be well, or to cancel it at once, and
give up whatever bargaining power its continuation commanded.
Before the fateful month of February was out the law clerk had been
instructed to arrange the postponement of the second reading of the
Bill for amalgamation with the Edinburgh & Glasgow Railway, and
negotiations were opened at once for a traffic agreement between the
two companies.

The financial crisis was as good as ended, so far as the shareholders
were concerned on February 25th, when a letter of reassurance was
sent to all debenture holders confirming the Company's intention to
honour to the full all its obligations, and stating that there was enough
coming in every week from traffic on the line to pay them all. At the
same time the most stringent economies were made in all matters

affecting day-to-day working expenses. In many localities there were more staff than necessary to do the job, and many men were dismissed. There was a general re-appraisal of staff salaries, and many more experienced cuts. Nor were the cuts and dismissals confined to the staff. By May, 1850, the economy drive had extended to the availability of passes and to the reduction of Directors' expense allowances to a very low level. The general tightening up of control, from end to end of the line had a very salutary effect, and from the brink of disaster the Caledonian Railway began its steady climb to prosperity and pre-eminence among the railways of Scotland.

IV

The Great Amalgamations

By the beginning of the eighteen-fifties a good deal of tidying up of the British railway network was in evidence. Business interests realized the disadvantage of having a large number of independent companies that had originated from enterprises that were in the majority of cases quite local in character. At the same time Parliament was keeping a very wary eye upon amalgamation projects, because it was felt to be against the public interest to allow any business concern, particularly one concerned with public transport, to assume a position of monopoly. There were arising, nevertheless, two different kinds of amalgamation project in Great Britain, those of parallel and potentially competitive lines, and those of railways making end-on connections.

No objection was raised to the great amalgamation that led to the formation of the London & North Western Railway, since it gave promise of co-ordination and better service to the public over a continuous line of railway from London to Lancaster and Carlisle. Every objection was, however, raised in later years when an amalgamation was proposed between the L.N.W.R. and the Lancashire & Yorkshire. However favourable such an amalgamation might have been to the business interests of the two companies it would have eliminated much of the local railway competition in Lancashire, and that was then considered to be a bad thing from the public point of view. The amalgamation that formed the North Eastern Railway came in 1854, and it was probably no more than the early financial embarrassments that delayed matters in Scotland until some ten years later.

The northern network of lines that eventually became part of the Caledonian Railway differed in most respects from enterprises that became included in some of the greater English amalgamations, in that they were all part of a single master plan for which the Grand Junction Railway was largely responsible. It would have been quite another matter with the Edinburgh & Glasgow Railway. Whatever the shareholders of the two companies may have thought about it, that deadly and ruinous competition for traffic between the two cities had given the public incredibly cheaper transport, and one feels that even if the two companies had eventually come to terms for amalgamation it is most unlikely that such a project would have received Parliamentary sanction. Had it done so it would have presented the Caledonian with a virtually impregnable monopoly over a belt of country more than 40 miles wide across the very heart of industrial Scotland.

At the time the amalgamation proposals were allowed to lapse the Edinburgh & Glasgow Railway did not constitute a very serious threat to Caledonian supremacy. It was an isolated enterprise and against the growing network of railways associated with the Caledonian had the appearance on the map of an intrusion. It is true that it was an older concern, and that it was associated with the East Coast 'alliance' at the Edinburgh end. The latter grouping at that time in railway history was a very uneasy association, far different from the strong friendship and understanding that already existed between the West Coast allies. The North British on many occasions adopted a policy of independence in railway politics that was a source of embarrassment and annoyance to the North Eastern, while the Great Northern was only just emerging from its position as the 'Ishmael of Railways' and had scarcely yet been accepted at York as a full and equal partner in the East Coast traffic.

Aware of all this, and faced with the urgent task of getting their own house in order one can well appreciate that the new Caledonian management could regard the Edinburgh & Glasgow Railway as no more than a local competitor. The advantages of eliminating that competitor did not appear sufficient to warrant all the time and expense that would undoubtedly be involved, quite apart from the risk of an abortive Parliamentary campaign. Nevertheless there was a serious point of contention between the two companies quite apart from the Edinburgh and Glasgow traffic. As early as 1844 the Edinburgh & Glasgow Railway shareholders had authorized their directors to promote a line to Stirling, and negotiations had been opened with the Scottish Central, then no more than a proposal. These were broken off, and the Edinburgh & Glasgow put forward a line of their own. Parliament, however, favoured the Scottish Central, and after the latter line was built there were several skirmishes between the Edinburgh & Glasgow, and the Caledonian to secure ownership. Although the Scottish Central was part of the great London–Aberdeen project fostered by the Grand Junction the Edinburgh and Glasgow people did their level best to block all attempts at amalgamation with the Caledonian.

Competition for the Edinburgh and Glasgow traffic was resumed for a time, at a more intense level than ever. Then, in 1853, came another attempt at reconciliation, with an agreement by which the management and working was put into the hands of a single set of officers, directed by a joint committee of the directors of the two companies. This arrangement was a precise forerunner of the working fusion of the London, Chatham & Dover, and South Eastern Railways in 1898. But in the Scottish case of 1853 Parliament refused to sanction the arrangement, and the Caledonian and Edinburgh & Glasgow managing committee was not only stillborn, but its demise led to an even more bitter competition for traffic. Once again the fare between Edinburgh and Glasgow was reduced to 6d. third class, and 1s. first class, and while the Scottish public enjoyed the benefits, and the Scottish shareholders looked on helplessly, the English shareholders of both companies took things into their own hands.

After several abortive attempts a meeting in London, in February, 1856, approved the arrangement whereby the two companies were pledged to enter an agreement to work for a common purse for a period of ten years. It was agreed that the net proceeds should be divided between the two companies in proportion to their probable earnings, and this was fixed at 30·64 per cent of the total to the Edinburgh & Glasgow, and 69·36 per cent to the Caledonian. Later, the Scottish Central was brought into the common purse arrangement, receiving 14·988 per cent of the joint net revenues. The remaining 85·012 per cent was divided between the Edinburgh & Glasgow and the Caledonian in the same proportion as previously. The fixing of the percentages to three places of decimals strikes one as amusing today, and one would like to have listened to the hard Scottish bargaining that led to the establishment of such fine limits of demarcation.

Heartened by this measure of agreement the three companies brought forward a Bill, in 1860, for their complete amalgamation. This was strongly opposed by the North British, and it was generally unpopular in Scotland where it was feared that the result would be a complacent monopoly. The Bill was rejected by Parliament, and a revised Bill suffered the same fate in the following year. The three companies made one last try, in 1864, and again failed. By this time the Caledonian must have realized the strength and determination of North British opposition, and instead of attempting any more working agreements with the Edinburgh & Glasgow attention was concentrated upon the more natural allies farther north.

So we come to the year 1865, when the first big amalgamation took place in Scotland; this, though not affecting the Caledonian as a company, was of immense importance for the future. The absorption of the Edinburgh & Glasgow Railway by the North British changed the whole railway position in Scotland. In a report to the shareholders it was stated that 'the whole character of the North British Railway had been regenerated by the incorporation of the Edinburgh and Glasgow and Monkland Railways within its system'. It had indeed! From being no more than a 57-mile link in the chain of communication between London and Edinburgh that link was now extended right across Caledonian territory to the heart of Glasgow, and provided a springboard for the launching of a whole series of highly competitive projects. The 45 years' 'war' between the North British and the Caledonian was on.

The very terms of the North British and Edinburgh & Glasgow Railways' Amalgamation Act of 1865 included the seeds of trouble between the enlarged company and the Caledonian. The latter company and its northern associates had naturally opposed the Bill, and they succeeded in getting inserted a provision that gave the Scottish Central Railway running powers between Larbert and Edinburgh. In that same year of 1865 the Caledonian absorbed the Scottish Central, and inheriting these running powers immediately began to work its traffic from Edinburgh to the north over this line. Until then the purely Caledonian service had been very roundabout, via Carstairs and Coatbridge. Moreover, for a period of nearly ten years they had to use the North British stations in Edinburgh. Waverley Bridge, as it was then known, was the scene of the most regular and chaotic unpunctuality to be found anywhere in Britain and the pressure of the Caledonian trains no doubt added to the congestion. It was not until 1874 that the short connecting line from Haymarket West Junction to Dalry Road was authorized, and Caledonian trains could thereby leave the North British line and arrive in Edinburgh at their own terminus.

The absorption of the Scottish Central by the Caledonian now took the latter company on its own metals to Perth, to Dundee, and to Newtyle, with branches to Denny, Alloa, Callander and Crieff. At Perth traffic for the north was handed over to the Scottish North Eastern Railway, which was an amalgamation dating from 1856, of the Scottish Midland Junction, and of the Aberdeen Railway, and of all the local lines north of Dundee. In the meantime a very important connection to the far north had been made by the opening throughout in September, 1863, of the Inverness & Perth Junction Railway between Forres and Dunkeld. The most southerly link in the chain soon to be known as the Highland Railway dated from

April, 1856, when the so-called Perth & Dunkeld Railway was opened between Dunkeld and its junction with the Scottish North Eastern at Stanley, 7¼ miles north of Perth. This little railway exercised running powers over the Scottish North Eastern in order to reach Perth.

Relations between the Highland Railway and the constituents of the Caledonian at Perth do not seem to have been very friendly at the outset. The Scottish Central owned the original station, but there had been a dispute over tolls, and the Inverness & Perth Junction, as it then was, had erected a temporary station beside the S.N.E.R. When the dispute was resolved the Highland sought permission to use this station as a carriage store. After the amalgamation of 1865, which brought the Highland Railway into being, the right of the company to exercise running powers over the S.N.E.R. from Stanley into Perth was confirmed, but it was soon considered that the tolls demanded were exorbitant, and by November, 1865, plans were being considered for an independent line into Perth, leaving the existing line near Murthly and following a direct course to the Highland engine sheds at Tulloch, just north of Perth.

The length of this proposed line was a little over 11 miles. It was to be double-tracked throughout, and matters progressed to the extent of a detailed survey and estimate. As matters eventually transpired this line would have been of considerable advantage to the Highland Railway in avoiding the blocks that came to occur in Stanley, but it would, of course, have transferred the blocks and congestion to the immediate approaches to Perth station. By the end of the year 1865 it was evident that the Caledonian and the S.N.E.R. would oppose the Bill for construction of the line, whereas the North British signified their strong support. The Highland thought it prudent to seek independent advice, and went to Mr Grierson of the Great Western. He agreed that the tolls paid to the S.N.E.R. for use of the Perth–Stanley section were exorbitant, but also felt that the construction of the independent line, with all the legal and Parliamentary charges that would be involved, was an expensive way out. He suggested trying to make a compromise.

The tolls paid during the year 1865 had amounted to over £10,000 and they were likely to increase rapidly in conformity with the increase in traffic. The Highland Railway management felt that the maximum they ought to be asked to pay was £5,000 per annum, and in May, 1866, a meeting was held with the Caledonian and the S.N.E.R. Clauses were included in the Amalgamation Bill of the two latter companies that the toll payable by the Highland Railway should be £5,000 in perpetuity, irrespective of the volume of traffic. In consideration of this, and an arrangement ensuring to the Highland Railway the entire traffic to the north passing through Perth, the Highland agreed to withdraw their Bill for the direct line from Murthly. The reference to the traffic to the north may not be fully appreciated at this point of time. From its very inception however the Highland was in conflict with the Great North of Scotland, and the latter company was doing its utmost to attract through business from the south via Aberdeen to the Morayshire towns. Before the construction of the Forth and Tay bridges all traffic from the south had to pass through Perth, and so by this agreement of 1866 the G.N.S.R. was cut out of any through traffic except to local stations on its own line.

The amalgamation of the Scottish North Eastern with the Caledonian was authorized in 1866, and together with the previous absorption of the Scottish Central gave the Caledonian a very snug and safe monopoly in Angus and the Mearns. Between the Firth of Tay and Aberdeen there was no railway that was not owned by the Caledonian. There was one fly in the ointment. As might be imagined North British interests were not blind to the effects of the Caledonian –S.N.E. merger, and they worked upon the susceptibilities of Parliament to anything that looked like a monopoly. As a result they secured the inclusion in the Act of 1866 of the following clause: 'The North British Railway Company may, for the Purpose of conveying Scottish East Coast Traffic, run over and use with their Engines, Trucks, and Carriages of every description, the Scottish North Eastern Lines, or any Part thereof, and the Stations, Watering Places, Works, and Conveniences upon and connected with the Scottish North-Eastern Lines.'

At the time this clause might have seemed to have little value, since the S.N.E. lines of the Caledonian were completely isolated from any part of the North British system. But the enterprise of the latter company knew no bounds, and they were determined to obtain a route of the own to Aberdeen that should be as independent of running powers over the Caledonian as possible. When, by absorbing the Edinburgh, Perth & Dundee Railway the N.B.R. reached the south bank of the Tay and secured authorization for the construction of the first Tay Bridge in 1870 the threat was obvious. The strategy of the North British became plainer still in 1871 when Parliamentary sanction was obtained for building a line northward from Arbroath to Montrose, and connecting with the Aberdeen main line at Kinnaber Junction. This was an astute move on the part of the

North British, for it not only cut out the westward detour that would have been necessary if the Arbroath & Forfar line had been followed to its junction with the Aberdeen Railway, but it put Montrose on the East Coast main line of the future.

In the meantime the Caledonian by its absorption of the Scottish North Eastern had, by the year 1866, a main line 241 miles long. By the amalgamations of 1865 and 1866 the company had indeed more than doubled its route mileage. Even so, the far-sighted management was not content. The manoeuvres by which the Caledonian had missed the chance of scooping the Edinburgh & Glasgow Railway into the fold left them weak on the shores of the Firth of Forth, and the opportunities of developing an export traffic to the continent of Europe were limited thereby. In mid-Victorian times Britain was enjoying a remarkably large export trade in coal to many European countries, including the Scandinavian group and Russia, and with its commanding position in the Lanarkshire coalfield the Caledonian Railway was able to collect the traffic direct from the pits. The need was felt for a port of their own on the east coast of Scotland, and the choice fell upon Grangemouth.

In 1866 the place consisted of nothing more than a tidal harbour, and two small docks having an area of seven to eight acres in all. It was then the property of the Forth & Clyde Navigation, which also owned the Forth & Clyde Canal, the Monkland Canal, two small connecting railways, and the harbour of Bowling on the River Clyde. The Caledonian Railway management was not interested in any of these properties, but to secure ownership of Grangemouth docks meant buying up the lot, and so in 1867, the Caledonian became a canal owner, and owner of the harbour of Bowling. The Forth & Clyde Canal had a long and fascinating history, and its eventual purchase by the Caledonian, by force of circumstances rather than desire, was in some ways appropriate enough seeing that it was this very waterway that had proved so troublesome a competitor in the early days of the Edinburgh & Glasgow Railway.

As the new owners came to use the canal extensively, not only for freight but also for certain pleasure sails, a brief note on the earlier history of the Forth & Clyde Canal will be of interest. The story goes back to the year 1761, when the Board of Trustees for the Encouragement of the Fisheries & Manufacturers in Scotland commissioned Thomas Smeaton, the celebrated civil engineer, to survey the route for a canal. Parliamentary sanction was obtained in 1768, and construction began from the Grangemouth end. By 1777 having reached the neighbourhood of Glasgow work came to a stop, with funds completely exhausted. For seven years the project hung fire, but then the Government of the day, having collected considerable sums from the forfeited estates of Highland chieftains and other big landowners who had supported Prince Charles Edward Stewart in the Jacobite Rebellion of 1745, decided to allocate £50,000 on loan, to enable the Forth & Clyde Canal to be finished. It was opened throughout from Grangemouth to Bowling in 1790.

It was in 1809 that the company began to operate the 'swift' passenger boats that were to prove such an embarrassment to the Edinburgh & Glasgow Railway. These were run between Glasgow and Falkirk, and covered the 25 miles in 3½ hours. This was quite a performance seeing that there were four locks to be negotiated *en route*. This service was eventually extended over the Union Canal, from Falkirk to Edinburgh and provided a through service between the two cities. The boats were beautifully appointed and were drawn by splendid horses galloping along the towing path. The riders were decked in scarlet coats and cocked hats, and up to the time of the first introduction of railways one can appreciate the enthusiasm of the Chairman at the opening ceremony when he said:

'I feel this to be the most remarkable day in my life, in inaugurating this grand national undertaking, by which means of locomotion in Scotland have at last been perfected.'

When the idea of a railway between Edinburgh and Glasgow was first mooted, following the success of the Liverpool & Manchester Railway, the Canal authorities pooh-poohed the whole thing, and even went so far as to issue the following statement to their own shareholders:

'The establishment of a railroad between Edinburgh and Glasgow on the principle of that now in active operation between Manchester and Liverpool never can be attempted with any hope of profit or will ever be undertaken by those who are acquainted with the cost of such enterprises.'

When the Edinburgh & Glasgow Railway developed from being no more than an idea to a definite project and a Bill was introduced in Parliament the Forth & Clyde Canal people put up the strongest opposition. It is strange to recall that it was this opposition that secured the inclusion in the Edinburgh & Glasgow Railway of that monumental piece of operating inconvenience, the Cowlairs Incline. At times of the fiercest and most troublesome competition with the North British the Caledonian people must sometimes have had cause for a little sardonic amusement that it was an early constituent of their own, albeit a canal, that had seen the North British saddled with

THE ALLAN INFLUENCE

One of the famous Conner 8 ft 2 in. singles, No. 83A as rebuilt by
Dugald Drummond.

Above: 2-4-0 mixed traffic engine, built 1872 as No. 586, here seen as numbered
in the duplicate list, No. 1586. This engine was renumbered *five times*, being
successively 586A, 1259, 1586, 127 and then 1586. She was scrapped in 1910.

Below: Conner 7 ft 2-4-0 No. 117 as rebuilt with Lambie type boiler in 1892.
[*Locomotive Publishing Co*

FREIGHT LOCOMOTIVES: ANCIENT AND MODERN

0-4-2 No. 1581, originally built by Neilsons in 1871, as running *circa* 1900.

[*The late W. J. Reynolds*

Above: Drummond standard 0-6-0 No. 686 built 1884, by Neilsons.

[*F. Moore*

Below: Pickersgill 0-6-0 No. 671, at Perth.

[*R. D. Stephen*

such a bugbear. It came about in a curious way. The route of the Forth & Clyde Canal itself lay well away from the proposed track of the railway, at the Glasgow end; but there was also the Monkland Canal, which connected up with the Forth & Clyde near Maryhill, and worked eastwards through the northern suburbs of Glasgow to Airdrie.

In 1839 when the Bill for the Edinburgh & Glasgow Railway was before Parliament the two canals were under quite separate management. The original survey for the new railway provided for a bridge over the Monkland Canal, about half a mile on the Glasgow side of Cowlairs, and for a terminus at high level, well up the hill from the city centre. The Forth & Clyde Canal fastened upon this feature of the survey. While they flouted the idea of the Lancashire example being a practical proposition so far as railways were concerned they were sufficiently impressed with the prowess of the Manchester ship canal to state they were intending to develop their own enterprise into a ship canal in conjunction with the Monkland Canal. If, they argued, the new railway crossed the Monkland Canal as proposed they would not be able to carry out the ship canal idea. And so the Edinburgh & Glasgow Railway Company was persuaded to carry its line downhill from Cowlairs on a gradient of 1 in 45 so as to pass under the Monkland Canal in tunnel. The Forth & Clyde Canal purchased the Monkland Canal in 1846, but the idea of the ship canal went no further.

We have discussed the relations of the Caledonian Railway with the Highland, and with the North British at the time of the great amalgamations, and there remains the Great North of Scotland. At one time there were scarcely any relations at all. The Great North saw to that! The Aberdeen Railway had built its northern terminus in Guild Street, near to the western end of the Upper Dock, whereas the Great North, using the track of an old canal had made their terminus at the junction of the Regent and Waterloo Quays, beside the Victoria Dock. The two stations were about half a mile apart, with no connecting services at all for passengers, and only a line of rails along the quayside for interchange of goods traffic. Connections between Scottish North Eastern and Great North trains were positively discouraged from the Great North side. True, there were margins of time between arrivals from the south and departures for the north, but they were impracticably tight, and there was no question of holding the Great North trains in cases of late arrival. Ahrons, indeed, tells dark stories of the officials at Waterloo holding their trains until the hurrying passengers from Guild Street hove in sight, and then slamming the gates and giving the right away to the driver!

All this makes good reading, but it was thoroughly bad railway business, and even before the amalgamation whereby the Caledonian took over the Scottish North Eastern Railway an important measure was undertaken to improve things in Aberdeen. From the S.N.E.R. point of view there was everything to be gained by first class facilities for interchange with the Great North. In 1864 the Scottish North Eastern made application to build a line from the G.N.S.R. at Kittybrewster through the Denburn Valley to join their own main line at a point immediately north of the Dee viaduct. The Act was obtained in the summer of 1864, and included authority to build a new Joint Station. Although the Act was obtained by the Scottish North Eastern Railway it laid down details of the ownership of the Joint Station and the lines leading to it. The station, through the provisions of the Act, became jointly and equally the property of the S.N.E.R. and the G.N.S.R. The line from immediately north of the station to the junction near Kittybrewster became part of the G.N.S.R., and the southern approach lines were correspondingly S.N.E.R. The North British were no party to this agreement, and when they did eventually come to Aberdeen they paid tolls for use of the station. It is of interest to recall that the total cost of the Denburn Valley Railway, 2,869 yards of line including the Joint Station was £232,558 of which £108,000 was contributed by the Great North and the remainder by the Caledonian as the successor to the S.N.E.R. The new line and the Joint Station were opened in November, 1867.

V

The Influence of Alexander Allan

THE close association of the Caledonian Railway with the Grand Junction, which Scottish interests tended to minimize, was most openly revealed in the locomotive history of the group of lines that came together to form the greater Caledonian of 1866 and onwards. In some ways this chapter might be titled 'The Influence of Joseph Locke', for although the development that had such a lasting influence was the outcome of collaboration, at various stages, of four distinguished engineers, Locke was the most senior of the quartet and provided the drive and the opportunity for the technical skill of Allan to flourish. The other partners in the development were W. B. Buddicom and Robert Sinclair. All four were men of the Grand Junction Railway. Locke was Chief Engineer; Buddicom was Locomotive Superintendent; Allan was Works Manager at Edge Hill, and Assistant Superintendent, and Sinclair was an assistant newly arrived from training under Robert Stephenson.

The origin of the Allan type of outside-cylinder locomotive, with its massively-built front-end framing is well known. Locke took a great personal interest in the way Allan had extricated the Grand Junction from its troubles with broken crank axles, while Buddicom, no doubt feeling that there was more to be gained in the manufacture of locomotives than by staying on the railway, supervising their running and maintenance, resigned and went into partnership with a former pupil of George Stephenson, William Allcard, forming the firm of Allcard, Buddicom and Company with works at Warrington. When Locke secured the post of Engineer to the Paris & Rouen Railway Buddicom got the contract for building the locomotives, and so bright were the prospects of the French business that his firm established works at Sottevillle and Chartreux, and Buddicom himself took up residence in France in 1841. Sinclair went too, and was made Manager of the Chartreux works.

So far this saga of four engineers has nothing directly to do with the Caledonian, except to note that Sinclair, from 1841 onwards, came under the influence of Buddicom rather than of Allan. The earliest engines for the Paris & Rouen Railway differed in one most important respect from Allan's Grand Junction design. In the latter the cylinders were strongly fixed to both inside and outside frames at the front end, whereas Buddicom's engines had the cylinders fixed only to the outside frames. This feature could be noted on the French locomotive exhibited at the Festival of Britain Exhibition in London in 1951. By this variation a great deal of the advantage of Allan's design was lost. I have not been able to discover whether any question of patent or copyright prevented Buddicom from following the Allan design in its entirety; but we do know that in 1844, at Locke's invitation, a party of French engineers visited Crewe works with the particular purpose of inspecting the drawings of the Allan 2-2-2 and 2-4-0 locomotives that were then being designed for the Grand Junction Railway. As a result of this visit permission was given for the English design to be built in France, at Buddicom's Chartreux works. In view of this it is interesting that one of the earlier Buddicom engines should have survived to become an historical relic, and not one of those built later and strictly on Crewe principles.

From this same year, 1844, the limelight begins to focus upon Robert Sinclair. The Glasgow, Paisley & Greenock Railway required a General Manager. This was another of the lines built by Joseph Locke, and through his influence, no doubt, Sinclair got the job, at the age of 28. Young as he was, Sinclair was no trumped up protégé of a famous man. He was possessed of great engineering ability, tact, and kindliness to a remarkable degree, and proved a great success, including supervision of the locomotive department among his other duties. Two years later Messrs Locke and Errington, as engineers to the Caledonian Railway, appointed him as their Locomotive Superintendent. He continued to act as their representative till June, 1849, when he was officially appointed as Locomotive Superintendent. In June, 1852, he became General Manager, while still continuing to hold the office of Locomotive Superintendent. In the meantime Allan had continued at Crewe, acting as 'Foreman of the locomotives' under the chieftainship of Francis Trevithick. But in September, 1853, he resigned, in order to become Superintendent of the Scottish Central Railway with headquarters at Perth.

And now with Sinclair on the Caledonian, and Allan at Perth the stage was set for the combined influence of the two men to settle upon Scottish locomotive practice something like an institution. Allan was by 7 years the senior of the two, and Sinclair in the first locomotives he built for the Caledonian followed Allan's practice in its entirety. There was no trace of the Buddicom variation used in the early days at Rouen. The complete history of the locomotives of the Caledonian

Railway down to 1895, including those of the earlier constituents such as the Wishaw & Coltness, the Greenock and the Garnkirk has been told in a remarkably comprehensive series of articles in *The Locomotive Magazine*, by J. F. McEwan, commencing in June, 1940, and running for 8 years – truly a monumental work! Here we can be concerned only with the general trend of events and a reference to the more notable designs.

No fewer than fifty-eight Allan-type 2-2-2 singles were put to work on the Caledonian in 1846–50. They all had 15 in by 20 in. cylinders, 6 ft diameter driving wheels, and differed only from the characteristic Crewe outline in their handsome bell-mouthed chimneys. The first three were built in 1846 at the Greenock works of the Glasgow, Paisley & Greenock Railway from drawings supplied from Crewe. Twenty-two of the remainder were built in England, twelve by the Vulcan Foundry, and ten by Jones and Potts of Liverpool, while no fewer than thirty were turned out by the Caledonian Railway at their Greenock works between 1847 and 1850. The remaining three locomotives of the class were also built in Greenock, by the shipbuilding firm of Scott, Sinclair & Co. The Sinclair in this concern was an uncle of the Caledonian Locomotive Superintendent, who had served his apprenticeship with the firm before going to Robert Stephenson for further training.

These pioneer Caledonian 2-2-2s had four-wheeled tenders, with hand brakes, and no brakes on the engines at all. They were painted light blue, and although the actual shade varied over the years they set the fashion for the very beautiful 'Caley blue' tradition which will always remain one of the most cherished memories of pre-Grouping days on the railways of Scotland. Originally they carried the name of the company and the engine number round the top of the driving wheel splasher, in letters not much larger than the names of their counterparts on the London & North Western Railway. The number came in the middle, so that the legend round the splasher would read 'Caledonian – No. 15 – Railway Co.' The Vulcan-built engines differed from the Jones and Potts batch in having steam domes on the raised firebox, as in Crewe practice. The Jones and Potts engines had domeless boilers.

At the time when the original Caledonian line was being surveyed Joseph Locke was more concerned about controlling trains descending the Beattock Bank than in providing adequate motive power to climb it. It would seem he had good grounds for his apprehension. When the line was first opened instructions were given that all southbound trains approaching the summit were to slow down to 10 m.p.h.;

that the guard was to screw down hard all available hand brakes, and that the driver must control the train on the descent purely on his tender brakes. With all train brakes screwed on from the start the driver was supposed to use no more than the tender brakes to stop the train in Beattock station. Drivers often found that their progress down the bank was too slow, and put on a little steam; then nearing Beattock station they used to pull up by the drastic process of putting their engines into reverse. The number of smashed cylinder covers soon brought this practice to the notice of authority, and extra brake vans were added to give additional brake power descending the bank.

Although the Allan design was followed very faithfully in the 2-2-2 passenger locomotives delivered to the Caledonian, Sinclair did not use the Crewe 2-4-0 design for heavy freight service. Instead a small class of 0-6-0s was built, having the 'Crewe' type of boiler, and mountings, but with inside frames throughout. It would have been a very awkward job to follow the Allan principle of double-framing around the cylinders in a 0-6-0, and Sinclair's goods engines had a more orthodox appearance at the front end, while retaining outside cylinders. These engines were not a success, and after a very short time were altered, not, as might be expected, to the 2-4-0 wheel arrangement but into 0-4-2s. One would imagine that some trouble was originally experienced with the long wheelbase of the 0-6-0s in negotiating sharp curves on the various mineral lines linking up with the Caledonian, and the alteration to the 0-4-2 type was one that could be readily and cheaply made.

This part of Caledonian locomotive history dates back to before the year 1850, yet the 0-4-2 type, arrived at by expedient rather than original design, proved to be one of the most generally useful on the line. With successive enlargements of boiler and cylinders the haulage capacity was gradually stepped up, until from 1866 onwards the dimensions reached something like a standard, at 17 by 24 in. cylinders, and 5 ft 2 in. coupled wheels. Construction of the type continued until 1881. Some of them were used for passenger working in the early days of the Callander & Oban Railway when Brittain's experiments with 2-4-2 tank engines had proved a failure. Although they cannot have been very comfortable riding engines on a route of such curvature they did well on the heavy banks, and when Brittain brought out his 4-4-0 'Oban Bogies' in 1882 the coupled wheel diameter was just the same as that of the 0-4-2 mineral engines, namely 5 ft 2 in. In connection with these engines it is interesting to recall that the famous blue livery was never used on the Caledonian for goods engines. The latter were painted in the early Crewe style, in light green with black lining out, until the time of Dugald Drummond, when the goods livery was changed to black with red lining.

On the northern associated lines of the Caledonian the Allan influence later came to be more direct and intimate, but at first it came only through Robert Sinclair. Although the Scottish Central was an independent company, and its relations with the Caledonian were to pass through some awkward phases, as told in the preceding chapter, there were a number of working arrangements from the start, one of which was that Sinclair supervised the locomotive department of the Scottish Central. As was natural he ordered locomotives that were the same as those going into service on the Caledonian itself: 2-2-2 'Crewe type' for passenger, and 0-4-2 for goods. There were forty-three of the 2-2-2 type put on the road between 1847 and 1849. These Scottish Central locomotives were painted light green, with lining out and panelling in dark green.

Turning for a moment from the locomotives to Allan himself one might have thought, in the early 1850s, that an outstanding career was ahead of him. He had only just turned 40 years of age, and although Francis Trevithick was the titular head of Crewe Works it was well known that Allan was the technical 'brains' of the establishment. It was perhaps this uneasy association, under a weak chief, that led him to resign from the London & North Western Railway in 1853, when he was 44 years of age, and go to Perth as Locomotive Superintendent of the Scottish Central Railway. Four years later Richard Moon forced the resignation of Trevithick, though whether Allan would have got the job if he had still been there, in preference to Ramsbottom, is a moot point. In Scotland the amalgamation of the Scottish Central, and the other northern lines, with the Caledonian was generally regarded as no more than a matter of time, and Allan probably took the Scottish Central post as a stepping-stone to a bigger appointment.

In any event Allan's influence in Scotland now became direct, and extended far beyond the confines of the Scottish Central. When the time came for new goods locomotives to be ordered Allan used the 2-4-0 'Crewe' design, in preference to the Sinclair 0-4-2 and these were followed by some enlarged 2-2-2 singles, with 17 by 22 in. cylinders, built by Sharp, Stewart and Co. in 1864. By this time Allan was acting as locomotive consultant to the Highland Railway, and not only were the earliest engines for that line of the traditional 'Crewe' type, but the massive double framing at the front end, surrounding the outside cylinders, persisted on the Highland longer than on any other railway. The last design incorporating this distinctive Allan feature was that of the Highland 'Strath' Class 4-4-0 of 1892.

In December, 1856, Robert Sinclair resigned. Since 1851 he had held the post of General Manager and Locomotive Superintendent of the Caledonian, but with his appointment as Locomotive Superintendent of the Eastern Counties Railway the chair at St Rollox was vacant. It might have seemed that Allan was the obvious man for the job, but the directors of the Caledonian preferred instead Benjamin Conner, a fine engineer, but one who had no railway experience up to that time. Hitherto his work had been entirely with locomotive builders, and at the time of his appointment on the Caledonian he was Works Manager at the Hyde Park works of Messrs Neilson & Mitchell, later Neilson and Co. and a constituent of the North British Locomotive Company. As to Alexander Allan, there were rumours at the time that he had been offered the job, but had declined. Perhaps the inducement was not enough for him to take a post that would probably curtail some of his activities as a consulting engineer.

Just over 2 years later the Caledonian took delivery from Neilsons of the first of one of the most beautiful and distinctive of all nineteenth-century Scottish locomotive designs, the Conner 8-ft 2-2-2 single. The merest glance at a photograph of one of these engines in its original condition is enough to show that it is a direct derivative of the Allan 'Crewe' design; the outside cylinders, double front-end framing, raised firebox, and dome over the firebox are all to be seen today in the little *Columbine* in York Railway Museum. They have always been referred to as the 'Conner' singles, though in *The Railway Magazine* for March, 1918, Ahrons quoted from an original letter in his possession, written by Alexander Allan in 1891:

'As to the Caledonian engine I say it was no new design. I was paid for the design by the Caledonian Railway Company, and it is of smaller wheel than the Crewe engine *Cornwall* and only 1 ft larger than *Velocipede* and *Courier*. When near Glasgow I called on Mr B. Conner at the Caledonian Railway works, where I met Mr Patrick Stirling, then on the Glasgow & South Western Railway, and one observation passed from Mr Stirling, which was the smallness of the axle for the 8-ft wheel. I afterwards heard they had all broken.'

In passing it is extremely interesting to learn from this letter that Patrick Stirling was on such good terms with Conner as to get a sight of the Caledonian 8-footer in its early days. His presence at St Rollox hardly suggests the cat-and-dog relations that developed later between the 'Sou' West' and the 'Caley'. Quite apart from the dimension of the driving axle however, it must be remembered that the Conner 8-footer preceded the famous Great Northern 4-2-2s by more than 10 years, and their success on the heavily graded line between Glasgow and Carlisle may have helped to settle the driving wheel arrangement of the No. 1 class on the G.N.R.

Originally the Conner 8-footers had the Allan type of boiler, but no mounting of any kind between the chimney and the firebox. The first twelve engines of the class, Nos. 76 to 87 were built at St Rollox between 1859 and 1865. They had 17 by 24 in. cylinders, a total heating surface of 1,169 sq ft and a grate area of 13·9 sq ft. In their original condition the working pressure was 120 lb per sq in. Four additional engines, Nos. 113 to 116 were built at St Rollox in 1875, and these had 'straightback' boilers without the raised firebox, a dome on the rearmost ring, and Ramsbottom safety valves over the firebox. The cylinder diameter was increased to $17\frac{1}{2}$ in. and the working pressure was raised to 140 lb per sq in. There were two other variations of these engines. The original batch all received 'straightback' boilers in Conner's time, with a dome forward of the driving axle, instead of in rear of it, as in the 113–116 series. To my mind, however, these engines reached their most handsome form when Dugald Drummond gave a few of them a heavy overhaul, and replaced the austere stove-pipe chimneys with his own distinctive pattern.

The relations between the Caledonian Railway and Neilsons were very cordial in the early 'sixties', and Conner's previous associates at Hyde Park works were evidently so interested in his activities at St Rollox that when the time came for the firm to exhibit a locomotive at the London Exhibition of 1862 permission was obtained to build a Conner 8-footer, although all the Caledonian engines of this class had hitherto been built at St Rollox. It was agreed that after the exhibition was over this engine would be purchased by the Caledonian, in fact it was exhibited with a nameplate inscribed 'Caledonian Railway Co. Exhibition Engine made by Neilson and Co. Glasgow, 1862.' However, the engine never reached Caledonian metals. In London it was so much admired by Said Pasha, the Egyptian Viceroy, that he purchased it, and afterwards two more were ordered direct from Neilsons. There is no evidence, however, that the influence of Alexander Allan spread further in the Middle East other than the running of these three locomotives.

With the advent of Conner the 2-4-0 type came into its own for goods and mixed traffic as surely and successfully as it had done on the North Western, and on other lines where the Allan influence was strong. There is, indeed, much to suggest that Conner relied a great deal upon Allan for the general design of Caledonian engines in the early 'sixties'. In 1860 the first of a long series of 2-4-0 locomotives was put into service. It could have well been considered an express passenger design, as the coupled wheels were as large as 6 ft 2 in. diameter. But the Caledonian, despite the heavy gradients on its main line regarded an 8-ft wheel as the hallmark of an express engine. These 2-4-0s were 'Allan' to the last cotter pin. There were superficial differences, as in the slotting of the splashers and in the stovepipe chimney, but otherwise they could well have come out of the Crewe of pre-Ramsbottom days.

The later 2-4-0s, of 1862, with 5 ft 2 in. coupled wheels, were true enough to the Allan tradition, and the Allan style was perpetuated in a small class of 7-ft singles built in 1864-5, which were in every way a smaller version of the famous Conner 8-footers. From 1865 onwards however, a new series of 2-4-0s with 6 ft 9 in. coupled wheels was commenced, and although they had the raised fireboxes there was a 6 ft 2 in. class turned out at about the same time in which one batch had flush-topped boilers, plain domes, and a safety valve casing in the style later made so familiar by Patrick Stirling on the Great Northern. At the time these Caledonian engines came out Stirling was still at Kilmarnock, and was apparently on the best of terms with Benjamin Conner. This last batch of 6 ft 2 in. 2-4-0s were easily the most handsome of all the earlier Caledonian locomotives. They were rebuilt in after years by Dugald Drummond, and while retaining the Allan framing received higher pitched boilers, with Ramsbottom safety valves on top of the dome, and a cut-away cab in the Patrick Stirling style. As such they were also most picturesque and distinctive engines. It is indeed rare that a locomotive design initially handsome and distinguished should be rebuilt by another engineer, have its characteristic lines completely changed, and emerge as an equally delightful, but quite different, entity.

The absorption of the Scottish Central and the Scottish North Eastern Railways by the Caledonian might well have raised a major problem so far as the personnel of the locomotive department was concerned. There is now no doubt as to Conner's indebtedness to Allan for the fundamentals of his engine designs. In view of this some might have expected that Allan would have secured the post of Locomotive Superintendent of the combined system. On the other hand Conner's past experience and his natural ability lay more in the direction of constructional work and works management, rather than the technical details of engine design, and it was he who laid the foundations at St Rollox on which his successors were to build so successfully. Whatever influences were at work behind the scenes Conner remained in the chair at St Rollox, and Allan left Scotland for the last time to become Manager of the Worcester engine works. Although he himself had gone his influence continued strongly, for after the amalgamation one of his most trusted assistants at Perth, George Brittain, was appointed Outdoor Inspector of Locomotives on that part of the line north of Stirling, and in 1870 he was appointed Outdoor Superintendent for the whole line. In 1876, on the death of Benjamin Conner, Brittain succeeded him.

Thus under Conner, and Brittain, the Allan traditions continued on the Caledonian, though the latter engineer broke away from the Allan front-end style, and the Allan wheel arrangements. Outside cylinders remained traditional, but the locomotives with which Brittain was particularly concerned, namely the 4-4-0 express passenger engines of 1877 and the 2-4-2 radial tanks for the Oban line were not far removed from failures. By far the best of the Brittain engines were the 4-4-0 'Oban bogies', which bore such a striking resemblance to the 'Skye bogies' of the Highland Railway. The five 4-4-0s of 1877, Nos. 125–129, had an inauspicious beginning. Following upon the success of the 7 ft 2 in. 2-4-0s of 1867 Conner had prepared designs for a still larger 2-4-0 ,which was intended to take over the principal duties on the main line south of Glasgow from the 8-ft singles. Authority for their construction was given, and Neilsons secured the order.

At the time Conner was a dying man, and when Neilsons raised a number of points in connection with the design it was Brittain who had to deal with them. The records do not reveal on whose authority the changes in design were made, save that the Caledonian refused to accept Neilsons suggestion that the coupled wheel diameter be reduced to 6 ft 8 in. How the engine got changed from a 2-4-0 to a 4-4-0 is wrapped in mystery, but from one cause and another the result was one of the poorest express locomotives ever put on to Caledonian metals. In service they were heavy coal burners, and so far as haulage capacity was concerned they could not touch the performance of the old 8-ft singles. They were bad steamers, and that was a failing that no good Caledonian engineman could condone. Drummond rebuilt them with his own type of boiler, but even he could not make much of them, and they worked out their short lives on very third-rate duties.

Although Brittain was brought into prominence under Allan one can say that the direct influence of the master engineer came to an end on the Caledonian with Conner's death. The Allan engines remained for many years. One of the most handsome of the Drummond rebuilds was that of the 7 ft 2 in. 2-4-os. The neat Drummond chimneys, and boiler mountings, enhanced their appearance, and as to their usefulness the six engines built by Neilsons in 1868 survived until 1913–5. All except one had Drummond boilers, but the first of the batch, No. 466, had a Lambie boiler, with plain dome and safety valves over the firebox. In their last days the six engines were numbered 1117–1122, and of these No. 1119 was the last survivor. With their large wheels and beautiful slotted splashers they were perhaps the most beautiful of all the Allan locomotives to survive into the twentieth century.

VI

The Callander & Oban Line

UNTIL the middle of the nineteenth century the Highlands of Scotland were regarded as a region into which few, except the most intrepid of travellers, dared to venture. Memories of the second Jacobite rebellion were still evergreen, and the classic account of his journey to the Hebrides, written by Dr Samuel Johnson, and the details filled in by Boswell in his journal were enough to put off all but the most venturesome of tourists. Then came Scott. In the series of historical novels that originally appeared under the general title 'Tales of my Landlord', he lifted the Highland scene out of the prevailing gloom, poverty and bitterness, and with that skilful touch that earned him the name of 'Wizard of the North' he created an aura of romance over the Highlands which shows no sign of lessening today.

But for all the wide circulation of the Waverley novels the Highlands themselves might have remained as remote as ever but for the work of two other Scotsmen, Thomas Telford and David Hucheson. Telford built the Caledonian Canal, and opened the way for Hucheson to extend and develop his steamer business among the islands and inlets of the west coast. By the year 1860, the frequency of service was as great as it was between the two World Wars. One could travel by steamer throughout from Glasgow to Inverness, via the Crinan and Caledonian canals; there were regular services to Mull, Skye, and the Outer Hebrides, and the mails from Glasgow and the south were all carried by water. The journey from Glasgow to Oban took 9¾ hours, but the enterprise of Hucheson did not end with his steamers. Having carried tourists to Oban and Fort William he arranged with local coach proprietors for circular tours to some of the more famous scenes inland, and altogether a very brisk tourist business was beginning to build up centred upon Oban.

The prejudice against railways through the Highlands had already been broken down with the construction of Joseph Mitchell's magnificent line from Perth to Forres. In the Parliamentary battles opposing counsels had attempted to ridicule the idea of carrying a railway through the Pass of Druimuachdar, just as earlier counsel had ridiculed Chat Moss, Box Tunnel, and other obstacles to the engineer. No great difficulty was experienced in obtaining Parliamentary sanction for the Callander & Oban Railway, which was authorized in 1865. Although promoted by an independent company this project was backed financially by the Caledonian, though the difficulties and cost of construction seem to have been much underrated. Previous experience existed in Scotland from the construction of the Highland main line, through very similar country; but at that stage in railway development there was little in the way of interchanging experience and ideas.

Probably Joseph Mitchell's paper, read before the British Association in Dundee in September, 1867, came too late. The Callander & Oban line, authorized in 1865, would have been well and truly committed by that time. Mitchell described the construction and works of the Highland Railway, dealing in considerable detail with the difficulties he encountered in places like the Pass of Killiecrankie, Huntley's Cave, and in crossing peat bogs on Dava Moor, and near the summit of the line in the Pass of Druimuachdar. Mitchell not only dealt with his engineering problems, but gave very full details of the costs. His paper did indeed constitute a remarkably comprehensive 'handbook' on the construction of railways in the Highlands. In comparison with such businesslike methods one can only feel that affairs on the Callander & Oban line were sadly mismanaged.

The line was laid out so as to keep cutting and embankment work to a minimum, and the gradients are heavy in places. There are, however, long stretches through the glens where the terrain looks deceptively easy; there the surveyors may have allowed for nothing more than ordinary soil excavation, whereas even the shallowest of cuttings had to be blasted from the solid rock. The start out of Callander, as seen from the footplate, is compelling in the extreme. One strikes out across green meadows for a frontal attack, as it were, upon a solid wall of mountains towering up to the summit of Ben Ledi. The rocky heights crowd so closely round the Pass of Leny, and are so thickly wooded that it is only when close at hand that the gap in the mountain wall can be descried, and the railway begins to wriggle its way uphill on a track that looks more like a sylvan country lane among the birch woods. The gradient here is 1 in 50, but is not long, and at the head of the pass level running commences, and continues for the entire length of Loch Lubnaig.

Through Strathyre and the Rob Roy country the scenery is that of a pastoral glen rather than of the wildest Highland country, but ahead lies one of the great obstacles of the route, the watershed between the streams flowing to Loch Earn and eastwards towards Crieff, and Glen Dochart. The ascent of Glen Ogle on a gradient of 1 in 60, providing a severe task for the locomotives of all but the lightest train, involved some heavy and difficult engineering work. Nearing the summit of the pass the line is carried on a ledge cut in the hillside; the profusion of great isolated boulders lying around tells its own tale of terrifying avalanches in the past, and the summit is reached through scenes of utter desolation all the more impressive in the contrast they provide to the placid beautiful countryside of Strathyre. Glenoglehead is no more than 17 miles from Callander, and here, in 1870, constructional work stopped for a while, presumably while the company took stock of its finances.

The temporary terminus could hardly have been more inconvenient as a railhead, perched at the summit of a most inhospitable mountain pass. The railway people named it 'Killin', though that pleasant village was a good 4 miles away, far below, at the head of Loch Tay. Having built the line thus far there came the question of how it was to be worked. The Caledonian had agreed to do this, but not over a distance of less than 20 miles. The Callander & Oban people found themselves in a quandary, for they had made no provision for engines or carriages, and all they could afford to build at this stage was 17 miles of line. In 1870 they appealed to the good nature of the Caledonian, and that company agreed to work the line between Callander and Glenoglehead ('Killin'), though reserving themselves the right to cease operations at any time.

Callander & Oban affairs were in a sorry plight at this stage, and things reached the stage of an Act of Parliament being passed in that same year of 1870, abandoning the section of line that had been authorized west of Tyndrum, and constituting the latter place as a general railhead for that part of the Western Highlands. It is a sufficient commentary upon the state of things prevailing that the relatively straightforward 15 miles of line between Glenoglehead and Tyndrum took 3 years to construct. By the abandonment Act of 1870 the Caledonian contribution to the capital of the Callander & Oban Railway was reduced from £200,000 to £162,000. The site of the railway station at Tyndrum led to some difficulties with the Perthshire County Council, as it lay a little distance away from the road leading up to the Argyll county march beside the present route of the West Highland Railway. The hapless 'C & O' was induced 'to relieve the County Council of all difficulties' – in other words, presumably, to build the connecting road!

The line had not been opened to Tyndrum very long before there

were complaints of unpunctual running. It is interesting to find, by
the way, that the term 'timetable' was not used. Instead reference
was made to the 'Scheme of Trains'. Anyway a certain director of the
Callander & Oban complained that in journeying between Edinburgh and Tyndrum his train was always late. It was discussed
around the board table, and the general consensus of opinion
decided that such lateness was the fault of the Caledonian, as the
trains were usually handed over late at Callander. A stiff, though
courteous letter was therefore sent to the Caledonian, asking them
to mend their ways. This was treading on rather delicate ground
seeing that the Callander & Oban depended not only for its locomotives and rolling stock, but for its very existence upon the good-
will of the Caledonian.

The reply came from James Smithells, the Caledonian General
Manager, who regretted that a report 'so unjust' should have been
made by a director of the Caledonian & Oban Railway. He
pointed out that the trains from Edinburgh were worked over the
North British Railway to Larbert, and laid the blame fairly and
squarely on that company's shoulders. In the period complained
of by the C. & O. director the average lateness of trains arriving at
Larbert off the North British was 19 min. He admitted that to this a
further 8 min., on the average, had been lost by the Caledonian
between Larbert and Callander, but he drew attention to the crowded
state of the line between Larbert and Dunblane, and pointed out
how difficult it sometimes was to provide clear running when trains
were arriving at Larbert out of their proper timetable paths, a
familiar enough cause of delay at the present time. So far as Larbert
is concerned, this took place before the construction of the Forth
Bridge when all North British trains for Perth, Aberdeen and the
Highlands travelled over the Caledonian line north of Larbert.

The abandonment of the western end of the line could not have
come at a worse time. Oban was not only a valuable prize from the
summer tourist point of view, but the steamer connections could
well provide a flow of traffic all the year round to the Hebridean
ports. It must have been with some dismay that the Caledonian
watched the efforts of its floundering protégé, while the rival concern
in the north, the Dingwall & Skye, strongly backed by the Highland
Railway, was being pushed rapidly forward to completion. Both
railways were authorized in the same year, and while the Callander
& Oban had reached no farther than Glenoglehead by 1870 the
Dingwall & Skye was through to Strome Ferry by August of that
year, and steamer services to Portree and Stornoway were commenced

Above: Connel Ferry viaduct.

WEST HIGHLAND VIADUCTS

Below: Creran Viaduct, Ballachulish branch.
[*both O. S. Nock*

Rothesay, Isle of Bute, with the Caledonian Steam Packet Co.'s steamer *Galatea* berthed at the nearest end of the pier, and with North British and G. & S.W. steamers in the background.

[*Annan, Glasgow*

Above: Eglinton Street Station. A striking
view of the platforms.
[*British Railways*

Below: Perth Joint Station. A view on the
down side, looking south.
[*British Railways*

WEMYSS BAY

Above: Interior of the old station.

Below: The beautiful concourse in the new station.
[*British Railways*

immediately. This was a sad blow to the prestige of the Caledonian, which had more than once felt the vigour, drive, and independent attitude of the Highland management. The dispute over the tolls payable for use of the Perth–Stanley Junction line will be freshly remembered.

Anyway, the Caledonian agreed to make a further substantial contribution to Callander & Oban finances, and a new Act was passed in 1874 authorizing, once again, the construction of the line west of Tyndrum. This time there was no faltering, and on July 1st, 1880, the line was opened throughout to Oban. Before leaving the eastern end of the line however, there are some interesting points to be noted at the stations between Strathyre and Tyndrum. It was not until 1905 that Balquidder became an important junction. The railway had reached Crieff as early as the year 1853 by a branch of the Scottish Central leaving the main line at Gleneagles. This latter name was not used until 1912, and until then the station was known as Crieff Junction. There was, by 1867, yet another way of reaching Crieff by rail, over the tracks of the Perth, Almond Valley & Methven Railway which branched westwards from the Scottish North Eastern at Almond Valley Junction, about $1\frac{1}{2}$ miles north of Perth. The link-up between these two early railways and the Callander & Oban line was promoted by the Caledonian Railway. Construction took place from the eastern end of the link, and the opening dates were, to St Fillans in 1901, to Lochearnhead in 1904, and to Balquhidder in 1905.

Until the construction of the line from Crieff the station at the present site of Balquhidder was known as Lochearnhead, even though it was nearly two miles from the remote Highland clachan of that name. After renaming, the station was even farther from the village of Balquhidder, which lay westwards in the mountains at the foot of Loch Voil. It is at Balquhidder station that the long and severe ascent to Glenoglehead begins, and in mounting the open hillsides the measured pace of the train gives a magnificent panoramic view over the whole length of Loch Earn, while the railway to St Fillans and Crieff is seen far below. The long, curving viaduct at Lochearnhead, which looks so massive at close quarters, appears a delicate, fairy-like thing from the height of the main line, set in its amphitheatre of wild mountains. We shall return to this interesting and picturesque line later in the story of the Caledonian Railway.

When the railway came to be extended westward from the temporary terminus at Glenoglehead the provision of a branch line running to Killin was considered. The location of such a line was a matter of no small difficulty owing to the difference in altitude between the main line at Glenoglehead and Killin itself, at the head of Loch Tay. The little town lies some 370 ft above sea level, whereas Glenoglehead is 940 ft up. The only way to avoid excessively steep gradients was for the branch to make a trailing connection with the main line after the latter had descended some way down the southern slopes of Glen Dochart. Even so the gradient throughout the $2\frac{1}{4}$ miles from Glenoglehead to Killin Junction is 1 in 69, and the branch itself descends at 1 in 70. This line belonged to a separate concern, the Killin Railway Company which was incorporated in 1883. It was opened to Killin and to the pier on Loch Tay in 1886. From the outset good connections were provided with all main line trains, and combined excursions were arranged in connection with steamer sailings on Loch Tay. Although worked by the Caledonian this little company was never absorbed till it became part of the L.M.S.R. in 1923.

At the time of the construction of the Callander & Oban Railway, Crianlarich was no more than a wayside station. It is true that the village itself was of some importance, lying at the junction of two main roads; but from the railway point of view it was of minor importance in comparison with Tyndrum, yet another temporary terminus of the line. Before the coming of the railway Tyndrum was an important coaching station, lying at the junction of roads to Oban and Fort William, and when the railway was built the need for providing terminal facilities involved the Callander & Oban in some additional expense. It became the railhead at which a surprising amount of West Highland tourist traffic was handled in the summer months and the extent of the railway terminal premises can be judged today by the remains. To the north of the line, and lying below the level of the present station is what appears to be a most unnecessarily large goods yard, with little, or nothing ever going on – veritably one of the ghost stations of the British railways.

Studying the maps, and still more so if one has any personal acquaintance with the country itself, it is not difficult to appreciate the readiness with which the Callander & Oban proprietors agreed to the abandonment of the western end of the line when their funds were exhausted. Whatever difficulties may have been experienced in the Pass of Leny, and in Glen Ogle were likely to be multiplied many times west of Tyndrum, where the line had to make its way round the head of Loch Awe, beneath the rough and boulder-strewn slopes of Ben Cruachan, and not least through the rocky and tumbled countryside of Lorne. It is surprising that in such geographical conditions the line is so free from curvature, and permits of quite brisk running. The worst alignment, curiously enough, comes when the railway has passed out of the mountain region proper and is wriggling its way beside the shores of Loch Etive. With the land rising to no great heights one might have imagined that with a judicious amount of cutting and embankment a direct line could easily have been secured. But in this countryside every cutting meant blasting from the solid rock, and expense in construction was still a prime consideration.

From Tyndrum one is travelling at first across sedgy moorlands over the watershed between east-flowing and west-flowing rivers, and the descent of Glen Lochy is on moderate gradients and taken at well over 50 m.p.h. After passing the intermediate crossing loop at Glenlochy, however, the descent steepens to an average of 1 in 55, and the 6¾ mile section down to Dalmally provides a piece of running that exceeds Glen Ogle in the severity of task set to locomotives in the ascending direction. I have several times been over this line on the footplate, and going over the brow of the hill, just to the west of Glenlochy loop is an extraordinary experience as seen through the cab glasses. The village of Dalmally is another centre of West Highland touring activity, and provides the nearest point on the Caledonian Railway to the Argyllshire capital of Inveraray. In the days of combined rail, coach and steamer tours in Scotland the Caledonian naturally emphasized the importance of Dalmally, and thereby hangs a tale. Although it belongs to a much later period, to the desperate year of 1940, in fact, it is worth retelling at this stage.

After the evacuation from Dunkirk the scattered and disintegrated units of the British Expeditionary Force were being sent by rail to various points of assembly all over Britain, for sorting out. There was no time, nor facilities for doing so at the Channel Ports, nor to any extent in the south of England. Well, on one of those anxious nights of June, 1940, when invasion was expected daily, a small detachment of Argyllshire L.D.V., as they were then known, sighted a mysterious party in Glen Aray. Cautiously the L.D.V. came up, and challenged these suspicious characters in British uniform, to find they were members of a British Regiment, survivors from Dunkirk, and now utterly lost in the wilds of Argyll. The poor fellows were so exhausted that they hardly knew or cared where they were going, but questioning established that they were supposed to be bound for Inverurie; but someone *en route* had mistaken the name for Inveraray, sent them to Dalmally, and told them to walk from there!

From Dalmally the railway passes round the head of Loch Awe, beside Kilchurn Castle, to run close to the water's edge at the foot of the mountain mass piling up to the five-pointed summit of Ben Cruachan. Within a mile is Loch Awe station, adjacent to the steamer pier, from which sailings were run in connection with the trains. Here again, as at Loch Tay, there were combined rail and steamer excursions. For almost the entire existence of the Callander & Oban Railway as a separate company the steamer services on Loch Awe were operated by private individuals. David Hucheson and Co., forerunners of David Macbrayne Ltd., operated a steamer named *Queen of the Lake*, from before railway days in the Loch Awe district, while the Earl of Breadalbane, who sponsored the Lochawe Hotel Company put on a vessel in 1882 named *Countess of Breadalbane*. Almost at the end of the pre-Grouping era, in July, 1922, this vessel was purchased by the Caledonian Steam Packet Company, which had been formed in May, 1889, to operate the shipping services of the Caledonian Railway.

One has to reach the foot of Loch Awe for a reminder of a combined coach and steamer service to Oban that operated before the building of the railway. Geographically, Loch Awe is a curiosity as its outlet is to be found not in the lower lying country at its southern end, but in the Pass of Brander, beneath the highest ridges of Ben Cruachan. Here, at the outlet of the loch, are some old piers that were used when there was an alternative service to the all-water route from Glasgow to Oban. Coaches ran from the steamer pier at Ardrishaig to the head of Loch Awe; one then sailed the length of Loch Awe, and transferred to coaches again for the last stage of the journey through Taynuilt, and Connel.

In the Pass of Brander the railway is carried high on the slopes of Ben Cruachan on a section of line completely exposed, and subject to the risk of damage from minor avalanches. The higher slopes of the mountain includes some rough and loose scree, and boulders have been known to come crashing down to the pass below. This part of the line was opened in July, 1880, and a year later the danger was sufficiently realized for the Board to be considering some means of protection. Only the most extensive and costly works would provide complete protection to the railway from the effects of such unwelcome descents. Had the Callander & Oban been a main trunk line something in the way of an avalanche shelter would have been essential, but in the circumstances it was considered enough to provide warning of any such danger. In August, 1881, the engineer was asked to propose a plan to prevent accidents 'from stones falling in the Pass of Awe'. Trials were made during the ensuing winter, on an experimental length, and these proving successful the installation was extended to cover the entire danger area in the pass. A fence of wires was erected parallel to the railway, some little distance up the slopes of the mountain, and to these wires are connected a series of semaphore signals, each having two arms on a post, one facing in each direction of running, and both arms normally at 'all clear'. If any of the warning wires up the mountainside should be broken by falling rocks all the special two-way semaphores are put to danger, and oncoming trains warned thereby. These semaphores were not connected in any way with the ordinary block signals.

The western end of the Callander & Oban line runs through a pleasant, deceptively lowland country, though the sharpness of the gradients, and the absence of any heavy earthworks is a sufficient reminder that solid rock is only just below the surface, and that there was every need to economize in the cost of construction. The line runs near to the tidal shores of Loch Etive between Taynuilt and Connel Ferry, and then climbs at 1 in 50 over the high ground by Glen Cruitten to make an equally steep and severely curved descent into Oban itself. This latter incline, which has to be tackled by locomotives starting cold from Oban has always been a gruelling proposition from the earliest days of the line. Not infrequently one could see trains double-headed only from Oban to Connel Ferry to help in surmounting this incline. For although there are gradients as steep farther, eastwards on the journey they could be tackled much more readily when the locomotive had warmed up.

So far as motive power was concerned the Allan era on the Caledonian was practically at an end when the line was opened throughout, and the locomotives that will always be associated with it in earlier days are George Brittain's 5 ft 2 in. 4-4-0s, the first 'Oban Bogies'. Strangely enough they bore a remarkable likeness to the famous 'Skye Bogies' of the Highland Railway, save in superficial details such as the shape of the chimney and of the cab. Both designs appeared in the same year, namely 1882, and had the same large sized cylinders for that period: 18 in. by 24 in. The Highland engines had the true Allan front-end framing, whereas the 'Oban Bogies' had inside frames throughout, and although the cylinders were steeply inclined and were partly above and partly below the running plate, this ensconcing of the cylinders was superficial, as they were secured only to the inside frame plates. The 'Oban Bogies' were ideal for this steeply graded line, and like their counterparts on the Highland they worked all trains, passenger and goods alike.

VII

The Firth of Clyde

FROM as long as historical records exist Greenock has been one of the most important towns in Scotland. In some ways it could be likened to a frontier point: a strongly-held bastion thrust out towards enemy territory. At the turn of the century, looking out over one of the most beautiful prospects in all Britain, Greenock played the part of the last outpost of lowland, commercial Scotland beyond which, across the Firth, lay the wild, remote, virtually unknown region of the western Highlands. In view of its 'strategic' position it is not surprising that a railway from Greenock to Glasgow was one of the earliest to be constructed in Scotland. The building of railways was only one manifestation of the tremendous growth of industry and commerce in Glasgow itself. The development of steam navigation was another, and the beautiful seashore, mountain, and estuarine scenery lying so close to Glasgow provided the strongest incentive for rail and steamer services to develop side by side.

The earliest steamships to operate anywhere in the world plied upon the Firth of Clyde, and from those quaint pioneer vessels with their incredibly tall funnels there had developed a veritable fleet of privately-owned ships sailing from the heart of Glasgow to primitive little jetties on both banks of the Firth, and into the remoter and more winding fiords branching north and westwards from the main waterway. It was a healthy 'free for all' among the steamboat owners, but with the establishment of the railway at Greenock, and the purchase of three steamers, which were operated thereafter by the Bute Steam Packet Company on behalf of the railway, a new factor entered into the competition on the Clyde. The combined rail and steamer services offered the inducement of speed in getting from Glasgow to Dunoon, Rothesay, or farther afield. The private steam-boat owners replied with a tremendous publicity campaign extolling the advantages of travelling 'all the way by water'. Rivalry between the steamers increased, and the intrepid captains developed the most audacious techniques in beating their opponents in navigating dexterously up to the piers and securing first place. In all but the most exceptional weather the little ships went through, though there is one recorded occasion of a skipper taken to task for not bringing his ship to Glasgow. He put in at Greenock, where, he said, the fog was so thick that the gulls were sitting on it!

In spite of heavy losses on their steamers, due to the intense competition, three new ships, the *Pilot, Pioneer* and *Petrel* were built in 1844–5; but as the results were still disappointing the railway associated company sold out in 1847 to Messrs G. & J. Burns. In 1851 the Glasgow, Paisley & Greenock Railway became part of the Caledonian, which at first operated in conjunction with selected private steamers. It was not long, however, before it was felt desirable, in the midst of such hot competition, to have everything in their own hands, and in 1852 the Caledonian had built for its own use three fine steamers, the *Helensburgh*, the *Dunoon* and the *Gourock*. To assist in what was hoped to be an increasing traffic from Greenock to Dunoon, the Gareloch, the Holy Loch, and to Rothesay, four others were subsequently acquired. The railway company had no power to operate steamers, and so these vessels were operated by the associated Railway Steam Packet Company. They sailed from Custom House Quay at Greenock, to which intending passengers from Glasgow had to make their way from the railway terminus at Cathcart Street station. Competition between the railway and the privately-owned steamers blazed away; but the railway control of steamers at this stage was not a success, and the Caledonian reverted for a time to the older practice of working in conjunction with private steamboat owners. In 1865 another step was taken to shorten the journey time, not merely between Glasgow and Rothesay, but also to the thriving towns and resorts farther down the firth, namely Largs and Millport. This step was the construction of the Wemyss Bay Railway, from Port Glasgow over the hills lying to the southwest of Greenock to what was then little more than a remote cove on the mainland, but right opposite to Rothesay Bay on the Isle of Bute.

Even before this development the Caledonian Railway had been the only concern, other than private steamboat owners, interested in passenger services on the Clyde, and with the establishment of a second port its position in 1865 might have seemed well-nigh impregnable. In that very same year however, the Greenock & Ayrshire Railway obtained authority to build a line to Johnstone, on the Glasgow & South Western main line to Ayr, which would not only introduce competition into the railway service between Glasgow and Greenock, but which included the great advantage of a terminal station at Greenock near to the water's edge, at Albert Harbour which was later to become so well known as Princes Pier. The

Caledonian management saw the danger, and saw equally the chance of turning the flank of their rivals even before the latter commenced operation. Westward of Greenock itself was the fine sweep of Gourock Bay. In 1865 there were no more than a handful of cottages and a little stone jetty, but the place held the key to a continuing successful competition.

Already the Caledonian Railway had come to appreciate that minutes counted in the cut-throat competition on the Clyde. The new railway route to Greenock, Albert Harbour, was going to include some very heavy gradients, and although the distance to a future packet station at Gourock would be slightly greater from the Glasgow terminus, the Caledonian reckoned they could do the railway journey in as good, if not better time, and their steamer would be able to cast off from a landing stage a good 3 miles farther down stream than that of her rival. This would give her a flying start in the dash across to Dunoon. So in 1866 the Caledonian Railway purchased the little jetty in Gourock Bay, and plans were formulated for an extension of the railway. Unfortunately the project was a very expensive one, involving the driving of a long tunnel; and the drawing up of these plans coincided with the onset of a serious trade depression and heavy decline in traffic. Because of this it was decided to abandon the Gourock project in 1869. Unfortunately for the Caledonian the timing of this abandonment, inevitable though it was, could not have been worse, for it was in that same year that the new route to Albert Harbour was opened for traffic.

The Caledonian soon came to experience the new competition in full measure, and the company was forced into the fighting of a defensive battle, losing traffic steadily to the Glasgow & South Western on the score of the inconvenience of the transfer arrangements between train and boat at Greenock. For how long competition on these manifestly unequal terms might have continued on the south bank of the Clyde is a moot point, if a second adverse factor had not arisen to affect still further the traffic earnings of the Caledonian. Consequent upon the amalgamation of the Edinburgh & Glasgow Railway with the North British, the latter company had secured control of the Glasgow, Dumbarton & Helensburgh Railway. Not content with developing a prosperous residential traffic on the north bank of the Clyde the North British must also enter the field of steamboat operation. In 1866 a service was introduced between Helensburgh and Ardrishaig, and although this proved unsuccessful and was later curtailed to Gareloch, the Holy Loch and Dunoon, a resolute new competitor was operating on the Firth. Plans were soon being formulated for the building of a first class steamer port at Craigendoran, a little to the east of Helensburgh. From the slowness with which the Caledonian took up this latest challenge it might have appeared that the Board did not fully appreciate the significance of what was happening, but as things turned out they had good reason for waiting.

When the Craigendoran project was authorized it would have been easy to have rushed in with a rival development. As it was it looks as though the Caledonian waited until both their rivals had laid their cards on the table, and then they came back with a project of the very first importance. The old Gourock scheme was revived, with all facilities for trains and steamers on the most spacious scale. The extension line was carried under the burgh of Greenock, in the longest tunnel in Scotland, and the approach lines ran through deep cuttings flanked by massive retaining walls. Craigendoran was opened in 1882, but it was 7 years later before the Caledonian steamers began to sail from Gourock. In readiness for this the Caledonian Steam Packet Company Limited was formed. The railway itself had no authority to own steamers, and for a time in the 1850s there had been another subsidiary the Railway Steam Packet Company, operating steamers in conjunction with the Caledonian trains.

Curiously enough, the situation at Wemyss Bay was quite different from that existing at Greenock. The Wemyss Bay Railway was from the outset worked by the Caledonian, and the former company also had a steamship owning subsidiary. The Wemyss Bay route was looked upon with the greatest disfavour by all the private steamship companies operating on the Firth of Clyde, save one; and ignoring the pier altogether, and refusing to run any trips in connection with the trains, they hoped to cause a collapse of the company altogether. Whether from this curious attitude or not, the railway-owned steamers were no more successful than those of the Caledonian Railway's own steamboat subsidiary at Greenock. The ships were sold, and the services to Rothesay and Largs worked henceforth by the one steamboat company that had been friendly, namely that of the Messrs J. Gillies and A. Campbell. This arrangement lasted until the year 1890, when the Caledonian Steam Packet Company took over the services.

The formation of this famous steamship company came about in a somewhat roundabout way. In August, 1888, the Caledonian Railway sent official notification to all steamboat owners operating on the Firth of Clyde that the new pier at Gourock would be ready in the following May, and invited co-operation. The response was discouraging. One of the biggest owners, MacBrayne, ignored the notice altogether; others surrounding their replies with so many conditions as to make them unacceptable, and, although the railway management was anxious to have as many connections as possible to its new services, there was every sign that if the private steamboat owners were to be relied on the whole enterprise might well flounder in muddle on the Firth. And yet the previous experiences of the Caledonian Railway in steamship owning had been unsuccessful. The Wemyss Bay Company, still independent, urged the Caledonian to try once again, and in that critical autumn of 1888, matters hung fire for a time. Many of the steamboat owners were one boat, or two boat men, remarkable characters in themselves, and outstanding seamen, but incapable of thinking as big as the needs of the Caledonian demanded. Captain James Williamson, of the *Sultana*, might have been no better than the rest, no more than a dashing young skipper; but he caught the eye not only of the public, but of the Caledonian management.

The Rev Wm C. Galbraith has written of his racing prowess with the *Sultana*:

'There was no monotony in those days – in fact as he said himself, the fun was excellent. It was the hey-day of competition; there were no pier signals to cramp one's efforts; any skeely skipper who could slip in his craft ahead of others waiting for a pier might do so. Captain James did so – to the loud applause of his passengers. Though one of the youngest of the Clyde navigators in the 'seventies, he became one of the high-lights of those days of unrestricted opportunity, as much admired by the Clyde partisans of the time as was Sir Malcolm Campbell or any other speed king in these days.' But beside all the excitement and the speed of competition, discerning men noted the punctuality with which his ship was run, the smartness of his passenger arrangements, and the courtesy and civility of his crew, and when the Caledonian Railway appointed him as their Marine Superintendent, as from 1st January, 1889, they gathered into their midst a man who was to prove as outstandingly successful an executive officer as Graham, Kempt, McIntosh, Matheson or any others among the Caledonian galaxy perhaps better known to railway enthusiasts. In May, 1889, the Caledonian Steam Packet Company was registered and on 1st June, 1889, Caledonian steamers berthed for the first time at the new Gourock pier.

There were no half measures about this later venture into steamship operation by the Caledonian Railway. The steam packet company, provided with magnificent new ships, began operations at the same time as the extension to Gourock was opened, and it is no exaggeration to say that the ensuing quarter of a century, till the outbreak of war in 1914, saw the working of the finest rail and steamer service the world has ever seen. From being the first in the field the Caledonian had seen its rivals establish themselves at points of vantage that sadly weakened the pioneer of combined rail and steamer services on the Clyde. In this competition, however, the Caledonian was like the 'scratch man' in a handicap race. The rivals at Princes Pier and Craigendoran were closely watched as they showed their respective hands, and their packet stations were developed; then the Caledonian came in like a thunderbolt, not only at Gourock, but in taking over the working of the steamer services at Wemyss Bay from 1890 onwards.

Not that the Caledonian swept the narrow seas from 1889 onwards – far from it! The Glasgow & South Western, and the North British had fleets every bit as good as those steaming from Gourock and Wemyss Bay. Competition was terrific. Every run across the Firth from Gourock to Dunoon was a race, with a steamer from Craigendoran closing in upon its Caledonian and G.S.W. rivals, to jockey in the manoeuvring for first place at the Dunoon pier. What beautiful ships they were! What stately high-sounding names they bore. *Marchioness of Breadalbane, Marchioness of Lorne, Duchess of Rothesay, Duchess of Fife*: with their low hulls, well-raked masts and funnels, and the casings over their great paddle-wheels streamlined back abaft of the wheel itself, they looked the greyhounds of the Firth they were. Many of those early ships of the Caledonian Steam Packet survived to carry the funnel colours of the London, Midland & Scottish fleet, but in pre-Grouping days the funnels were yellow throughout, with no black top.

The incidents of one particular day's racing between the Caledonian and the 'Sou' West' bring out vividly the spirit of the Clyde, and the way passengers entered into the partisanship as keenly as the steamboat crews. Again to quote Galbraith: 'Trains were very carefully scheduled to receive clear runs; no sooner did the passengers alight than they were hustled on to the steamers and the gangways almost pulled out from their feet as they stepped aboard. At Gourock all eyes turned east to watch Fort Matilda and the grey craft from whose red lums billowed up clouds of smoke.

'On the 7th August, 1894', Galbraith continues, 'it was the *Minerva* that was on the 4.3 St Enoch run; she was well down Gourock Pier and began poking her nose up as she led off by about three boat lengths. Soon twin spirals of Caley smoke were forming a pillar of cloud by day for the *Minerva* to follow, and follow she did, always keeping on the starboard quarter to avoid the moving wash. Gradually the *Minerva*'s bow wave grew nearer and nearer to the watching eyes on the *Galatea*. For the lochs run Captain Duncan Bell preferred to take Kirn from the south but he saw that such a manoeuvre on this occasion would lose him the pier, so he instructed the *Galatea*'s pilot to make for the north side. Captain Archibald Henderson on the *Minerva* kept her just to the northward, pulling slowly up. At last, 300 yards from the pier he had her bow on the *Galatea*'s paddle-box; he had the inner berth; still no signal showed; believing he had lost, he rang down "Stop", no sooner had he done so than the signal winked white for him and over to "Full Ahead" he went. But the *Galatea* was holding straight on; he slowed; he stopped; he was not risking anything. The *Galatea* swung in and Captain Bell attempted to land his passengers, but the piermaster, Frederick Brown, refused to take his ropes and ordered him off. So in came the *Minerva* and off came her passengers. The *Galatea* took a swing round and came in at the moment the *Minerva* was off. The pierman took her ropes this time but hooted and jeered at her discomfiture. "Why don't you black that man's eyes?" queried ex-Bailie Colquhoun, LL.D., one of the passengers on the *Galatea*, from the sailor on the ropes: "These boys on Kirn Pier are backing the Sou' West against the Caley".'

The *Galatea*, beautiful two-funnelled ship though she was to look upon, was not one of the most successful of Caledonian steamers. She was a little underboilered, and although her engines were a powerful set they developed greater power than the hull could stand, and therefore she was rarely run all-out. It was said that her paddles were set slightly too far astern. One of the finer points of paddle-boat design where speed was a maximum consideration was to have the hull so proportioned that the wave from the bow rose to its maximum height at the paddle-wheels so that the blades were in contact with the largest possible volume of water. The proportions were not ideal in the *Galatea*, and her speed was not much over 17 knots. She was sold in 1906.

In 1893 the Caledonian absorbed the Wemyss Bay Railway, and at once work was put in to improve the line itself, and to rebuild the terminus station. The railways of Great Britain are not famed for either the spaciousness or beauty of their stations, but among them the Caledonian was a noble exception. It is true that there are some archaic examples still surviving, as at Buchanan Street, Glasgow, but against this can be set Stirling, Gleneagles, Callander, Oban, Perth and Aberdeen, not to mention, of course, Glasgow Central and Edinburgh Princes Street. More of these, however, in a later chapter. At Wemyss Bay the Caledonian substantially excelled its own high standards. The platforms are long and spacious, with ample verandah roofing, and the glass-covered circulating area is not only most attractive in its bright cleanliness but in the distinguished architectural styling. All through the summer this pleasant glazed 'ceiling' was plentifully adorned with hanging baskets gay with geraniums in full bloom. The glazed covering is extended down the approach way to the steamers, and the pier itself has accommodation for five steamers at once. This new station and pier was completed in 1903.

The relentless, unending competition between the steamers, railway-owned and otherwise, was matched on land by the very fast running of the rival boat trains. In the half hour following 4 p.m. the Glasgow terminal stations between them despatched no fewer than eleven boat trains, and with these trains were associated thirteen steamers! On the Caledonian no luggage was permitted at all on the Clyde boat expresses. When no more than 2 minutes was scheduled at Gourock between arrival of the train and departure of the boat one cannot be concerned with such trifles as luggage! The regular passengers entered into the spirit of this amazing competition, and were just as eager as the railways and packet company men to beat the Glasgow & South Western. At the very height of the rivalry the Caledonian booked the 4.8 p.m. from Glasgow Central to run the 26·2 miles to Gourock in 32 minutes. Although the line is on a fairly easy gradient the run was complicated by the need to slow down at the junctions of Paisley, and again over the continuous curvature of the extension line from Greenock Central through Fort Matilda, to Gourock.

Dugald Drummond built a class of 4-4-0 tender engines specially for the Clyde services. They were similar in appearance to the famous main line express passenger 4-4-0s, but having coupled wheels 5 ft 9 in. diameter and somewhat smaller boilers. The first six of these pretty little engines were built in 1887–8 in readiness for the opening of the Gourock extension, and another six were built in 1891 after Drummond himself had departed. In later years the fastest of the Gourock trains were judged of sufficient importance for the famous 'Dunalastairs' to be put on to the job. In 1897 when the train left Glasgow at 4.13 p.m. and was allowed 35 minutes Rous-Marten clocked a 'Dunalastair II', No. 767, to make the run in 31 minutes 44 seconds with a load of 200 tons, even though she was severely held in until after Paisley.

In the combined rail and steamer services centred upon the Firth of Clyde there was at first no rationalization, no agreed territories, no pooling arrangements. Each of the rival companies ran just where it pleased, and far from there being any systematic spacing out of departure times the competitors were away simultaneously, as from the shot of a starter's pistol, from Glasgow Central and St Enoch. It was at Greenock perhaps that the fight was hottest, but for all that things could be pretty lively at Ardrossan, whence the steamers sailed to Arran. The mere presence of the Caledonian at Ardrossan was a piece of outstanding railway audacity. A glance at the map is enough to show that this packet station lies in a territory that looks as though it should be exclusive to the 'Sou' West'. The Caledonian, however, secured control of the nominally independent Lanarkshire & Ayrshire Railway, and they proceeded to wage a rare battle for the Arran traffic. This was never on such an intense scale as the sailings from Princes Pier and Gourock, but tales are told of the boat trains racing neck and neck along the sand dunes to Ardeer, with the drivers shaking their fists at one another!

When the Lanarkshire & Ayrshire Railway came into existence as a very minor concern, empowered by Act of 1883 to make a railway from Barrmill to Kilwinning, a distance of about 6 miles, it originally had the title of Barrmill & Kilwinning Railway. What happened in the intervening 12 months has never been fully disclosed, but in 1884 a further Act was obtained, changing the name, and authorizing an extension from Kilwinning to run cheek by jowl with the Glasgow & South Western line to Stevenston, Saltcoats and Ardrossan Pier, the whole to be worked and maintained by the Caledonian. The latter company had access to Barrmill over the Barrhead joint line from Glasgow, and so the Caledonian was through to Ardrossan Town by September, 1888, and to Ardrossan Pier by June, 1890.

Some of the curves on this difficult route were taken at speeds that would not be appreciated by *all* the passengers, and as on the Gourock route there were representations to the Caledonian to ease the speeds of the more tightly-timed of the boat trains. On the Firth, however, the arrival of the Caledonian at Ardrossan was signalized by the introduction of a magnificent new steamer for the Arran service, the *Duchess of Hamilton*, which immediately began to make inroads upon the traffic previously carried by steamers operated in connection with the Glasgow & South Western Railway. In this handsome ship the promenade deck was, for the first time on a Clyde steamer, extended right to the bow, and another innovation was the use of the first-ever Parsons steam turbine, not for propulsion, but to generate electricity for lighting. The *Duchess of Hamilton* was a paddle steamer, and was the forerunner of the similar *Duchess of Rothesay* and the *Duchess of Fife* in both of which I travelled many times.

Whatever faults there may have been in previous Caledonian steamers Captain Williamson secured a veritable 'Queen of the Firth' in the *Duchess of Hamilton*. Her contract speed was 18 knots, and exceeding this on her trials by 0.1 knot she earned for her builders, Denny of Dumbarton, a premium of £3,000. Next day, in celebration of her success, a party of distinguished visitors were taken for a cruise through the Kyles of Bute. On the return they waited off Kirn for MacBrayne's famous *Columba* to come up on her return mail run from Ardrishaig. When she was nearly level the *Duchess of Hamilton* went away, 'all-out', raced the *Columba*, and comfortably beat her to Gourock. For the Arran run the *Duchess of Hamilton* was commanded by Robert Morrison, an Anchor Line man, new to the Clyde passenger services. In the narrow confines of Ardrossan harbour he found difficulty in swinging the ship and resorted to a tug. This would never do for Captain Williamson; so down to Ardrossan he went and personally demonstrated to Morrison how a large paddler could be turned entirely under her own power.

The Glasgow & South Western reply to the *Duchess of Hamilton* was the two-funnelled paddle steamer *Glen Sannox*, to my mind one of the most beautiful ships ever to sail on the Clyde. Beautiful ships or not, neither side could afford to rest long upon its laurels, and the year 1906 saw the next stage in this intense competition. Marine engineering history had been made on the Clyde in 1901 by the commissioning of the first turbine-driven passenger steamer in the world, the *King Edward*, run by the Turbine Steamer Syndicate Ltd. and managed by Captain John Williamson. Later he was associated with Williamson-Buchanan Steamers Ltd., one of the largest non-railway owners. Five years later the Caledonian Steam Packet Company put on their new *Duchess of Argyll*, a turbine of very similar design to the *King Edward*, and a faster ship than the *Glen Sannox*. On the score of speed the last round before the outbreak of war in 1914 fell to the Caledonian, but splendid ship though she was the *Duchess of Argyll* never seriously won traffic away from the very popular *Glen Sannox*. In 1909 certain pooling arrangements were made whereby the two competing services provided the Arran services in alternate years, and from the period of the First World War the *Glen Sannox* had the Ardrossan–Arran run to herself, while the *Duchess of Argyll* operated a daily trip to the island via the Kyles of Bute.

In dealing with steamer services on the Clyde the longevity of the
steamers inevitably brings in references to activities far ahead of the
general period of the story so far reached in this book, and in some
ways I have been putting the cart before the horse in this chapter by
leaving until the last the great development in Glasgow that contributed so greatly to the efficient handling of the Clyde Coast
services of the Caledonian. This was the building, and the extension
of the Central station. By the 'seventies' of last century it was evident
that the two stations on the south of the river, South Side, and
Bridge Street, were too far away from the commercial centre of the
City of Glasgow to be adequate. Furthermore, the completion of the
City of Glasgow Union Railway, sponsored and backed by the
Glasgow & South Western was approaching, not in its final form,
but sufficient to bring the trains of the 'Sou' West' to a station on the
north side of the river, Dunlop Street.

Still bigger things were brewing on what might still be called the
'Nithsdale' route. Construction of the Midland direct line to Scotland, the far-famed 'Settle & Carlisle' was in full swing, and the City
of Glasgow Union project included the building of a fine terminus
and hotel in St Enoch square. The prospect of direct competition for
the English traffic to and from Glasgow, from a terminal station sited
far more advantageously than any of their own no doubt strengthened
the resolve of the Caledonian Board to apply for Parliamentary
powers to bridge the Clyde and establish a terminus of their own in
the heart of the city. Up to this time the English traffic had been
handled at Buchanan Street. The Act was obtained in 1873, and
subject to some amendments authorized in 1875, the work was pushed
ahead.

As on the shores of the Firth of Clyde, the rivals of the Caledonian
brought their improvement schemes to completion first. St Enoch
station was opened in May, 1876, ready for the new express service
from St Pancras which was inaugurated at the same time. Public
attention was drawn to the new route and terminal station in October
of that same year; and when the Prince and Princess of Wales paid
an official visit to Glasgow, they arrived and departed from St Enoch.
For a short time, as at Greenock, the honours were with the 'Sou'
West', particularly as a number of hampering restrictions were placed
in the way of the Caledonian advance across the Clyde. On the other
hand geography favoured the railway engineers in that the ground
rose quickly from the north bank of the River Clyde, and the main
entrance to the Central station could be made at street level, in
Gordon Street, while the rails could cross the Clyde at a sufficiently

The *Caledonia* at full speed.

FAMOUS
STEAMERS

Below: 'Twin spirals of Caley smoke'! A striking view of the *Ivanhoe*.

The turbine-driven *Duchess of Argyll*.
[*Courtesy Graham E. Langmuir*

MARITIME ACTIVITIES

Above: The *Duchess of Rothesay* swinging in to Brodick Pier, Isle of Arran. Goatfell in the background.

Below: Wemyss Bay: one of the five steamer berths.

[*Courtesy, Graham E. Langmuir*

high level to satisfy the needs of navigation. Nevertheless the Clyde Trustees limited the width of the bridge to 55 ft, and with this limitation it was not possible to provide more than four running lines across the river.

The work was completed, and the new station opened in 1879, and at once the English traffic was transferred from Buchanan Street. At first the Clyde Coast traffic continued to be dealt with at Bridge Street; but this feature of the working put the Caledonian at just as much of a disadvantage in Glasgow as they had experienced at Greenock. Passengers by the 'Sou' West' route could travel conveniently from St Enoch and transfer quickly from train to steamer at Princes Pier. If travelling Caledonian they had to cross the Clyde to reach the station at Bridge Street, and then walk from the old Cathcart Street station in Greenock to the Custom House quay. In 1890, however, following the completion of the extension to Gourock, Glasgow Central station was enlarged by widening the bridge over Argyle Street, and lengthening certain of the platforms. This gave the additional accommodation necessary to work the Gourock and Wemyss trains from 'Central', and part of Bridge Street for a time became a through station.

While the platform accommodation in the station was increased there remained only four running lines across the Clyde, and there was congestion at times. While there is no evidence to suggest that the Caledonian ever got tangled up to the extent that the South Eastern got itself virtually strangled outside Cannon Street, delays of any kind could not be tolerated in the working of the Clyde Coast traffic, and in less than 10 years from the 1890 enlargement the Caledonian had embarked upon one of the largest schemes of station and track improvement seen anywhere in Great Britain, until the time of the B.T.C. Modernization Plan. The strictures placed upon bridge width by the Clyde Trustees were relaxed to the extent that an entirely new bridge was authorized, alongside the old one, and one that would be no less than 110 ft wide, carrying nine lines ot railway abreast. Such indeed was the carrying capacity of this new bridge that today, when the original bridge of 1879 is no longer serviceable and has had to be closed, the entire traffic into and out of Central station is being handled over the new bridge erected under the scheme of 1899.

Engineering details of this great constructional work are referred to in the succeeding chapter. Here I am concerned with its effects upon the Clyde Coast traffic. Bridge Street station was completely demolished, and the area used for carriage sidings. Over the space once occupied by the station there were seventeen lines of rails – eight running lines and nine carriage sidings. These latter were made long enough to accommodate whole trains, and the proximity of these sidings to the Central station was exploited in a particularly interesting and expeditious method of operation. Although the track and platform capacity in the station and its approaches had been so enormously increased everything possible was done to minimize the number of light engine movements. After unloading at the platforms the empty stock was propelled by the train engine out to the carriage sidings. In later years this practice was extended to provide for the propelling of empty stock trains to sidings considerably farther from the terminus than Bridge Street.

Studying Caledonian engineering developments at the turn of the century, and nowhere more so than where concerned with the Clyde Coast traffic, one is deeply impressed with the careful attention given to all matters in connection with terminal station working. Just as its great English partner, the London & North Western, was concerned in the improvements of its great junctions and its marshalling yards, the Caledonian could be considered a model of terminal station practice. At Wemyss Bay, for example, quite apart from the beauty of the station itself, the traffic facilities provided in the reconstruction of 1900 are remarkable in themselves. The enterprising timetables of the day required that a train and a steamer should arrive simultaneously, and exchange passengers. Although the changeover did not need to be done at the lightning speed demanded by the most competitive services at Gourock, there was to be no dawdling about. The station platforms, and the approach ways to the steamer berths, were therefore made exceptionally wide, so that two opposing streams of pedestrians could pass without interference. From the railway point of view, while the two long island platforms provided four platform faces for trains, a third line was laid in between the two island platforms to enable the locomotives of incoming trains to be released immediately on arrival, and 'run round' their trains.

On the Clyde, as nearly everywhere else, the Caledonian was beset by competition, and that competition was countered by large and wise expenditure on new works and equipment that was to put the company in the very forefront of British railway practice. The shareholders, no less than the travelling public, had little cause to be dissatisfied with the results; for if the dividends were not quite so princely as those Richard Moon was able to secure for the proprietors of the North Western the holders of Caledonian 'ordinary' between the years 1882 and 1900 never received less than $3\frac{5}{8}$ per cent, and often got more than 5 per cent. The Clyde Coast was an exciting, spectacular, and remarkably successful part of Caledonian Railway operation, though it merely served to highlight an attitude to the job that was typical of the Company as a whole.

VIII

Dugald Drummond at St Rollox

In one of his inimitable articles on 'Locomotive and Train Working in the Latter Part of the Nineteenth Century', contributed to *The Railway Magazine* nigh 40 years ago, the late E. L. Ahrons wrote: 'There are few brooms that sweep so clean as the new locomotive broom.' He was referring to the results that followed Adams's retirement from the locomotive chair at Nine Elms, and the appointment of Dugald Drummond to take his place, but it could equally have been written of affairs on the Caledonian 13 years earlier when George Brittain resigned owing to ill-health and the directors appointed in his place the still young, and extremely able engineer who had wrought such a transformation on the rival North British Railway since his arrival from Brighton in 1875.

In 1882, when at the age of 42 he was appointed Locomotive Superintendent of the Caledonian, the star of Dugald Drummond, magnificently in the ascendant, was already one of the first magnitude. Trained under Stroudley he was a perfectionist in engineering detail; but his days on the Caledonian were to suggest that he had an altogether broader and grander conception of the capacity of the steam locomotive for development than ever Stroudley was able to display within the narrow confines and muddled operating conditions of the Brighton Railway. One pauses to wonder how the course of Caledonian locomotive history might have progressed had not Drummond been tempted by the offer of an exceedingly lucrative post overseas, and by his ill-starred experience as a locomotive manufacturer afterwards. Although his subsequent management of the locomotive department of the London & South Western Railway was extremely successful, as an engine designer he never seemed to regain the heights he touched in the eight eventful years he was at St Rollox.

So far as outward styling was concerned there was quite a strong parallel between the locomotive stock Drummond took over at St Rollox in 1882 and that which caused Ahrons to write about new locomotive brooms. The Caledonian up to this time was exclusively an 'outside cylinder' line, and like the South Western of the Adams era boasted nought but stove-pipe chimneys at a period when beauty not only of line and livery, but also of individual detail counted for much with the majority of locomotive engineers. Even the austerely minded F. W. Webb went to almost fastidious lengths in designing the profile of the chimney cap that was to remain standard on the North Western for nearly 50 years. Dugald Drummond, while showing many evidences of his early associations with Stroudley, developed a style that could be described as neat and workmanlike, rather than beautiful. His most picturesque achievements on the Caledonian were to be seen in his rebuilds of some of the older engines rather than in his own standard classes.

His rebuilds of the Conner 8-ft singles, and of the 7 ft 2 in. 2-4-0s have already been mentioned in the chapter dealing with the influence of Alexander Allan. These reconstructions came as part of the ordinary programme of repair work, as boilers needed renewal. On taking over at St Rollox, however, Drummond was faced with a locomotive situation not far removed from an emergency. The later stages of the Conner–Brittain period were less distinguished than the earlier ones, so far as main line locomotives were concerned, and with steadily increasing weight of trains on the main line, and the need for double-heading with the Conner singles there was an acute shortage of motive power. There is an interesting parallel here, and in the measures taken to meet the situation, to the case of the London & North Western Railway after George Whale had succeeded Webb. There was no time to wait for the working out of a new design, and for building it; Drummond did as Whale was to do in 1903, take the most serviceable existing class and modernize it in the quickest possible way.

On the Caledonian no rebuilding, however drastic, could appreciably enhance the tractive power of the Conner 8-footers, while the 7 ft 2 in. 2-4-0s were too few in number. So Drummond took the 6 ft 2 in. Conner mixed traffic design, and fitted a number of them with considerably larger boilers. In these days a wheel diameter of 6 ft 2 in. would be considered no detriment to the use of a locomotive in the very fastest of express passenger work, but in the 'eighties' of last century the rebuilt 2-4-0s of the '420' Class were in many quarters regarded as rather unsuitable stopgaps. Nevertheless they did a good deal of hard work between Carlisle and Glasgow before the new Drummond express engines came upon the scene. By the end of 1884 ten of these rebuilds were at work, and they were of such general usefulness that a further fifteen were rebuilt, even after Drummond's own express locomotives were at work. So far as styling was concerned they were unique in the whole range of locomotives designed by Dugald Drummond, and his brother Peter, in having the Patrick Stirling type of cab. It was used afterwards on the North British, by Matthew Holmes, but while Drummond himself was at Cowlairs he used a type that was almost pure Stroudley. In the '420' Class rebuilds the characteristic Drummond chimney replaced the plain stove pipe of the Conner–Brittain period, and a pair of Ramsbottom safety valves were placed on top of the dome.

The interest centred upon steam locomotives, their design, construction and running tends to high-light that part of a railway chief mechanical engineer's duties to the virtual exclusion of all else, at any rate in the eyes of the enthusiast. Although Drummond's work on the Caledonian as an engine designer was outstanding it was not pre-eminent among the manifold duties he undertook so vigorously and enthusiastically. First of all there was the matter of automatic continuous brakes. There was no dodging the issue where Drummond was concerned: no hoping to 'get by' with cheap palliatives of doubtful reliability. He recommended using the Westinghouse automatic air brake from the start, and the Board, to their credit, sanctioned the expense readily enough. Again, while the interior appointments of the main line carriages were spartan enough by present-day standards we find, as early as April, 1883, Drummond proposing to use some of the exhaust steam from the locomotives for warming the carriages. The Board were interested and instructions were given to fit up one of the Edinburgh & Greenock train-sets as a trial. In November, 1883, authority was given to equip a second train, and the success of the system was such that a further and more extensive trial was proposed on some of the West Coast Joint Stock for the comfort of through Anglo-Scottish passengers, though this project could not be so readily put into effect because the agreement of the ultra-conservative London & North Western Railway had to be obtained.

So far as the Caledonian Railway's own coaching stock was concerned Drummond was sufficiently satisfied with the system that in the spring of 1885 he wrote to the Chairman recommending that the entire stock be equipped 'before next winter'. While it is evident that by this time the Board had gained the utmost confidence in their Locomotive Engineer they hesitated before this sweeping proposal, and while they agreed to it in principle Drummond was asked to report upon the total number of engines and carriages concerned. The cost was reasonable enough, amounting to no more than £12 per locomotive. In another amenity, the lighting of carriages, the Caledonian was well to the fore, thanks again to Drummond. While the experiments with steam heating were in progress the specifications drawn up for new carriages called for gas lighting. As it turned out none of the firms tendering for the new stock put in satisfactory proposals for lighting, and so Drummond obtained separate estimates for the lighting from three specialist firms.

The system that was eventually adopted was that of Messrs Pintsch, using compressed oil gas. It served the Caledonian well enough for a number of years, though its dangers were most vividly revealed in later years in the disastrous accidents suffered by the Midland Railway at Hawes Junction in 1910 and near Ais Gill in 1913, when escape of the gas led to very destructive fires. The Caledonian was fortunate enough to experience no such catastrophes so far as its own coaching stock was concerned, though to be sure one must not forget Quintinshill, the crowning railway tragedy of all time on British metals. The stock mainly concerned in that holocaust was Great Central. Gas lighting apart, however, the introduction of automatic continuous brakes, of steam heating, for the carriages, and of improved lighting – all in the middle 'eighties' of last century – is enough to show how widely Dugald Drummond was spreading his influence and his talents.

At the time he took over control of the department the Caledonian had locomotive shops at Greenock and Perth, in addition to St Rollox. But Drummond recommended the concentration of all major work at St Rollox, and a large amount of new machinery was installed to bring the shops into line with the tasks of new construction that they would shortly be expected to undertake. At the same time as he was concentrating facilities for the building and heavy repair of locomotives Drummond was giving equal attention to facilities for the daily servicing of engines at the out-stations, and new sheds were built at Greenock in 1884, and Dundee in 1885. The attention given to Greenock is significant, for the Caledonian was then entering upon the phase of ruthless, all-out competition with the Glasgow & South Western, and with the North British for the Clyde Coast traffic. The new locomotive shed, located at Bogston, was designed to house thirty engines of the largest contemporary passenger type.

In those early years of his chieftainship at St Rollox hardly a Board meeting passed without some recommendation, or suggestion from Drummond, and it was well thought out, economic proposals like the closing of the shed at Eglinton Street that brought him into such high esteem with the directors. Drummond showed that by closing Eglinton Street as an engine shed, and transferring the locomotives concerned to Polmadie, the space vacated could be used as a carriage shed. By having the carriages stabled close to the Central station the empty stock train mileage would be reduced, and he could do with one less station pilot, the annual saving on this one item alone being £3,000. The proposal to transfer all new engine building facilities from Perth to St Rollox caused much concern in the northern city, particularly as it was intended to transfer a number of the workmen. The case was taken up by the civic authorities, who demanded that they should be heard in person. The Caledonian Board readily agreed to see a deputation representing the magistrates and traders, and accordingly, at the end of April, 1884, the Provost of Perth, the Dean of Guild, one of the bailies and four other gentlemen travelled to Glasgow to meet the full Caledonian Board. The discussion was long, and at times heated, but the railway company could not be moved from their decision, and it was pointed out with some cogency that even when that new constructional section of the Perth works had been removed to St Rollox, and the men with it, there would still be left more men in the repair and maintenance shops than were employed there at the time of the absorption of the Scottish Central by the Caledonian, in 1865. Right down to the time of Grouping in 1923, engines were repaired at Perth, and these could usually be distinguished by a slightly darker shade of Caledonian blue than that of engines repaired and repainted at St Rollox.

Next we come to the locomotives themselves. In Drummond's time only four new designs were worked out in the drawing office at St Rollox namely:

(a) 6 ft 6 in. 4-4-0 express passenger
(b) 5 ft 9 in. 4-4-0 passenger, for Clyde Coast
(c) 0-6-0 goods
(d) 0-4-4 small suburban tank

The two classes marked 'b' and 'd' were relatively small machines for local work, and though good in themselves they were soon replaced by larger engines. Of the 0-6-0s it is enough to say that they proved so excellent and so generally useful that many of them are still in service today. No fewer than 210 of them were built to the original design. The first hundred or so had the Drummond boiler, but after the year 1893 the Lambie type of boiler was fitted, with plain dome, and safety valves over the firebox. As they were displaced from the heaviest freight duties on the main line they undertook many light branch passenger jobs, and in the late 1930s a number of them were engaged on piloting work on the Callander & Oban line. In their heyday, their express passenger counterparts, the

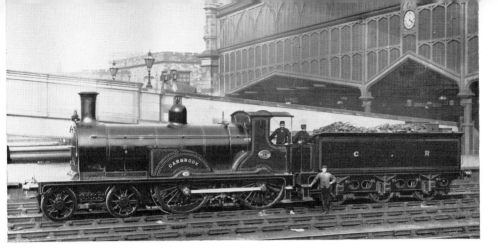

FAMOUS
4-4-0
LOCOMOTIVES

Above: Drummond 4-4-0 No. 79 *Carbrook* at Carlisle.

Below: The *Dunalastair*, pioneer of McIntosh's very famous series of 4-4-0 designs.

[*F. Moore*

A 'Dunalastair II', No. 775 on the turntable at Perth, 1921.

[*R. D. Stephen*

St Rollox works. The erecting shop as it was in 1890, with one of the Brittain Oban 2-4-2 tanks in the foreground.

[*British Railways*

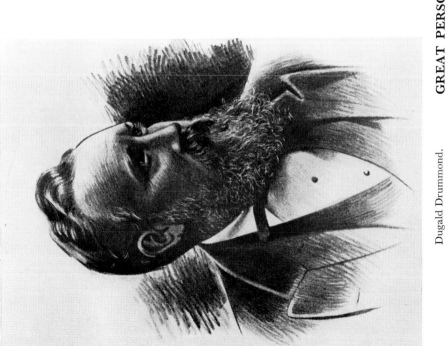

Dugald Drummond.

GREAT PERSONALITIES

Both from pencil portraits in *The Baillie*

Donald A. Matheson.

Above: 2-6-0 No. 36 at Perth.

McINTOSH
FAST GOODS
LOCOMOTIVES

Below: 0-6-0 No. 32 on a Gourock train in Glasgow Central.

[*R. D. Stephen*

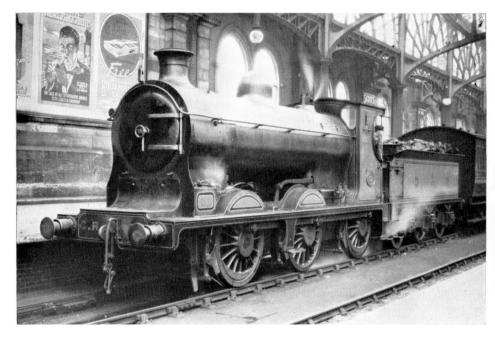

'66' Class, were putting up such brilliant work and attracting almost world-wide attention, that it was no more than natural that the solid reliability of the o-6-o 'Jumbos' – as they became known – should have been taken for granted, even if it was noticed at all.

Dugald Drummond's 6 ft 6 in. 4-4-os the first ten of which were completed in 1884, at Neilson & Co. works, can be put down as one of the really outstanding locomotive designs of the nineteenth century. They were outstanding enough in what they actually did, but in the conception of their design they were many years ahead of their time. The critics may ask at once whether there was anything so wonderful in a simple, straightforward 4-4-0 locomotive, with 18 by 26 in. cylinders, and a boiler pressure of 150 lb per sq in. Behind those seemingly innocuous 'leading dimensions' were many design features that made those engines far faster than many of their contemporaries having considerably larger driving wheels. Again, while the boilers fitted to the original ten, and to the subsequent six engines of 1885 were pressed to no more than 150 lb per sq in. the later engines of 1889 and 1891 had steel boilers designed for a working pressure of no less than 200 lb per sq in., and Drummond's experiments with four of these engines are referred to later in this chapter.

The boilers were relatively small, but Drummond in his scientific approach to the utilization of steam in the cylinders was in many ways anticipating the classic work of Churchward on the Great Western, some 20 years later. To quote Drummond's own words regarding these Caledonian 4-4-0 locomotives: 'The design of the cylinders is a departure from the normal arrangement with a central valve face. The steam ports were moved to the cylinder ends, and the slide valve was divided, each having its own exhaust port. In this way the port clearance was reduced to a minimum and a reduction in back pressure was effected. The weight of the valve, however, was increased by 70 per cent. The exhaust passages were increased so that the belt from the lower and top valves extended along the whole length of the cylinder, thus forming an exhaust steam jacketed cylinder. The blast pipe, which was of the Vortex type, had likewise a large exhaust capacity with a nozzle equal to a 5 in. opening.' Having thus reduced back pressure in the cylinders to a very small amount Drummond intended that the locomotives should be worked with a wide open regulator, and short cut-offs. Unfortunately, as the trials of 1889 were to show, the Caledonian drivers were not yet ready for such modern methods of handling.

The most famous of all Caledonian engines built during the

Drummond regime was neither designed by Drummond himself nor built at St Rollox. How the beautiful 4-2-2 we now know so well as No. 123 actually came to take the form she did it is difficult to say at this distance in time. It is certain that when she was laid down at the Hyde Park works of Neilson & Co it was not to any order from the Caledonian Railway. The firm wished to exhibit an engine at the forthcoming Edinburgh Exhibition, in 1886, and No 123 was designed in close agreement with Drummond's '66' Class 4-4-0, and provided with standard Caledonian fittings throughout. She provided a strikingly parallel case to that of 1862, when Neilsons obtained permission to build a Conner 8-ft single to exhibit as an example of their craftsmanship at the London Exhibition of that year. The difference lay only in the sequel, for as I have already told the exhibition engine of 1862 went to Egypt.

The exhibition engine of 1886 began her career in spectacular fashion. In the first place she was built in the short space of 66 days from the time the order was given to Hyde Park works. She was given a superb finish, and Neilsons were so proud of her that not only was she photographed from every angle, but all the managers and foremen concerned in her construction were photographed in front of her. Through the courtesy of the North British Locomotive Company I have had an opportunity of studying a large print of this latter picture. It presents a wonderful series of portraits of locomotive building men in their workaday clothes, and their earnest, serious faces could not epitomize more faithfully the expression, 'pride in the job'.

If Neilson's men were proud of her, the citizens of Edinburgh, or at least some of them, must have regarded her arrival in their midst with mixed feelings. There was no railway approach to the exhibition grounds. The nearest line of rails was a level crossing with the Lothian Road, and the method adopted was to bring her on the rails until she was athwart the roadway, and then to swing her gradually round until she was facing up the 1 in 20 gradient of the road, and then to tow her towards the exhibition ground supported on trolleys tunning on the horse-tram tracks. There was little railway publicity in those days, so just imagine the astonishment and thrill experienced by that great Edinburgh enthusiast of the day, Norman D. Macdonald when, one fine Sunday afternoon, he found this glittering new engine, of a design hitherto unknown in Scotland, completely athwart the Lothian Road! Her magnificent exhibition finish was not in the true Caledonian style, for gold leaf was used instead of the usual white lining, and she had a gilt cap to the chimney.

She was purchased by the Caledonian Railway after the exhibition, and soon proved she was no mere ornament. Indeed, by the summer of 1888 it is no exaggeration to say that she was the pride of the line, and was entrusted with the task of running the Edinburgh portion of the 10 a.m. West Coast express from Euston during the racing days in the late July and August of that year. That Drummond should have used her – a single-wheeler – in preference to the 6 ft 6 in. coupled engines he had designed specially for the Beattock Bank was a most significant point. I have discussed the technical details of her running during that exciting time very fully in *The Railway Race to the North*, but here I cannot refrain from emphasizing again that her fast overall times were regularly achieved not by any fast running downhill, as one might expect from a single-wheeler, but in the uphill work. The load of 105 tons that she conveyed throughout the race in relation to her own weight, and more significantly to her adhesion, was indeed no featherweight. For ready reference I have tabulated again the log of her fastest run from Carlisle to Edinburgh. (*See p. 92.*)

In 1889 a further batch of 6 ft 6 in. 4-4-0 express locomotives was turned out, and with four of these Drummond carried out an interesting series of experiments, described in a paper he read before the Institution of Civil Engineers in 1896. I have already mentioned that the boilers of these engines were designed to carry a pressure of 200 lb per sq in. In these trials, conducted on the 10.15 a.m.express from Edinburgh to Carlisle, and the 4.30 p.m. Carlisle to Edinburgh, two of the four engines had their safety valves set to blow off at 200 lb per sq in., while a third was set for 175. The fourth engine carried the normal working pressure of 150 lb per sq in. Apart from any discussion of the results obtained it is extremely interesting to study the testing methods that Drummond employed. Indicator diagrams were taken at a number of pre-arranged locations *en route*, the same for all four locomotives, and smokebox temperatures were taken at the same time. In addition to measurements of indicated horsepower the drawbar pull was measured. No dynamometer car was available, and so Drummond designed a dynamometer of his own, consisting of two hydraulic cylinders. The pressures registered in these cylinders were shown on a gauge mounted in the locomotive cab, and the readings were noted by an observer on the footplate.

In these days, when poor performance of steam locomotives is so frequently excused on the strength of poor coal, it is interesting that all these important trials of 1889 were conducted with coal described by Drummond himself as 'of very inferior quality; 50 per cent of that used would have passed through a ⅜-in. mesh riddle'. A coal strike was in progress at the time of the tests and no fresh coal was available; the tenders were loaded with coal that had been stacked for over 12 months. In consequence the evaporation of the engines on test was much lower than normal on the Caledonian Railway. Drummond had no hesitation in saying that 25 per cent of the coal fired went straight up the chimney without exaporating 1 lb of water per lb of coal. The normal Caledonian evaporation rates

9th August, 1888
C.R. 4.8 p.m. CARLISLE–EDINBURGH
Load: 4 bogie coaches, 80 tons
Engine: Drummond 4-2-2 No. 123

Dist. Miles		Actual m. s.	Speeds m.p.h.
0·0	CARLISLE . . .	0 00	—
4·1	Rockliffe . . .	5 35	62
8·6	Gretna Junc. . .	9 38	72
13·1	Kirkpatrick . .	14 07	57
—	*Brackenhill* . . .	—	54½
16·7	Kirtlebridge . .	17 46	65½
20·1	Ecclefechan . .	21 04	57
—	*Castlemilk* . . .	—	57
25·8	LOCKERBIE . .	26 46	64½
28·7	Nethercleugh . .	29 22	70
31·7	Dinwoodie . .	31 54	72
34·5	Wamphray . .	34 26	65/72
39·7	BEATTOCK . .	39 13	60
42·0	*Milepost 42* . .	41 44	52
44·0	,, 44 . .	44 20	43
46·0	,, 46 . .	47 17	39
48·0	,, 48 . .	50 23	38½
49·0	,, 49 . .	51 58	37½
49·7	*Beattock Summit* .	53 04	36½
52·6	Elvanfoot . .	56 05	70
55·3	Crawford . .	56 42	64
57·8	Abington . .	59 52	70/64
63·2	Lamington . .	65 35	71½
66·9	SYMINGTON .	69 04	62
68·5	Thankerton . .	70 29	73
70·0	*Leggatfoot* . .	71 45	65
72·0	*Milepost 72* . .	73 28	72
73·2	*Strawfrank Junc.* . .	74 44	slack
74·8	Carnwath . .	77 16	—
78·0	*Milepost 78* . .	80 51	64
79·1	Auchengray . .	81 55	61
80·0	*Milepost 80* . .	82 51	58½
81·0	,, *81* . .	83 54	56½
82·2	Cobbinshaw . .	85 13	54½
85·3	Harburn . .	88 16	74
89·3	*Midcalder Junc.* . .	91 45	60
95·1	Currie Hill . .	96 58	70
98·4	Slateford . .	99 58	60
100·0	*Milepost 100* . .	101 28	66
100·6	PRINCES STREET .	102 33	—

were then around 8 lb per lb of coal, and in these trials the figure fell to little over 6 lb. The locomotives all appear to have steamed freely enough; it was just that the firemen had to shovel about 30 per cent more than normal to get the same results, and this the worthy men did readily enough.

With the two locomotives carrying a boiler pressure of 200 lb per sq in., namely Nos. 76 and 79, a definite attempt seems to have been made to induce the drivers to work at short cut-offs, and engine No. 76 in particular was frequently linked up to less than 20 per cent. On the other hand the 150-lb engine, No. 78, afterwards famous as the regular engine of the great Tom Robinson of Kingmoor shed, Carlisle, was driven in the traditional Caledonian style of the day, with nothing less than 33 per cent cut-off, and relatively narrow openings of the regulator. The finest performance was put up by No. 79, one of the 200-lb engines, and a selection of her power outputs, together with the relevant speeds and footplate details are given in the accompanying table.

CALEDONIAN 4-4-0 LOCOMOTIVE No. 79

Speed m.p.h.	Regulator Opening	Cut-off per cent	Indicated Horsepower
51	Full	27	940
65½	Full	19	553
57½	Full	21	766
65	Full	22	770
37	Full	33	856
33¼	Full	33	806

The output of nearly 1,000 i.h.p. at 51 m.p.h. strikes one as remarkable from a locomotive of 1889 vintage, and of such relatively small proportions, but no less excellent are the two results tabulated at 37 and 33¼ m.p.h. during the ascent of Beattock Bank. The second 200-lb engine, No. 76, also did well, and in her corresponding power outputs in the same two locations were 830 and 781 i.h.p. The latter engine also produced the fastest running of the whole series of trials with a maximum speed at one point of 82 m.p.h. Engine No. 76 was worked at one stage in as short a cut-off as 13 per cent. As a result of this experience Drummond claimed, as Churchward demonstrated later, that there was no advantage to be derived from compounding, as 'five expansions' – as he termed it – could be obtained within a single cylinder.

Drummond concluded his paper to the Institution of Civil Engineers, describing the tests, with a strong advocacy of simple propulsion, against compound. He claimed that comparative tests which had purported to show the superiority of compounding had not been made on equal terms and were usually between simple and compound locomotives in which the boiler pressure of the compound was considerably higher. He stressed that in any such comparative tests the boiler pressure should be alike, again anticipating what Churchward actually did on the Great Western with the Atlantic engines *Albion* and *La France*. Drummond presented this paper some years after he had left the Caledonian Railway, and his concluding paragraph may therefore be regarded as retrospective so far as his former responsibilities were concerned at St Rollox. He had found a very real difficulty in getting the drivers to work expansively. Whether he would have had greater success in later years, had he stayed on we are not to know. We do know, however, that he waged his campaign with renewed vigour on the London & South Western Railway, which appointment he had taken not long before the presentation of his paper at the Institution of Civil Engineers.

He concluded the paper thus: 'Viewing the question of steam pressures broadly, the author has come to the conclusion that for the present, until drivers appreciate the value and take advantage of higher pressures for ordinary locomotive engines working main line traffic economically in all respects, the pressure should not be less nor more than 170 lb per sq in. Pressures of 200 lb per sq in. can, he believes, only be economically used with engines working heavy suburban passenger traffic whereby speed can be got up quickly when leaving stations. By this means a larger amount of traffic can be worked in a given time, than by engines with pressure of 140 lb per sq in., which is the average now used in working such trains.'

High pressures or not, Dugald Drummond had provided the Caledonian Railway with a stud of the fastest and most economical express engines running anywhere in the country, and which proved invaluable to the West Coast Route in the second great race to the north. Then, apart from the Caledonian, it was only the North Eastern that was attempting, without water troughs, non-stop runs of around 120 miles, and there is no comparison in running difficulties between the Newcastle–Edinburgh road, and that between Carlisle and Stirling. When the Caledonian essayed the run from Carlisle to Perth non-stop, 150 miles, with some hard going between Stirling and Crieff Junction, they were displaying an innate confidence in the Drummond 4-4-0 locomotives, both in their speed and in their economy; and when Driver Crooks and engine No. 90 made that long run at an average speed of 60 m.p.h., start to stop, it was a combined demonstration of superb enginemanship, and locomotive efficiency of the highest order of the day.

Drummond must have been one of the most highly prized locomotive engineers of the day. In October, 1884, he received a substantial increase in salary, and yet another in 1888. Then, in 1890, he received an offer of a most attractive position in Australia. The inducement must have been great for him to consider forsaking the high salary and tremendous prestige he enjoyed on the Caledonian, and the prospect of still greater things to come. But forsake it he did, and on 15th April, 1890, his letter of resignation was placed before the Board. The minute concerning this reads: 'Resolved that Mr Drummond's resignation be accepted, the Board at the same time desiring to express their great regret that the Company should thus lose the services of an officer of whose value they are very sensible, attested as it is by the admirable state of efficiency of the Locomotive Works and of the Rolling Stock under his charge. Mr Drummond carries with him the warm regard of the Directors and their sincere wishes for his future happiness and prosperity.'

His forthcoming resignation was evidently no surprise for at the same meeting applications for the vacant post were considered and Hugh Smellie, then Locomotive Superintendent of the G. & S.W.R., was appointed, at a salary, I may add, less than two-thirds of that Drummond was receiving. It is of interest to note that in the records of the appointment the new Locomotive Superintendent's name is spelt Smillie. From the moment of his resignation Drummond's good fortune deserted him. The Australian position fell through, and he was left without a job. He went into industrial management, but after five troubled years was glad enough to take the Locomotive Superintendency of the London & South Western, at a salary less than he was receiving from the Caledonian, in 1890. At St Rollox, Smellie died within a year, and was succeeded by John Lambie. Apart from a change to round-topped domes and the use of a neat closed-in safety valve mounting over the firebox he continued the Drummond traditions for another 5 years. In the years 1882–95 the Caledonian came into the very forefront of British locomotive practice. This epoch might have been merely the stepping stone to still greater things in a continuous line of development. As it was, the year 1895 proved the end of a chapter and the great things that followed sprang from a different line of development altogether.

IX

New Lines and New Stations

THE turn of the century approached with the Caledonian in fine fettle. The Clyde Coast services were geared up to the pitch of highest efficiency; the locomotive and traffic departments had won great renown in the Race to the North, in 1895, and it was only in respect of one large new undertaking that the results had been disappointing, namely the Glasgow Central Railway. The disappointment was, however, no more than relative, and on the personal side also it brought to Glasgow, and ultimately to the staff of the Caledonian Railway one of the most distinguished twentieth-century officers, Donald A. Matheson. Hitherto, after the struggles of the earliest days the only personalities that have come into this account have been those of the locomotive department, and before passing on to a description of the many fine new works put into commission from 1888 onwards it is time to say something of some of the other great men of the Caledonian Railway.

On the operating side there was that colourful and striking personality Irvine Kempt, whose drive for better services and higher speed was a constant stimulus to successive generations of locomotive engineers at St Rollox, and who was one of the principal architects of the resounding West Coast successes in the Race to the North in 1895. In his famous work on the railways of this country, written in 1893, J. Pearson Patterson singled out six lines that then stood out prominently from the rest through the excellence of the speed maintained by their principal expresses. It is interesting to find that of these six, two, the Caledonian and the Glasgow & South Western were Scottish. The four English railways in this select company were the Great Northern, the Midland, the North Western, and the Manchester, Sheffield & Lincolnshire. It is significant that all these lines operated under the stimulus of severe competition, and that the fastest running was not necessarily found on the railways with the easiest gradients. So far as Scotland was concerned the Glasgow & South Western was certainly giving the Caledonian a tremendous run for its money so far as the English traffic was concerned.

In the seventh chapter of this book reference was made to the traffic effects of the large engineering works in Glasgow, and in the extension from Greenock to Gourock. All these works were planned and carried through by George Graham, the veteran Engineer-in-Chief of the company. There are times when one is inclined to use the word 'veteran' in a relative sense, but Graham was a veritable patriarch. His associations with Caledonian affairs went back to the very first surveys in his native Annandale, yet it was only by a personal misfortune that he happened to be there at all when Joseph Locke was in the neighbourhood in 1845. As a youth Graham had been apprenticed to Robert Napier, the famous marine engineer, in Glasgow; but he had a breakdown in health, and he returned to Annandale to recuperate. Reasonably fit once more he secured a job on Joseph Locke's staff. His ability soon made its mark, and on 10th September, 1847, it fell to him to start the first passenger train ever to run on the Caledonian Railway. Six years later, when the triple task of General Manager, Locomotive Superintendent, and Civil Engineer was proving too great for Robert Sinclair, and he had to be relieved of at least some of his duties, George Graham was appointed Engineer-in-Chief, and he held that office from 1853 till his death in 1899.

At the time of the Caledonian Railway Jubilee, in 1897, a celebration dinner of the engineering department staff was held in Glasgow, not only in honour of the railway itself, but of the career of their own chief, and of the historic event in which he had played so prominent a part. At that dinner Graham was presented with a silver commemoration cup and two companion vases, each bearing the following inscription:

'Presented to George Graham Esq., M.I.C.E., by the staff of the Engineering Department of the Caledonian Railway company, as a mark of esteem, and to celebrate the jubilee of the occasion of his starting the first passenger train run on the Caledonian Railway on September 10th, 1847. Glasgow, September 10th, 1897.' At that time Graham was still in office, but he died 2 years later.

One of the least openly spectacular works that he planned and carried through was the Glasgow Central Railway, authorized in 1888, and vested in the Caledonian Railway Company in the following year. Its construction was to a large extent prompted by the success of the underground lines of the Metropolitan, and of the Metropolitan District Railways in Central London, though the Caledonian had additionally in mind the need for a direct freight connection between the heavily industrialized area south-east of Glasgow, so well served by the main line to the south and its numer-

ous colliery and other branches, and its canal and dock properties
lying west of Glasgow on the north bank of the Clyde. Quite apart
from any use as a freight line, the popularity of the new Central
station in Glasgow was already proving something of an embarrassment, and it was hoped that the underground line would provide a
relief for some of the shorter distance traffic.

The Glasgow Central Railway makes a triangle junction with the
main line to the south at Rutherglen, and then running north crosses
the Clyde before turning westwards and going underground at
Dalmarnock. Thence, passing under some of the busiest streets of
the city it has stations at Bridgeton Cross, Glasgow Green, Glasgow
Cross, and Glasgow Central where the underground station is
immediately below the main line terminus. Then comes Anderston
Cross, and then at Stobcross the line forks, with the left-hand connection being that of the Lanarkshire & Dunbartonshire line. The Glasgow Central proper turns rightwards to serve Kelvingrove, Botanic
Gardens, and the northern suburbs. The possibilities for local passenger work, and for through freight connections were enormous, and
it is not surprising that the Caledonian hoped for rich rewards. On
the streets above all traffic, including the trams, was horse-drawn,
and with the rapid growth of the city and its industries progress on
the streets was both slow and congested.

It was realized at the outset that engineering work of an exceptional
and specialized nature would be involved. It was not only a case of
underpinning the closely-packed houses that lined the highways of
Trongate and Argyll Street, but that the proposed line of the tunnel
was near enough to the north bank of the Clyde for the sandy ground
to be affected by the rise and fall of the tide. It was a task greater than
anything the railway company's own engineering staff could be
expected to tackle without specialized assistance, and accordingly
Mr, afterwards Sir, John Wolfe Barry was appointed as consulting
engineer. Wolfe Barry had already had much experience with underground railways in London. The contract for the work was let to
Messrs Forman & McCall, probably better known as the constructors
of the West Highland Railway.

It was a time of much expansionist activity on the Caledonian
Railway, and all available staff of the engineering department were
fully engaged. Despite the employment of a consultant, and contractors of such proved ability, it was of course essential to have on
works of such magnitude a resident engineer, representing the
Engineer-in-Chief of the Caledonian Railway, and to this important
post Donald Matheson was appointed. A Perthshire man by birth,

Matheson, still young, had already acquired a variety of experience as a civil engineer before he joined the Caledonian in this special capacity. That previous experience included some service on the London & North Western Railway. He certainly had a task of the utmost importance in watching over the construction of the Glasgow underground line. Buildings in their hundreds had to be underpinned; the tunnels crossed the tracks of the foul and primitive sewerage system of Glasgow, and in more than one place the route took the engineers through quicksands.

Except in some of the outlying districts where ordinary tunnelling methods could be followed and a simple arch construction used, the line for the most part ran at such a shallow depth below street level that a special form of construction had to be adopted. Work commenced from street level with the driving of sheet piling down on either side of the roadway. Everything had to be done with a minimum of interference to traffic, and a gantry pile-driver was used that straddled the roadway. Inside the piling thus driven the earth was excavated, and in the cavities thus created were built the tunnel walls. The roadway was then taken up, piece by piece, and replaced by a temporary timber staging to carry the road traffic, and support the tram lines. Beneath the timber work the ground was excavated, and the large cross-girders of the tunnel roof could be manoeuvred into position. All in all it was a tremendous task. The distance from Dalmarnock to Stobcross is less than 4 miles, and although work was commenced in June, 1890, it was not until August, 1896, that the line was opened for traffic throughout.

In the meantime Donald Matheson, the Resident Engineer, had by his care and vigilance over this difficult work so impressed all concerned that on the death of George Graham, only 3 years after the completion of the underground line he was selected to fill the post of Engineer-in-Chief to the company. Eleven years later he succeeded Guy Calthrop as General Manager. His experience in the construction of the underground was to prove invaluable in the early years of this century when the great enlargement and reconstruction of Glasgow Central station involved some highly intricate underpinning and foundation work in ground lying between the underground railway and the River Clyde. Before coming to this work, reference must be made to some interesting new lines in rather more salubrious districts.

The construction of the West Highland Railway from Craigendoran to Fort William put all railways serving the west coast on their mettle, and in 1897 the Caledonian obtained Parliamentary sanction to improve the steamer berthing facilities at Oban, and to construct a single line branch running northwards from Connel Ferry through the Appin country to Ballachulish. There may have been undisclosed intentions to bridge the narrow entrance to Loch Leven and continue northwards to Fort William at some future time. For the moment, however, Ballachulish was the goal, and attempts were intended to be made to build a tourist traffic including combined rail and coach tours through Glencoe. It must be admitted that the cost of the line proved out of all proportion to the traffic immediately offering; for while the Appin country was full of historical and romantic interest at the turn of the century it was little more than a remote, depopulated, stretch of West Highland wilderness. Though not presenting perhaps the difficulties to a railway engineer that were encountered later in the extension of the West Highland line from Fort William to Mallaig, it was mighty hard and expensive going for all that.

On the Ballachulish line two major engineering works were called for, the crossing of Loch Etive at Connel Ferry where this beautiful inlet of the sea narrows to a width of about 500 ft before it debouches into the Firth of Lorne, and in crossing Loch Creagan. The latter involved a viaduct of two spans of 150 ft each, with a central pier in the waterway. The main spans are of the N-girder type, but the piers, and the single-arch approach spans are massively and picturesquely built in granite, harmonizing very happily with the wild and rocky hills that rise on either side of the loch. The viaduct is a narrow one carrying no more than a single line of rails. At Connel Ferry things were different, and from ancient times the way from Fort William to Oban had included the crossing of Loch Etive by a primitive ferry boat. Although rowed by hand the boat was large enough to convey carriages, and the ferrymen were always ready to rig up supports to carry a motor car if required.

The ferry traffic had been duly noted by the Caledonian Railway, and to obviate the delays and risks of a crossing by such primitive means the proposal was made that the new railway bridge at this point should be made wide enough to carry both railway and road. The tolls derived from road traffic would help to pay for the cost of the bridge. The viaduct built for this purpose is one of the most striking to be seen anywhere on the railways of Britain. It is built on the cantilever principle with the uprights of the two cantilevers inclined vertically towards the centre of the bridge. The clear span is 500 ft and the height of the roadway 50 ft above high water mark. Although the railway was opened for traffic in August, 1903, a dispute arose between the Caledonian Railway and the local authority as to the method of charging tolls for road traffic, and because of this it was some years before road users were able to make use of this excellent facility.

Then there was a time when cars and other road vehicles were required to be run on to flat trucks, and hauled across by a motor tractor with wheels adapted to run on rails. It was not until some considerable time after the bridge had been in service that the seem- ingly obvious course was adopted, of making the track across the bridge suitable for road vehicles to be driven across under their own power. Owing to the restricted width it was necessary to confine road traffic to such times as when no train was signalled. The gates pro- vided at each end were interlocked with the signalling in a similar way to the safe-guarding of ordinary level crossings.

Before the Ballachulish line was completed another section of the Caledonian Railway in the Highlands had been brought into use. This was the first section of the connecting link between Comrie and the Callander & Oban line, at Balquhidder. As far as St Fillans, to which the line was opened on 1st October, 1901, the going was not so tough from an engineering constructional viewpoint as in the wilder and more remote parts of the Highlands, but even so some substantial works were needed. At the beginning of this century the districts around Crieff, Comrie and St Fillans were rapidly becoming one of the most fashionable parts of the Highlands – indeed some advertisements apostrophied Crieff as 'The Montpelier of Scotland'! In any case, on this new railway every care was taken to build stations in the best possible taste, and in several places trees were planted to screen the railway from view. At St Fillans, one of the most delightful of Highland villages, the carrying of the railway through a short tunnel was much appreciated as preserving the amenities of the district. As on all contemporary extensions of the Caledonian Railway the masonry work put into the viaducts was extremely fine.

The continuation of the line along the northern shores of Loch Earn provided a picturesque journey and a pleasant foretaste of the grander scenery to be enjoyed if the trip was being continued west- ward from Balquhidder to Oban. At Lochearnhead the line curves round on a graceful viaduct as the foot of Glen Ogle is crossed, and then comes a stiff climb southwards up the hillside to join the Callander & Oban line, running in the direction of Callander. This line was completed in 1905, and from that time some of the through trains from Glasgow to Crieff were extended to Balquhidder. These trains left the Aberdeen main line at Gleneagles, or Crieff Junction as it was then known, but some local trains to Balquhidder came from Perth, and others from Dundee West. It must be admitted that this route never attained any real popularity as a tourist line, and the majority of the trains were of light formation and of a purely local character.

This chapter, which chronicles a collection of important new works on various parts of the line, is bound to involve some rapid changes of scene, though the great projects taken collectively give an impressive picture of the way in which traffic facilities were being improved over the line as a whole; and if it is recalled that all this civil engineering activity was in progress while the 'Dunalastair' locomotives were achieving unparalleled fame for the express trains it will be well imagined how much the Caledonian Railway and its affairs were in the news at the end of the Victorian era. So then, our next move is from the Highlands to Edinburgh where work on the new Princes Street station was commenced in 1890. If the earlier Caledonian stations in Glasgow were cramped, inadequate and inconveniently situated the Edinburgh terminus was a disgrace, though the reasons for its long continued existence were, to put it mildly, a little complicated.

The original headquarters of the Caledonian Railway was in Edinburgh, and after the fashion of the earlier railways plans were drawn up for a grand terminal station in the Scottish capital city that would completely eclipse, in sheer splendour, the London terminus of their English allies. On 9th April, 1847, the foundation stone was laid with full Masonic honours, by the Grand Lodge of Scotland. The Duke of Atholl, who was then Grand Master Mason officiated, assisted by other officers of the Grand Lodge, in the presence of the Lord Provost and magistrates of the city of Edinburgh and the directors of the Caledonian Railway. The proceedings were concluded by a speech from J. J. Hope-Johnstone, in his most flowing style, saying that the new station would be on a scale of magnificence appropriate to the city of Edinburgh. The station had been designed by one of the leading architects of the day, Tite, who had designed the Royal Exchange in London, and Princes Street station was apparently to have had a classical façade some 370 ft in length.

Unfortunately, that foundation stone, laid with so much ceremony and speech-making, was the only thing that did get laid. Nothing further had been done when the line was opened in February, 1848, and in the financial crises that followed it was unlikely that £100,000 would be forthcoming for a grand terminal station. Instead, the Scottish capital had to be content, so far as the Caledonian Railway was concerned, with a wooden shanty 180 ft long and 54 ft wide at the south-western extremity of the city, in the Lothian Road. For 22 years this glorified shack did duty, and then in May, 1870, the line was extended a short distance to reach the western end of Princes Street, and another temporary structure was erected, this time much larger and more commodious from the traffic point of view but still little removed in appearance from a wooden shanty. Due to the angle at which the railway approached these important thoroughfares the station, in plan, was of parallelogram shape, 500 ft long and 100 ft broad. It was in these unpretentious surroundings that the great runs of the 4-2-2 single No. 123 in the race of 1888 terminated.

Part of this station was destroyed by fire in 1890, but by that time the Caledonian management was sweeping away all traces of its past vicissitudes, and the contracts had been let for a really fine new station. Once again the limitations of space between the three main roads that flank the railway property might have been a serious handicap, but the design was worked out to give a most imposing exterior and a spacious layout inside. In plan the site tapers to a very narrow wedge facing Princes Street, and inside the fine entry arch the platforms are set some way back so as to provide for a large circulating area and a wide cab road. Structurally, there is a fine bayed roof, 850 ft long, springing from the stone walls that enclose the station on either side, while from the operating viewpoint there are seven platforms, varying in length from 460 ft to 800 ft in length. Although not all the work was then complete the station in its enlarged and final form was in use by the year 1893. The Caledonian Hotel, which was built over the station entrance was added later.

Around Edinburgh the end of the nineteenth century found the Caledonian with a number of branch lines, though not constituting a serious competitor with the North British for the local traffic. There were two connections with the main line of the North British near Haymarket: via Haymarket West Junction and Dalry Junction trains ran direct from Larbert and Falkirk into Princes Street, while Caledonian trains from the Carlisle direction taking the leftward fork at Slateford Junction could run direct to Haymarket and Waverley. This spur line was used on at least one memorable occasion during the severe winter of 1946–7 to run the 'Flying Scotsman' to the south via Carstairs, when both the East Coast and the Waverley routes were blocked with snow drifts. From this same spur, at Granton Junction, branches the line to Leith, and the short branch to Granton and the Western Breakwater. This gave the Caledonian access to the ferry across the Firth of Forth, by which traffic was conveyed to Burntisland, before the construction of the Forth Bridge.

Although not a new line in the period now under review the Solway Junction Railway was one in which the Caledonian had been interested, from its inception in 1870, and in 1895 they took over absolute control and responsibility. As early as the 'sixties' of last century there were proposals for by-passing the traffic congestion of Carlisle, and proposals were made for a line running almost due north and south, connecting the Caledonian at Kirtlebridge with the Maryport & Carlisle at Brayton. There was more in it than a mere by-pass. A first class traffic was waiting to be picked up in the iron-ore from Cumberland that was needed by the ironworks in Lanarkshire. Although no more than $21\frac{1}{4}$ miles long it was a complex affair, crossing the Solway Firth on a viaduct second only in length to the Forth Bridge. On the English side it made a junction with the Silloth branch of the North British Railway at Kirkbride Junction, exercised running powers for $3\frac{3}{4}$ miles over this line, and then continued on its own metals for a final 5 miles from Abbey Junction to Brayton Junction where it joined the Maryport & Carlisle Railway.

The traffic in iron-ore flourished for a time, but the disposition of the steelworks to import increasing amounts of ore from abroad, and the working out of the mines in Cumberland brought the inevitable decline. The Solway viaduct was always a cause of anxiety, for although it was strongly built the waters of the Solway Firth, which might be imagined as placid and sheltered, are in fact, treacherous. At times the tide runs very strongly, and in wild and severe winters the rivers debouching into the Firth are often in spate, and add to the stresses to which the bridge was subjected. In one particular winter, when a period of intense frost was experienced, ice floes from the river set up such a bombardment of the piers of the bridge that some collapsed, and no fewer than thirty-seven girders collapsed. Fortunately no train was involved, though this misfortune, in 1881, caused the suspension of through traffic for more than 3 years. It was from this time that the decline in traffic set in, though even before the Grouping, in 1923, the Caledonian had ceased to run a through passenger service between Kirtlebridge and Brayton.

While on the Solway Firth reference must also be made to the Portpatrick & Wigtownshire Joint line, which from 1885 was worked under the joint ownership of the London & North Western, the Midland, the Caledonian, and the Glasgow & South Western. The joint line began at Castle Douglas and ran through Newton Stewart to Stranraer and Portpatrick, with a branch from Newton Stewart to Whithorn. The Irish boat expresses of the Glasgow & South Western from Glasgow and Ayr used a short length of this joint line between Challoch Junction, near Dunragit, and Stranraer. In pre-Grouping days most of the traffic on the joint line was worked by Glasgow & South Western engines and stock, though an interesting through carriage service was operated between Whithorn and Edinburgh Princes Street. The Caledonian coaches used were worked over the eastward continuation of the line – purely G.S.W.R. – from Castle Douglas to Dumfries, and thence over the Caledonian branch to Lockerbie.

It is of interest to recall that the Portpatrick & Wigtownshire line originally began as a most grandiose project, as part of a proposal for a new fast route to Ireland. The first title was, indeed, the 'British & Irish Grand Junction Railway.' It was proposed that Portpatrick should be the packet station on the Scottish side and Donaghadee on the Irish. The Government mail packets crossed the channel regularly by this route, and despite the rather primitive facilities on either shore there was a brisk trade in livestock. This project, incorporating railway service on both sides of the North Channel was never to materialize; the channel crossing eventually took a somewhat different form, and it was only as a result of substantial advances from other railways that funds were raised to build the line through Galloway. The North Western, the Caledonian, and the G. & S.W.R. contributed from the start; the Midland came in later.

Reference to joint lines leads us naturally on to joint stations. Carlisle and Aberdeen have been mentioned earlier in this book; the situation at Perth was in many ways the most complicated of all. It was in 1863 that the Perth General Station Joint Committee was set up, and although the Caledonian amalgamations of 1865 and 1866 reduced the number of companies involved there remained three right down to the time of the Grouping. While the approach lines from both north and south are Caledonian, the ownership of the station itself was shared with the Highland and the North British. From an early date in the history of Scottish railways Perth occupied a special place in connection with Queen Victoria's journeys to and from Balmoral. On the northward journey the Royal train stopped for the Queen and her entourage to take breakfast, and for these auspicious occasions, apartments were set aside in the adjoining station hotel. It was probably this Royal patronage that caused Perth station to be one of the first on the Caledonian Railway to be modernized.

From an early date much of the express passenger traffic dealt with at Perth involved marshalling and remarshalling of long and heavy trains. Expresses from the Highland Railway had separate sections for the East Coast, Midland, and West Coast route into England. Trains for Glasgow often had portions from Dundee and Aberdeen, to be combined, and in the modernization of the layout opportunity was taken to provide very long main line platforms on each side of the central 'island'. The down main platform is 1,415 ft long, while that on the corresponding up side is 1,672 ft long. Scissors crossings are provided at the middle of each platform road, so that two trains or two portions to be combined in one train can be worked from the same platform. The convenience of having all the station offices on the one central island platform is much appreciated, and it is only the Dundee traffic that is not handled under the main roof.

X

Twentieth-Century Splendour

THE zenith of Caledonian Railway express speed achievements had definitely passed with the end of the summer service of 1896. The great Race of the previous year had left some remarkable timings on the down night expresses which were maintained with the utmost regularity by the 'Dunalastair' engines. I am not going to add that they were maintained with ease, for the down 'Tourist' express involved some very hard running. The derailment of this train, however, in most alarming circumstances at Preston, had repercussions on railways all over Great Britain, and from competition in sheer speed the emphasis changed to a competition of travel and luxury of passenger accommodation. The austerely-minded J. F. McIntosh, who had once pooh-poohed the suggestion of armrests in third class carriages, found himself designing some of the most luxurious bogie corridor stock ever to run on the British railways in pre-Grouping days.

On the Caledonian in particular the new century ushered in an age of splendour, and an account of this beautiful, colourful period may well be commenced with some notes on the new carriages. On the services to England the West Coast Joint Stock was used, and this was all of London & North Western design and construction. The Caledonian also used white upper panels, but the bodies were of a rich purple-lake, several shades lighter, and with much more red in it than the body colour of the North Western and West Coast Joint carriages. The purely Caledonian coaches were frequently used in strengthening the regular West Coast sets at times of heavy traffic, and so they were frequently seen in England, but to see the Caledonian stock at its grandest one had to travel on the highly competitive services, such as the Glasgow–Aberdeen, Glasgow–Edinburgh and the Clyde Coast 'flyers'. The new coaches, introduced from 1905 onwards, were known by the generic title of 'Grampian' stock, from the name given to the 10 a.m. express from Glasgow to Aberdeen, but there were variations to suit the requirements of other services.

The stock designed specially for the trains in hottest competition

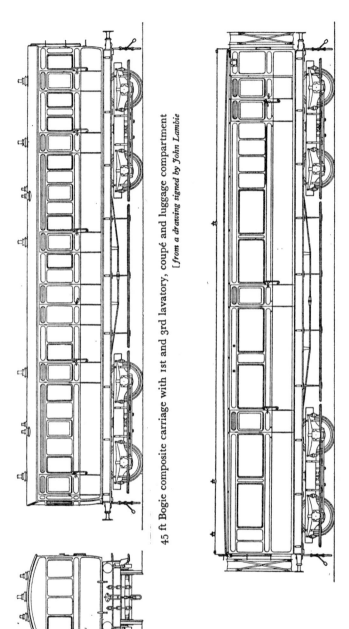

45 ft Bogie composite carriage with 1st and 3rd lavatory, coupé and luggage compartment

[from a drawing signed by John Lambie

50 ft Corridor brake composite carriage (pre-Grampian style)

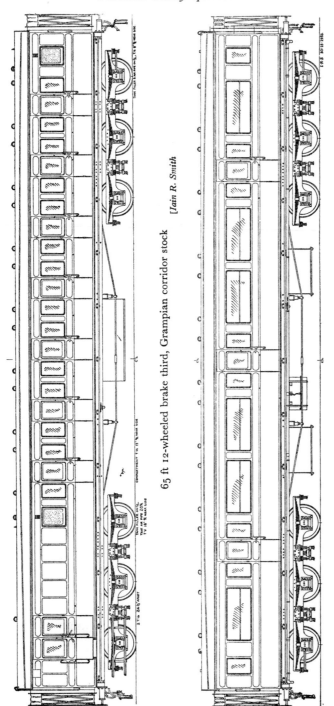

65 ft 12-wheeled brake third, Grampian corridor stock

[*Iain R. Smith*

65 ft 12-wheeled, corridor third, Grampian stock

[*Iain R. Smith*

with the North British was all twelve-wheeled, and measured no less than 68½ ft over the buffers. They were among the very first coaches in Britain to be built to the utmost width and height permitted by the loading gauge, and to have a high curved roof. Until then the largest and most luxurious coaches on the Anglo-Scottish trains had clerestory roofs, and it was only on the Great Western that the high curved roof had begun to appear. Quite apart from the furnishings these new Caledonian coaches gave an air of spaciousness that was indeed novel to those who had been accustomed to travel in the old flat-roofed straight-sided stock of later Victorian times. It was on the trial trip on 6th April, 1905, that J. F. McIntosh suggested the name of 'Grampian Express', though as turned out from St Rollox works the new coaches were permanently lettered, just above the windows: 'Corridor Express – Glasgow, Perth and Aberdeen' or 'Corridor Express – Edinburgh, Perth and Aberdeen' according to the section of the train.

It is not surprising that the vast length and elegant appearance of these coaches caused something of a sensation in Scotland. The standard Caledonian colour schemes had never been shown off to better advantage. The magnificent coat-of-arms was displayed twice on each side of each carriage, and the distinctive lettering was rendered in bold gilt capitals. Add to this the spotless white roofs, the red wheel-centres, and one of the famous blue engines at the head of the train and one had an ensemble to take the eye of the dullest and most unimaginative of travellers. As introduced to the public, on 10th April, 1905 the train included four coaches from Glasgow to Aberdeen, and two from Edinburgh. The two sections were combined at Perth.

The third class accommodation was sumptuous, yet it is strange to recall that this was the first British stock to provide four seats a side in any side-corridor carriages. Very careful attention was paid to the springing and the upholstering of the seats, while the colour scheme was in peacock blue, with ceilings covered in Lincrusta panelling to give a rococo effect. A number of 'gadgets' were introduced, such as a recently patented device for keeping the window blinds fixed in any desired position, automatic draught excluders, and an arrangement for drawing moisture away from the window panes without running down the coat sleeve of the passenger in the corner. Whether any of these 'gimmicks' were really successful is another matter, but their inclusion is enough to show how much attention was being given to the comfort of the third-class 'penny-a-miler' passenger of those days.

The first class compartments, seating three a side, were proportionately more luxurious, but particular interest concerns the engineering details of the train: in the elaborate springing of the six-wheeled bogies, the measures taken to reduce noise in running, the novelty of hot water as well as cold in the lavatory basins, floor racks for bicycles in the guard's vans, and the provision of a safe locker for consignments of special value. As an insulation against noise a special hair felt-layer was included in the carriage construction, under the floors, in the side walls, and along the roof. Similar coaches were introduced on to the Clyde Coast services, including corridors, but in addition, some twelve-wheeled non-corridor 'Grampian' stock was built for other duties, including the highly competitive inter-city service between Edinburgh and Glasgow. The very long twelve-wheelers were naturally found to have a somewhat limited application, and some similar eight-wheeled vehicles were built at a later date. Two of the latter have recently been restored to their original condition and are now used on certain special trains in the Scottish Region.

Although the locomotives are discussed more fully in the next chapter one cannot take the story of the Caledonian into the twentieth century without reference to some of the tasks performed by the 'Dunalastairs'. These engines were based upon the highly successful Drummond 4-4-0s of 1887, but with very much larger boilers, and some of the work they did was amazing. Their introduction enabled the Caledonian Railway to be the first company in Great Britain ever to have a 60-m.p.h. start-to-stop run published in *Bradshaw*. This was from Forfar to Perth with the up West Coast Postal express, 32½ miles in 32 minutes. From the locomotive point of view, this was an easy run compared with that of the down Tourist express in 1896, when that train was scheduled to run the 117¾ miles from Carlisle to Stirling, over Beattock summit, in 125 minutes. The 'Dunalastairs' took loads of up to 200 tons on this train, and with such a tonnage no driver ever dreamed of stopping at Beattock for rear-end banking assistance. On one memorable occasion, with engine No. 728, driven by Tom Robinson who did such magnificent work in the 1895 race with the Drummond engine No. 78, the train reached Stirling on time despite 12 *minutes* lost by delays from a Royal 'horse and carriage' train.

The net time of 113 minutes on this journey represents a phenomenal piece of work when the size of the engine is considered; but although exceptional it exemplifies the spirit of the Caledonian at that time, when nothing was too great, or too arduous for its men to undertake, those men were the rank and file or the highest executive officers. The engineering staff of the Caledonian never had a greater task than in the rebuilding and enlargement of Glasgow Central station, as referred to briefly in the chapter dealing with the Clyde Coast services. The music hall joke of Scottish parsimony recoils like a boomerang upon its persistent perpetrators when one regards some of the larger Caledonian stations. While the North Western, for all its wealth, was content to add bits and pieces to historic, grimy, and inconvenient Euston, while the Midland sat smug in its primeval headquarters at Derby, and the Great Northern struggled in its narrow confines at Kings Cross, the Board of the Caledonian took an altogether broader view and gave their engineer-in-chief authority to rebuild Glasgow Central on a scale fully comparable with the grandiose projects now incorporated in the British Railways Modernization Plan. The result was the finest station in Great Britain, both from the passenger and the operating point of view; and in the years that followed this great work only Waterloo has seriously challenged its supremacy.

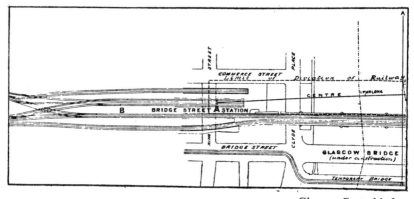

Glasgow Central before

The need for expansion can be readily appreciated from the following figures of trains and passengers handled at the 'Central' since its first opening.

Year	Number of trains daily	Passengers using the station per annum (millions)
1880	173	$4\frac{3}{4}$
1888	300	$9\frac{1}{4}$
1893	374	$13\frac{1}{2}$
1897	486	$15\frac{3}{4}$

The above figures do not include traffic handled at Glasgow Central low-level underground station. The decision to enlarge was taken when the passenger figure had just reached the 16 million mark, and Parliamentary sanction for the very heavy work involved was obtained in 1899. In view of the complexity of the engineering and the temporary work involved in the successive stages it is remarkable to record that *before* the work was finished the number of trains dealt with per day had still further increased, to 512, a wonderful feat of operation.

Glasgow Central station, in 1899, was completely encompassed on all sides, by three main streets – Gordon Street to the north, Hope Street to the west, Union Street to the east – and by the River Clyde to the south; before reaching the river bank the railway had to cross another thoroughfare in Argyll Street. Encompassed or not, there were to be no half measures about the enlargement, no hole-in-corner methods, adding bits here and bits there. The accommodation for both passengers and trains *was to be doubled*. It was typical of the magnificent spaciousness of Caledonian policy at the time not only

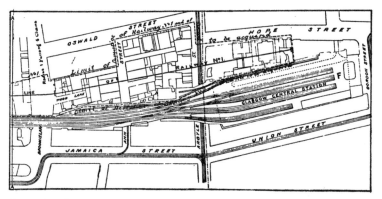

the great enlargement.

to double the length of platform faces at which trains could be berthed, but to double the area of the concourse leading to the platforms, so as to make things easier and much more pleasant for passengers passing to the trains. The question was, how *could* it be done? Encroachment upon streets to west, north and east of the company's property was out of the question; the only outlet was towards the river.

The great lengthening of the platforms that was envisaged would make access to the original four-track bridge impossible, and in any case line-occupation over the bridge itself was approaching saturation

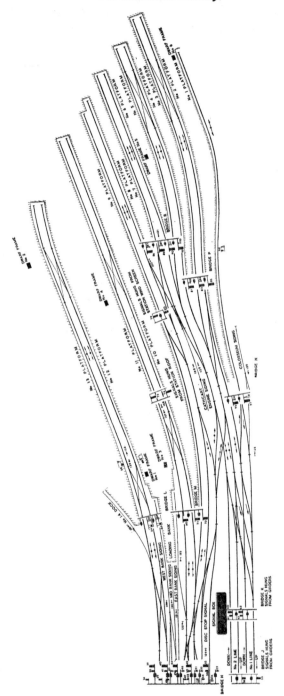

Glasgow Central as completed and newly signalled, 1908.

point. Once again there was no cheese-paring in the way this need was met. It was not enough to double the track capacity across the Clyde, it must be *trebled,* and the scheme included the construction of a fine new viaduct that would accommodate no fewer than nine tracks abreast. Finally, although lavish provision was thus to be made for increased capacity in every way the operating authorities took no risks of letting the train working sprawl haphazardly over all the increased space available. A great increase in business was hoped for, and plans were made for signalling the new layout on the most up-to-date methods known at that time. All concerned had the intense gratification of seeing the passenger figures jump from just over 16 million to nearly 20 million in a year from the completion of the scheme.

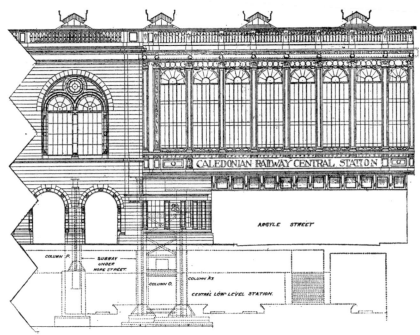

Glasgow Central station at the crossing of Argyll Street.

The broad conception of the station rebuilding scheme is similar to the new layout at Edinburgh Princes Street, but on a much larger scale. The general line of the concourse is set athwart rather than square with the line of the railway itself, thus bringing the main line departure platforms nearest to the Gordon Street entrance. The suburban, and shorter-distance passenger platforms are in the centre, and the very long main line arrival platforms on the western side, from which the cab roads lead out into Hope Street. The Clyde Coast trains are dealt with on the extreme western side, whence they can take the most westerly of the tracks across the river and branch off at Bridge Street Junction without interfering with any other traffic. The main line departure platforms were made 900 ft long, while the two main line arrival platforms were 700 and 800 ft long respectively with no less than 70 ft between platform faces to provide the 30 ft wide cab rank. The accompanying sketch map shows how cleverly the varying requirements of platform lengths were provided. The lengthening of the platforms was made possible only by the complete reconstruction of the bridge over Argyll Street. In so doing, the foundations had been carried down to a depth of 45 ft below street level, in order to be below the disturbing effects of the drainage system of the underground line.

The new viaduct over the Clyde was a very massive structure of five spans, the three over the river itself being 160, 200 and 178 ft respectively. Two of the piers had to be sunk in the river, and these are supported on caissons sunk to a depth of 50 ft in one case and 66 ft in the other, below high water mark. The great pillars are lintelled in order to provide a bearing for the main girders, above which a handsome upward extension was built in each case. On these extension pillars were supported some of the large signal gantries spanning all the tracks on the bridge, while at the present time these are being used for supporting the overhead wires for the electrification now in progress. The bridge was 110 ft wide, and because of this all the main girders had to be beneath the flooring. So as not to encroach upon the permissible headroom required for navigation the rail level over the new bridge became some 3 ft higher at the station end than that of the original bridge. This of course would have led to many difficulties, and so an incidental feature of the rebuilding work was the raising of the level of the old bridge to correspond with that of the new. All in all, the station rebuilding, and the remodelling of the approach lines was a colossal task of which the photographs reproduced between pp. 120 and 121 give a vivid impression. That it was completed in a little under 6 years is a resounding tribute to the engineer-in-chief and his staff; and during this time of upheaval the traffic in the station continued to increase!

Traffic working during this transition period can have been kept going, on an increasing scale, only by a masterpiece of organization, and it is significant that from 1902 onwards the post of General

Superintendent had been held by Guy Calthrop. Trained on the North Western under Findlay and Harrison, the new Superintendent of the Caledonian was no more than 32 years of age when he recieved the appointment, and he very quickly applied himself to the particular problems of Scottish operating. No very novel, or exceptionally fast passenger train services were introduced in the early years of the century, but emphasis was laid on the development of the express parcels traffic. Calthrop himself attributed much of the growth of this business to the increasing availability of telephones. Tradespeople in the vicinity of large towns were tending to keep smaller stocks, to purchase oftener, at short notice and in small quantities, and he organized the Parcels Department of the Caledonian to give quick, reliable deliveries, sending the many small consignments by regular passenger trains. Such was the traffic at Glasgow Central that it was quite usual for more than fifty lorries to leave before 9 a.m. laden with goods for all parts of the city.

The first decade of the twentieth century saw the business of the Caledonian Railway expanding in every direction. And it was a gracious expansion. Here was no sprawling, uncontrolled commercialized growth, but a careful process of evolution. Floral displays were not confined to the spare-time efforts of country station men, or to a delightful coastal terminus like Wemyss Bay. Stirling was gay with baskets of geraniums hanging from the awnings; the concourse at Oban was a delight, and at Strathyre there was that exquisite figure of a heron, carved in granite from Ben Cruachan. The advertising was beautifully and tastefully done, by the posters on the stations, and just as today the French railways stress the 'exactitude' of their train running, so the Caledonian was bold enough to put this claim on to their hoardings: 'Punctuality is the courtesy of Kings. It marks the line that leads to England.'

A piece of Caledonian publicity such as to delight the hearts of all railway enthusiasts was the distribution in magazines, circulating libraries and such like, of some 3 million copies of the famous 'Bonnie Scotland' bookmarker in full colour, showing a view of Loch Katrine, a view of the 'Grampian Express' passing Stonehaven and – a flagrantly competitive touch! – Alloway Kirk, Ayr. It was not only the obverse side that was so attractive. On the reverse was a gradient profile of the line from Carlisle to Glasgow, a table to show the speed of trains, and the method of calculating them and details of the longest and fastest runs on the system. As *The Railway Magazine* commented at the time this bookmarker was issued: 'This information cannot fail to be an excellent advertisement. The traveller will naturally be interested to know at what speed the heavy train will ascend the formidable Beattock Bank, and by means of the speed table and his watch he will be able to find this out during the ascent. So powerful are the Caledonian Railway's locomotives, that passengers cannot fail to be impressed by the feat performed, and to talk about it to their friends when relating incidents connected with the journey.'

Signalling practice on the Caledonian had a number of features that were distinctive, if not to be termed unique. The semaphore arms had a spectacle that had an adjustable attachment to the hub casting, so that it could be moved to a certain extent inwards or outwards if it were necessary to sight a particular signal to a location on a curve. Like the older semaphores of the Great Western the arms moved through an angle of 60 degrees. The details of the posts and other items were derived from the practice of one of the oldest signalling manufacturing firms, Stevens & Sons, who had a works in Glasgow in addition to the famous 'Darlington Works' in Southwark Bridge Road, London. The Caledonian did not, however, use the very distinctive Stevens shape of spectacle glass, which was standard on the North British down to the time of the Grouping, and was to be seen in large quantities on the London, Chatham & Dover Railway. Evidence that the Caledonian did not skimp things in any direction was also provided by the signalboxes. While some of the largest and wealthiest English railways provided little better than wooden shacks to house many of their smaller locking frames, the massive brick cabins of the Caledonian, with their great overhanging eaves, looked as though they had been built to withstand a siege!

On the long stretches of single line on the Callander & Oban Railway an interesting practice was in use for many years to economize in the manning of the boxes. During the night there was no traffic at all, yet in the ordinary way the boxes would all have had to be manned to signal through the early morning mail train. This would have been the only job the night shift signalmen would have to do, and the following arrangement was adopted to avoid having any men on the night shift at all. After the last train in the evening had passed, before the late-shift man went off duty, the road was set for the down early morning mail, and at each box the signalman going off duty withdrew a tablet for that train, by correct co-operative action with the man in the box ahead. The tablet was then left on the table. When the train came through, at each block post the fireman entered the signal box and exchanged tablets, leaving the one for the section they had just passed through and picking up that for the section ahead. The first job of the day man coming on duty was to insert the tablet in the appropriate instrument, and so prepare for the regular single line working. This practice was only possible when it was known definitely that there would be no other trains.

Another interesting piece of signalling, that shows the ingenuity of the engineering department, was installed at Stobcross shortly after the opening of the Glasgow Central underground line. At the junction with the Lanarkshire & Dunbartonshire Railway, where the line is mostly in tunnel, it was not possible to sight the signalbox to give the man a very good view of trains passing over the junction. After a little experience of working the traffic it was considered essential to move the signalman to a point of greater vantage, and this entailed the construction of a small cabin so narrow that an ordinary locking frame could not be accommodated. A system of remote control was introduced, using a locking frame of miniature levers that actuated hydraulic valves. These valves controlled a pressure-water supply to hydraulic rams by which the full-sized levers were operated. It was the earliest instance of power being used in the actuation of points and signals, and was carried out jointly by Stevens & Sons, and the Kilmarnock firm of Glenfield.

The 'show piece' of Caledonian Railway signalling was the very large electro-pneumatic installation at Glasgow Central, put into commission in 1908. For sheer size the miniature locking frame, with its 374 levers in one row, has never been surpassed, and it remained in service for 52 years. In the early nineteen-hundreds the electro-pneumatic system had already been adopted for a number of large installations in Great Britain, notably on the North Eastern Railway. After the First World War there was a pronounced swing towards all-electric operation, but nowadays the wheel has come full circle, and when the time came for the modernization of the signalling, in conjunction with the forthcoming electrification of the Cathcart Circle line the electro-pneumatic system in its most modern form was chosen again. The 1908 installation covered the entire station area, and the tracks across the Clyde. The first mechanical box was at Bridge Street Junction, where the Gourock and Wemyss Bay lines turn away to the west.

In the 1908 installation compressed air was used for the points and for the operation of the lower quadrant semaphore signals. These were all of the standard Caledonian pattern, on lattice posts, with the air motors fixed just above the balance weights. The number of

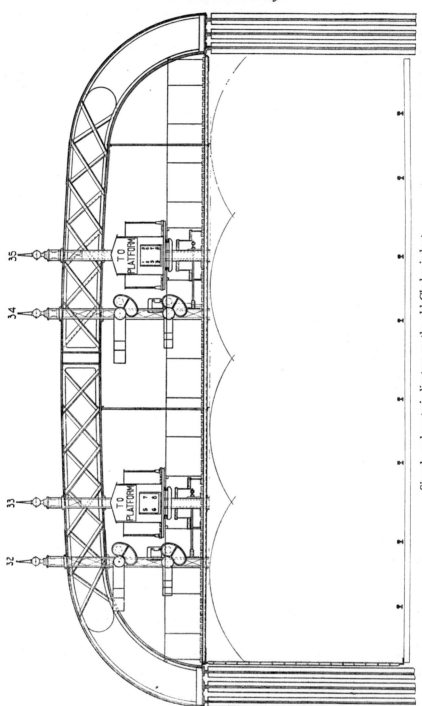

Signals and route indicators on the old Clyde viaduct.

Above: City workers arriving from Clyde coast and suburban trains.

[*British Railways*

GLASGOW CENTRAL

Below: A fine view of the approach tracks.

Above: The new Clyde viaduct finished; laying the permanent way.

GLASGOW CENTRAL

Below: Gantry of electro-pneumatic signals adjacent to the new power signalbox, 1908.

[*British Railways*

Above: View looking northwards across the Clyde during the construction of the new viaduct, July, 1902.

Below: New arches, in the widened approach to Glasgow Central. Photo taken in July, 1902.

[*British Railways*

Testing the new floor, in the enlarged part of Glasgow Central station. A remarkable photograph taken on 22 May, 1904, showing a great assembly of locomotives, including two 0-8-0 mineral tanks, Nos. 495 and 494 and an 0-8-0 tender engine.

[British Railways

semaphore arms was very much less than it would otherwise have been through the use of route indicators. These latter were also pneumatically worked, with a letter or figure being drawn from an obscured position in front of a display ground as shown in the typical example illustrated in the accompanying drawing. A further drawing shows one of the imposing signal gantries mounted on the new Clyde viaduct. At Glasgow Central, as everywhere else on the Caledonian the green glasses used in the semaphores were a beautiful shade of grass-green. While this was a much prettier colour than the more usual blue-green used in signalling it had the disadvantage of giving a distinctly yellow shade to the clear indication as seen at night.

Like the majority of British railways in pre-Grouping days the Caledonian derived the greater part of its revenue from the conveyance of freight. In the early years of the century export business to the continent of Europe was flourishing, particularly in coal to the Baltic countries and to Russia, and the Caledonian Board decided upon an expansion of their dock facilities at Grangemouth on a scale commensurate with the other great new works to which reference has already been made. In the year 1867, when the Caledonian acquired Grangemouth, the tonnage of freight dealt with amounted to 464,160 tons. Seven years later the traffic had very nearly doubled and in 1876 authority was obtained to construct a new dock and to dredge the River Carron, which provides access to the docks from the Firth of Forth. It was intended to keep this dredged to a depth of 25 ft below high water mark, so as to permit the entry of large vessels. After long and strenuous efforts the task of maintaining such a depth was given up as hopeless, such was the speed at which the dredged portion became silted up. But the Carron Dock, as it was named, was nevertheless a great success, and by 1896 the traffic through the port had risen to 2,418,878 tons.

Even this was not anything like enough to meet the demands of traders, and in 1897 Parliamentary sanction was obtained for another substantial increase in dock area. The Carron Dock had an area of 20 acres. The new project provided for a new dock of 30 acres, a canting basin of 10 acres, a new entrance lock on the south shore of the Firth of Forth, a channel between the entrance lock, the canting basin, and the new dock, and another channel between the new dock and the existing docks. In addition to this there was to be a timber basin of 23 acres. This made a total of nearly 100 additional acres of water in the port area. This vast enterprise was thus thoroughly typical of all Caledonian new works of the period. The contracts for the work were let in 1898, and although practically all the area

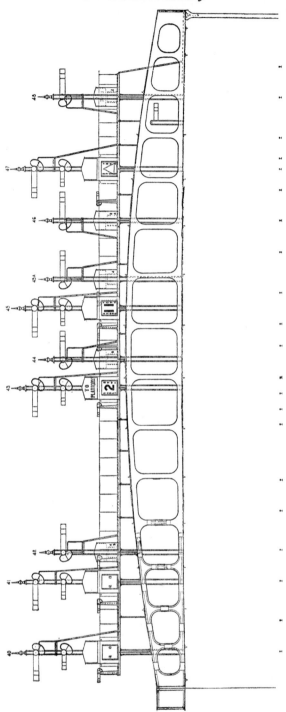

Bridge of signals and route indicators on the new Clyde viaduct, 1908.

concerned was foreshore and required reclaiming, the progress was swift, and the complete group of new docks, channels and basins, was brought into service in October, 1906.

The quaysides were equipped with cranes and hoists of the latest pattern, for rapid loading of cargo steamers and colliers, and in the railway approaches a large marshalling yard was laid in at Fouldubs, specially for classifying export traffic outward bound through the Grangemouth docks. In addition to this marshalling there was some 60 miles of running lines and sidings on or near the quaysides. The effect of this great enterprise was very quickly shown in the tonnage of freight passing through the port. Even before the Grange Dock had come into operation the tonnage had increased to 3,100,000.

Thus, in the first few years of the twentieth century the Caledonian Railway made notable strides in almost every direction of its activities: in its stations, its civil engineering, its steamer traffic, its main line coaches, its signalling, and not less as a dock owner. But the department that caught the imagination of the travelling public more than any other was of course that of locomotives, and the stately blue engines of John F. McIntosh's design provided the 'neon lights' display of a railway that was outstanding, into whatever facet of its equipment one cared to enquire.

There are some enthusiasts, no doubt, whose tastes will differ from mine, but I will be bold enough to assert that never was there a more beautiful locomotive livery than that of the Caledonian. There are some, in totally different colour that come near to equalling it according to one's particular fancy; but there has never been one to surpass it. And yet its astonishing beauty was to a large extent accidental and unofficial! The basic colour was 'Prussian Blue', set off by purple lake underframes and black and white lining, a handsome, dignified livery, appropriate to the railway that included the Royal arms in its crest. The blue was an expensive paint, and to make it go further the practice grew up at St Rollox of mixing white with it. The result was an exquisite, ethereal sky-blue, with which the colour of the underframes blended delightfully. Although there have been several liveries of bright blue since the days of the Caledonian Railway: the G.N.R. of Ireland, the Garter blue of the L.N.E.R. streamlined Pacifics, and the blue of the British Railways Class '8' express locomotives, there has never been one to match the limpid softness of the Caledonian. Engines repaired at Perth came out in a darker shade, very rich, full-bodied and beautiful, but nevertheless not to be compared with the sky-blue of St Rollox. As Caledonian locomotives grew progressively larger and more massive they lost none of their grace, and Mr McIntosh's Pacific if it had ever been built would have been a breathtaking sight. From colour and aesthetics it is indeed time now to take a look at the McIntosh locomotives in more detail.

To conclude this chapter details of the best and longest runs called for in the timetable are included in two tables. These relate to the summer service of 1906 when competition with the North British for the Aberdeen traffic was at its height.

SUMMARY OF CHIEF RUNS, SUMMER SERVICES, 1906

Station and Station		Direction	Distance (miles)	Time (min.)	Number of Trains	Speed m.p.h.
Carlisle .	Lockerbie .	Down	25·8	28	1 (s.c.)	55·3
				30	5	51·6
		Up		28	2	55·3
				30	3	51·6
Carlisle .	Beattock .	Down	39·7	43	3	55·4
				44	7	54·1
		Up		43	1	55·4
				44	2	54·1
Carlisle .	Carstairs .	Down	73·5	84	1	52·5
		Up		81	1	54·4
				83	1	53·1
Beattock .	Lockerbie .	Up	13·9	16	1	52·1
„ .	Carstairs .	Down	33·8	39	1	52·0
Crawford .	Symington .	„	11·6	13	1	53·5
Symington .	Carlisle .	Up	66·9	75	1	53·5
„ .	Glasgow .	Down	35·5	42	1	50·7
Carstairs .	Motherwell .	Down	15·9	17	1	56·1
				18	1	53·0
Carstairs .	Stirling .	Down	44·2	50	1	53·0
Perth . .	„ . .	Up	33	37	1	53·5
Perth .	Forfar .	Down	32·5	36	2	54·2
		Up		32	2	60·9
				34	1	57·4
Perth .	Aberdeen .	Down	89·8	96	1	56·1
„ . .	Magdalen Green	Down	20	23	2	52·2
Coupar Angus .	Perth . .	Up	15·9	18	1	53·0

(s.c.) by slip coach

RUNS OVER 100 MILES WITHOUT ADVERTISED STOP

From	To	Train	Distance (Miles)	Time (Min.)	Speed	Remarks
Glasgow	Carlisle	2.0 p.m.	102·3	135	45·5	Non-stop
Carlisle	Glasgow	5.46 a.m.	102·3	124	49·5	Beattock stop for bank engine
,,	,,	4.0 p.m.	102·3	135	45·5	Beattock stop for bank engine, also two conditional stops
,,	,,	8.13 p.m.*	102·9	123	50·2	Stops at Beattock (bank engine) and Strawfrank
Edinburgh	Carlisle	10.5 a.m.	100·6	120	50·3	Non-stop
Carlisle	Edinburgh	3.53 p.m.	100·6	134	45·0	Non-stop
Carlisle	Perth	1.20 a.m.	150·8	185	48·9	Beattock bank engine stop
,,	,,	1.40 a.m.	150·8	180	50·3	Beattock bank engine stop
,,	,,	2.17 a.m.	150·8	180	50·3	Beattock bank engine stop and one conditional stop
Stirling	Carlisle	9.50 p.m. ex-Perth	117·8	159	44·1	Non-stop

* This train, the 2 p.m. down 'Corridor' from Euston, took the Holytown route, which is 0·6 mile longer than the main line via Motherwell.

XI

The McIntosh Locomotives

THE foundations of twentieth-century Caledonian locomotive practice had been well and truly laid with the Drummond 4-4-0s of the '66' Class. John Lambie followed in the Drummond tradition, and then, when McIntosh had succeeded to the chair at St Rollox he began, in some ways, to reverse the policy of his predecessors. Drummond was forever advocating the practice of expansive working, using high pressure steam, a wide open regulator, and a relatively short cut-off. Despite the excellent results he obtained in the comparative trials between the four engines 76, 77, 78 and 79 he seemed inclined to give up the quest, because of the reluctance of drivers to pull their engines up to short cut-offs. The 4-4-0 locomotives Nos. 76 and 79, with 200 lb per sq in. pressure produced some astonishing outputs of power, having regard to the size of their boilers and cylinders; but Drummond was before his time and Caledonian development did not progress on the lines of these engines.

McIntosh was no scientific theorist. Like his great counterpart on the London & North Western, George Whale, he had grown up on the footplate. An engineman himself he knew his men, and he set out to give them machines that were, in every sense of the word, 'drivers' engines'. He built upon the very sure foundation of the Drummond chassis and machinery, at a time when speed was the watchword of the Caledonian, but instead of going in for higher boiler pressures, and preaching the cult of expansive working, he gave his men bigger boilers and bigger firegrates. So, in 1896, came the first of the immortal 'Dunalastairs'. The outstanding merit of these engines lay not only in their almost unlimited capacity for generating steam but that they were not susceptible to any particular method of working. They could be thrashed for hours on end if need be. In the meantime the engines and their feats of haulage and speed became household words among thousands of travellers and enthusiasts, most of whom remained happily oblivious of the origin of the famous class name. Dunalastair is a remote clachan on the shores of Loch Rannoch, where the Chairman of the Caledonian Railway, J. C. Bunten, had a country estate.

The first class of 'Dunalastairs', Nos. 721–735, came out early enough in 1896 to participate in the running of the down night 'Tourist Express' in the height of the holiday season. It is a pity that they were built too late to take part in the Race to the North; had they been available, heaven knows what times might have been achieved, for in 1896 they were running from Carlisle to Stirling, night after night, in overall times almost as fast as those achieved by the Drummond engines in the race, but generally with about double the loads! What a fascinating and exciting time it was. The 'Dunalastairs' were not universally acclaimed in the technical press, and when Rous-Marten went into panegyrics of praise in *The Engineer*, a host of correspondents turned upon him, extolling the merits of other contemporary locomotives and for a week or so Rous-Marten found himself defending the 'Dunalastairs' against those who backed *Jeanie Deans*, *Greater Britain* and the whole galaxy of Webb three-cylinder compounds! Quite a number of correspondents wrote as though the two-cylinder simple locomotive was quite out-moded, and as though the only designs worth considering were compounds.

It is interesting to set out the basic dimensions of the McIntosh non-superheater 4-4-0s down to the very handsome '140' Class or 'Dunalastair IV' type. With these four McIntosh designs are included the corresponding figures for the Drummond and the Lambie designs that preceded them. From this table can be seen the gradual increase in heating surface and working pressure from the first 'Dunalastairs' of 1896, to the '140' Class. While the grate area of the later engines showed a tendency to grow less, rather than greater, the firebox heating surface was increased, and this gave what McIntosh was constantly striving for, a capacity for burning coal. All four groups of 'Dunalastairs' were outstandingly successful as hard runners, and heavy weight pullers. Tradition has it that they were heavy on coal, but they cannot have been outrageously so, from the plain fact of the long non-stop runs they performed regularly.

It is true that the tank capacity was increased from 3,570 gallons in the first 'Dunalastairs' Class to 4,125 in the second and third, and to 4,300 in the '140' Class; but even if the tanks were topped up at Stirling the non-stop runs of the night expresses over the 117 miles from Carlisle would permit of little more than 35 gallons per mile. Non-superheater locomotives with such excellent boilers as those carried by all four groups of 'Dunalastairs' would show an evaporation of at least 9 lb of water per pound of coal, thus indicating a consumption of about 40 lb per mile, from Carlisle to Stirling. In view of the work done by the 'Dunalastair III' Class and the '140s',

CALEDONIAN RAILWAY

Comparative Dimensions of non-superheater 4-4-0s

Date	Design	Cylinders dia. stroke in.		Heating surfaces, sq in.			Grate Area, sq ft	Working pressure p.s.i.	Nominal T.E. 85 per cent B.P. lb
				Tubes	Firebox	Total			
1884	Drummond . . .	18	26	1,088·7	122·0	1,210·7	19·50	160	14,720
1894	Lambie . . .	18	26	1,071·50	112·62	1,184·12	19·50	160	14,720
1896	Dunalastair I . .	18¼	26	1,284·45	118·78	1,403·23	20·63	160	15,100
1897	Dunalastair II . .	19	26	1,381·22	118·78	1,500	20·63	175	17,900
1899	Dunalastair III . .	19	26	1,402	138	1,540	22	180	18,411
1904	Dunalastair IV . .	19	26	1,470	145	1,615	21	180	18,411

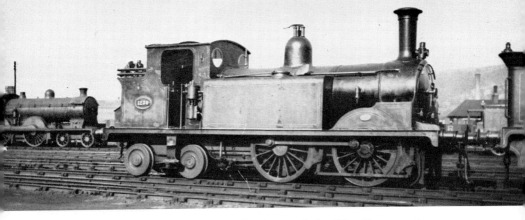

Drummond 0-4-4 tank engine No. 1230 at Perth, 1921. Built 1886 as No. 230 and used for a time on the Methven branch.

Above: Lambie 4-4-0 tank No. 7, built 1893 for the Glasgow Underground line. Later station pilot at Perth.

Below: McIntosh 0-4-4 tank No. 426 at Perth south shed.

[*all R. D. Stephen*

Above: Liverpool and Manchester – Glasgow express passing Kingmoor yards, Carlisle. 'Dunalastair II' Class 4-4-0 No. 766.

[*B.T.C. Historical Relics*

Below: Up West Coast express approaching Beattock Summit. 'Dunalastair IV' Class 4-4-0 No. 148.

[*H. Gordon Tidey*

this is a very moderate figure. With superheater engines of the fourth 'Dunalastair' Class, there were several trains, prior to 1914, run non-stop from Carlisle to Perth. The superheater engines which did such excellent work from 1910 onwards were a direct development of the '140' Class. None of the various 'Dunalastair' Classes were very numerous, improvements and enlargements being incorporated as successive batches of 4-4-0 express locomotives were authorized.

Class	Number built	Year
Dunalastair I . .	15	1896
Dunalastair II . .	15	1897–8
Dunalastair III . .	16	1899–1900
Dunalastair IV .	19	1904–1910
Superheater type .	22	1910–1914

Apart from their technical excellence, and their almost unfailing dependability in fast and heavy traffic, all the McIntosh 4-4-os were very pleasing to look upon. The design staff at St Rollox most skilfully contrived to keep a most graceful appearance, while all the time the height of the centre line of the boiler was going up, and the diameter of the barrel was getting larger. In some schools of design, as more modern products were evolved the result merely assumed a massive appearance, impressive in mere bulk but little else. At St Rollox, on the other hand, the larger the engines, the more care the drawing office seemed to put into the overall design, and their handling of the big 4-6-0 projects was nothing if not masterly from the viewpoint of lineaments.

The boiler of the 'Dunalastair I' Class passenger engines was used without change in a large class of fast goods and mixed traffic engines, 0-6-os turned out from 1899 onwards. These engines had 18½ by 26 in. cylinders and 5 ft diameter coupled wheels. While the passenger engines throughout McIntosh's time were all built at St Rollox works the majority of these 0-6-os were built by outside firms. The first seventeen were fitted with the Westinghouse brake, and painted blue. This batch were used in passenger service, including the fast coast trains to Gourock and Wemyss Bay; the remainder had steam brakes and were painted black. In all there were seventy-nine of this class built between 1899 and 1900, while a further seventeen were built at St Rollox in 1908–9. Some of these latter, although fitted with steam brakes, also had vacuum ejectors and through pipes for working fitted goods trains from England. In these heavily utilized, workaday goods engines, nothing of the traditional Caledonian grace in design was missing. They must rank as one of the most handsome 0-6-0s ever built.

One cannot impart the same degree of elegance to a suburban tank engine of the 0-4-4 type, especially when the service demands high capacity water tanks. Nevertheless the Caledonian 0-4-4s were a neat, workmanlike lot, which did their work so admirably that new construction of them continued until 3 years after Grouping. There were three broad categories of these engines: those with condensing equipment, painted black, and used principally on the Glasgow underground lines; the standard general service tanks, and the Cathcart Circle Class. The leading dimensions were:

	Condensing type	General service	Cathcart Circle
Coupled wheels ft in.	5 – 9	5 – 9	4 – 6
Cylinders dia. str. in.	18 × 26	18 × 26	17 × 24
Total heating surface sq ft	1095·76	1085·9	1085·9
Grate Area sq ft	17	17	17
Boiler pressure p.s.i.	150	160	150

There were some variations in boiler dimensions among the condensing engines, the earlier ones dating from 1896 having smaller tank capacity. Construction of the general service variety began in 1900. A total of sixty-eight was built in McIntosh's time; fourteen more, with larger cylinders and 180 lb pressure were added between 1915 and 1922, and a further ten, generally similar to the Pickersgill developments were built to the order of the L.M.S.R. by Nasmyth, Wilson & Co, in 1925. The Cathcart Circle engines, with 4 ft 6 in. coupled wheels were designed for rapid acceleration between the closely-spaced stations, on a suburban line having many sharp curves.

The development of the 4-6-0 type on the Caledonian Railway, under J. F. McIntosh, presents one of those episodes in British locomotive history over which those clever fellows who can always be so wise after the event can shake their heads and write it all off as a monument of wasted effort. Between 1902 and 1913 no fewer than six different classes of considerably varying dimensions were built, mustering a total of no more than forty-two locomotives between them; and students of locomotive history will recall, rather sadly perhaps, that some 25 years later a single 4-6-0 design was introduced on to L.M.S.R. metals 2 tons lighter than the largest of the six built between 1902 and 1913, that could tackle anything that any of the McIntosh 4-6-0 type did, and could do it a great deal better, and more economically. For my own part I would not presume to criticize the practice of St Rollox in any way. The building of the various 4-6-0s from 1902 onwards was entirely in keeping with the sentiments and traditions of the time, and as one also who never ceases to delight in the variety and styles of the engine designs of old I would be the first to assert that railway history would be very much the poorer without those forty-two behemoths that bore so clearly the stamp of J. F. McIntosh.

At the time the Caledonian development began 4-6-0 locomotives were few and far between on the railways of Great Britain. The much longer main frames were not without their troubles. A boiler design that was completely successful on a 4-4-0 could not be enlarged by rule-of-thumb methods to suit a 4-6-0. The drawing office had to advance in stages, and it is not without a certain significance that the first 4-6-0 was a relatively small one. If much double-heading was to be avoided on the Oban line something much more powerful than the Brittain outside-cylinder 4-4-0s was needed. The ordinary main line passenger engines could not be used owing to weight restrictions, and it is probable that the idea of a small-wheeled 4-6-0 may have been suggested by the success of David Jones's famous goods 4-6-0s on the Highland Railway. By the use of the 4-6-0 wheel arrangement McIntosh was able to get greater adhesion weight without exceeding the axle-load limit of the Oban line, while the use of 19 by 26 in. cylinders in conjunction with coupled wheels of no more than 5 ft diameter and a boiler pressure of 175 lb per sq in. gave the high nominal tractive effort of 23,269 lb.

The boiler proportions on these engines were interesting. The barrel was considerably longer than on any of the 4-4-0 classes, and provided 1,800 sq ft of heating surface in the tubes. On the other hand the grate area was no bigger than that of the first 'Dunalastairs', and the firebox heating surface was no more than 100 sq ft. Here was a clear case of designing to suit the road. None of the very severe banks on the Callander & Oban line was of very long duration; an all-out effort was needed in spells of 10 minutes or a quarter-of-an-hour at the most, and in between times there would be far longer spells when the engine would be steaming lightly or coasting. For such duty the long boiler and small firebox were ideal. The boiler could be used as a reservoir for building up a large head of steam in readiness for a

big, though brief effort. While the small firebox ensured the minimum
of coal consumption in light steaming conditions, when coal can be
wasted merely in keeping the bars covered! These Oban 4-6-0s were
a great success, not only climbing well, but running up to 60 m.p.h.
on favourable stretches of line.

The next 4-6-0s were a very different proposition. Excellent
hill climbers though the 'Dunalastairs' were, the rapid increase in the
weights of the London–Glasgow expresses was leading to much
assistant engine mileage, between Carlisle and Beattock Summit on
the down road, and between Glasgow and Carstairs on the up.
Having so brilliantly mastered the tasks of 1896–7 it is not surprising
that every effort was made to keep pace with the increasing demands
of the traffic, and that a great new express engine should have been
put on the road in 1903. Until that time the largest main line express
passenger engines in service were the 'Dunalastair III' 4-4-0s, and
a comparison of the leading dimensions is illuminating.

	Dunalastair III	4-6-0s 49 and 50
Cylinders dia. by stroke in.	19×26	21×26
Total heating surface, sq ft	1,540	2,323
Grate area, sq ft	22	26
Boiler pressure p.s.i.	180	200
Total engine weight tons	51·7	70
Nominal T.E. 85 per cent B.P. lb	18,411	24,990

There were no half measures about this advance in power; Nos. 49
and 50 were in fact the most powerful locomotives in Great Britain
at the time of their construction. And what superbly proportioned
locomotives they were! As if to increase the impression of vastness the
initials 'C.R.' on their great tenders were made nearly twice the
normal size and the coat of arms was ringed with gilt thistles and
leaves instead of the usual scrolls. It is amazing to recall that these
two locomotives, with their tenders, were built for no more than
£3,100 apiece, which, even when the difference in price-levels today
is taken into account, is a mighty low figure!

These engines did excellent work from their very inception, but
for the servicing facilities then available they were ahead of their
time. For one thing, the length of engine and tender over buffers was
65 ft 6 in. and there were no turntables large enough to take them.
At Glasgow they were run round the Cathcart Circle, but at Carlisle
engine and tender had to be uncoupled. Incidental difficulties like

this, and the fact that some time elapsed before any further express 4-6-os were built led to rumours getting around that Nos. 49 and 50 were relative failures. Certainly, in comparison with some of the work that was being done by the 4-4-0 locomotives the big 4-6-os did not show a proportionate superiority; but when a non-superheater 4-4-0 works a load of 404 tons tare from Strawfrank Junction, passed slowly, to Carlisle, 73¼ miles in 76¾ minutes pass to stop, over Beattock Summit, the 4-6-os would have to perform prodigies to justify their increased weight and tractive power to the fullest extent. Again, a 'Dunalastair III' took a load of 412 tons tare northbound from Carlisle, without assistance and reached Beattock 39·7 miles in 46 minutes 4 seconds start to stop, an astounding piece of work.

By the year 1906 70-ft turntables had been installed at the principal locomotive depots, and the experience obtained with Nos. 49 and 50 was embodied in the five new express passenger 4-6-os built in that year. The boilers were larger in diameter, though a re-arrangement of the tubes to give better circulation of the water, resulted in slightly less tube heating surface. Also, the cylinder diameter was reduced to 20 in. Whatever doubts anyone might have had about the success of Nos. 49 and 50 there was no room for any lurking suspicions about the '903' Class. It can be well and truly said that these huge, but wonderfully graceful engines represented the summit point of McIntosh's work as an engine designer. There was a subtle point to be noted about these engines, which they shared with Nos. 49 and 50. As originally built they had no brake hoses on the front buffer beams. The folks at St Rollox evidently considered they would never need to be double-headed! They, more than any other class on the line, epitomized the twentieth-century splendour of the Caledonian, and the regular daily working of the afternoon West Coast corridor trains between Glasgow and Carlisle by No. 903 *Cardean*, made that engine a veritable institution on the Scottish railways.

When the London & North Western Railway built the special twelve-wheeled corridor stock for the afternoon West Coast expresses the minimum load of the 8.13 p.m. down from Carlisle became seven of these palatial vehicles, and a paragraph in *The Railway Magazine* of August, 1932, vividly recalls the spirit of the day:

'A handsome combination *Cardean* made with seven cars of the "two o'clock", all twelve-wheelers of a special design, and some of the smoothest-riding stock that has ever run over West Coast metals. And so, on a typical winter's night at Carlisle, with half the city – or so it seemed – making the Citadel station the *venue* of its evening promenade, and *Cardean* the centre of attraction, the same ritual would be gone through after *Cardean* had backed down; the fireman, usually from high up on the great tender, would wave to and fro an improvised torch consisting of an oil-can, whose spout contained a blazing wick of oily waste, to show to officials farther down the platform that the brake test had been made satisfactorily, then would come a thrilling blast on the great foghorn that *Cardean* carried in place of a whistle, and the shapely form of the "two o'clock" vanished into the night. Yes, those were great days.'

Here is a personal memory, dating back to the autumn of 1923. At that time, some nine months after Grouping, it was generally understood that Midland lake was to be the colour for all L.M.S.R. passenger locomotives; but it was surprising what large stocks of the old colours seemed to be on hand at the various works, and none of the constituents were anxious to accelerate the change! Nevertheless, by that time change was definitely in the air, even on the Caledonian, and I remember being rather shocked to see the 10 a.m. up West Coast express from Glasgow arrive at Carlisle behind a shabby and dirty 'Dunalastair IV' – on time, all the same. But this more precious memory is of an afternoon at Glasgow Central. At that time the working of the afternoon express to Euston had been changed from that of *Cardean*'s days. It still conveyed the Liverpool and Manchester portions, but instead of running non-stop to Carlisle, as of old, a stop was made at Symington, and there remarshalling took place with the corresponding train from Edinburgh.

Superheater 4-4-0 locomotives were usually employed from both Glasgow and Edinburgh, and the pre-*Cardean* arrangement was revived, whereby the heavy Glasgow train was assisted, in this more recent instance, to Symington. Because of this working there was little chance in those post-war years of seeing one of the big engines on the up 'Corridor'; but the 4.10 p.m. express to Liverpool and Manchester nearly always had a 4-6-0, more usually one of the Pickersgill '60' Class. On the afternoon in question I was bound for Rothesay, and although my train left before the express for the south there was usually time to cross over to the long No. 8 platform, which, extending far beyond the short suburban platforms and the Cathcart engine siding, provided a grandstand from which the main line departures could be seen with little or no interruption. While I watched, there came into sight far across the Clyde bridge a light engine coming tender first towards the station. Even at that distance there was no mistaking what it was! No other Caledonian engines had such huge tenders, and it only remained to see if it was one of the 'Cardeans', or 49 or 50. It proved to be No. 50, and whatever falling off there might have been in other directions, this engine, still a monster even in 1923, was gloriously turned out. After she had coupled on, and stood there at No. 2 platform in the full afternoon sun, against the dark buildings in the background she made a picture that a railway enthusiast never ceases to delight in recalling. I nearly missed my train to Wemyss Bay.

Two other classes of 4-6-0 were built at St Rollox in 1906. One was a large-boilered version of the Oban type, having exactly the same wheel base, cylinders and motion, but a boiler of the same diameter as that of *Cardean*; the other, although designated 'mixed-traffic', was really a passenger class, used on heavy shorter distance traffic, and having 5 ft 9 in. coupled wheels. There was a high degree of boiler standardization between the three 1906 classes of 4-6-0, all having the same diameter barrels, and thus permitting of common flanging plates. The leading dimensions of the three classes were:

Class	903–7	908–917	918–922
Coupled wheel dia. ft in.	6 – 6	5 – 9	5 – 0
Cylinders dia. × stroke in.	20 × 26	19 × 26	19 × 26
Heating surface sq ft			
tubes	2,117·5	2,050	1,895
firebox	148·25	128	128
total	2,265·75	2,178	2,023
Grate area sq ft	26	21	21
Boiler pressure p.s.i.	200	180	175
Nominal T.E. at 85 per cent			
B.P. lb	22,667	20,812	23,269
Wt. of engine only in work-			
ing order (tons)	73	64	60·4

Both the '908' and the '918' Classes had six-wheeled tenders, and all the engines of both classes were painted blue. The '908' Class, which was very handsomely proportioned, were regularly used on express trains. Several of them worked between Glasgow and Gourock, where their capacity for rapid acceleration enabled the sharply-timed boat trains to be run without excessive speeds. It was also customary for many years to have a '908' on the 'Grampian Corridor Express' between Glasgow and Perth and earlier editions of the *Wonder Book of Railways* included a fine colour plate of one of them, thundering out of Stirling on that job. Two of the 'Cardeans', Nos. 904 and 905, were stationed at Perth, and one of them usually took the train northwards to Aberdeen. It is significant of the top-link express status of the '908' Class that two of them were named. No. 909 was *Sir James King,* after a former Chairman of the Board, and

No. 911 was *Barochan*, the residence of Sir Charles Renshaw, who was Chairman at the time the locomotives were built. *Cardean* was named after the Perthshire estate of Edward Cox, Deputy Chairman, and one can only assume that the name *Barochan* was bestowed on the lesser of the two engines because of the running of No. 911 on the Gourock trains, and thus passing near to Sir Charles Renshaw's home, which lay about a mile from the line between Paisley and Langbank on the Firth of Clyde. Cardean is near Meigle on the Alyth branch, and about a mile from the Aberdeen main line at Alyth Junction.

In 1910 engine No. 917 was fitted experimentally with a cab having side-windows, one might say in North Eastern style, but there was an example far nearer to St Rollox in the North British 'Atlantics'. This change was made to give greater protection to the enginemen in bad weather. It must be admitted that the McIntosh cabs in their wide, sweeping downward curve of the side sheets were somewhat exposed, and I well remember the comments of some North Eastern men anent the Great Central '04' 2-8-0s which had similarly shaped cabs. At York the '04s' were known as 'the pneumonia engines'! Humanitarianism or not, however, it is extraordinary how the change of one single feature can upset what Mr Henry Maxwell has termed 'the balanced plastic symmetry' of a locomotive design, and in the superheated version of the '908' Class, built in 1913–4 and numbered 179 to 189, it only needed the addition of an extended smokebox, plus the side window to remove practically all the grace of the earlier McIntosh engines, and to give instead the impression of a massive cart-horse of a locomotive, even though the shapely boiler mountings and pleasingly curved splashers remained.

Superheating was added to Nos. 49 and 50 and to the 'Cardeans', in 1911–2 without any change in their external appearance. In both classes the boiler pressure was lowered from 200 to 175 lb per sq in., and although in the case of the '903' Class the cylinder diameter was increased to $20\frac{3}{4}$ in. the nominal tractive effort was slightly reduced. McIntosh was one of those engineers who used superheating as a means of reducing boiler pressures and thus reduce his boiler maintenance charges, and although this change was probably reflected in the running and repair costs of the engines concerned, little change was to be noted in the work of the engines on the road. Mr Cecil J. Allen, who travelled many times behind *Cardean* on the down evening 'Corridor Express' from Carlisle to Glasgow, wrote, in 1914, 'the addition of the superheater has had no marked effect on the performance of these engines, which always has been, and still remains, of the finest quality'.

The Caledonian Railway had always been partial to the use of 0-6-0 locomotives on certain of the Clyde Coast trains, despite the availability of passenger engines of both 4-4-0 and 4-6-0 types, but the introduction of a small new class of 0-6-0 superheater engines in 1912 specially for the Clyde Coast traffic always seemed to me a little odd, to say the least of it. Nos. 30 to 33, with their 5 ft wheels and and 19½ by 26 in. cylinders, were brisk, powerful machines, with a nominal tractive effort greater than that of the '908' Class! Still, one can hardly regard them as an ideal type for the job, or a comfortable one for the enginemen to handle on such sharply timed services. A further five were built in the same year, specially for goods traffic, and these were of the 2-6-0 type, though otherwise identical so far as the boiler and machinery were concerned. The 2-6-0s, Nos. 34 to 38, were used for fast goods trains between Carlisle and the Glasgow district.

The 2-6-0s of the '34' Class were the first Moguls to work in Scotland, but before that McIntosh had scored two other 'firsts' in Scottish locomotive design. In 1910 he had built the first superheater engine, No. 139 of the 'Dunalastair IV' Class and 9 years earlier he had built the first Scottish 0-8-0. The latter engine, No. 601, was the first on the Caledonian to have a boiler larger than those of the 4-4-0s of the day, and preceded by a year the design of the Oban 4-6-0s. Two of them were built in 1901, and a further six in 1903. With 21 by 26 in. cylinders, 4 ft 6 in. coupled wheels, and a boiler pressure of 175 lb per sq in. they had the very high tractive effort, for that period, of 31,584 lb. They were specially designed to work in conjunction with the 30-ton bogie open wagons that McIntosh was building at the time, and proved capable of handling *sixty* of them, loaded. To provide proper control of these huge trains both engines and wagons were fitted with the Westinghouse brake, and thus afforded what was probably the first instance in Britain of continuously-braked heavy freight trains.

Throughout his tenure of office McIntosh gave continual evidence that he was a man who 'thought big', and one can well imagine his dislike of the situation at Beattock where with increasing train loads, even his largest and most powerful express locomotives had to take rear-end banking assistance. But for the onset of war in 1914, he might have added another very spectacular 'first' to his notable record of achievement, nothing less than the first Scottish Pacific. Locomotive history is full of fascinating 'might-have-beens', and in 1905 a De Glehn four-cylinder compound 'Atlantic' had been designed at St Rollox, very similar in general lineaments to the

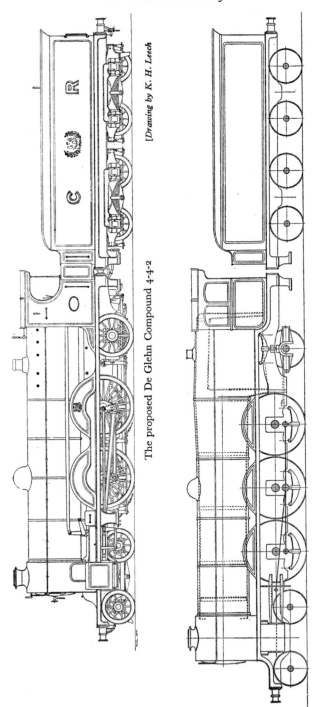

[*Drawing by K. H. Leech*

The proposed De Glehn Compound 4-4-2

The proposed 4-cyl. simple Pacific of 1913

4-6-os Nos. 49 and 50, and similar in nominal tractive effort. The design was prepared at a time when intense interest was being displayed in the work of the De Glehn compounds in France, and when the famous trials of the Atlantic engines *La France*, *President*, and *Alliance* were in progress on the Great Western Railway. No Atlantic was ever built for the Caledonian Railway, but quite recently a beautiful O gauge model of the stillborn McIntosh engine was on show at one of the model railway exhibitions.

Through the good offices of several friends I am able to include herewith an outline drawing of the proposed Pacific. I have had the opportunity of studying a St Rollox drawing dated 8th October, 1913, signed by McIntosh, which gives the following dimensions:

Cylinders (four)	16 in. diameter by 26 in. stroke
Coupled wheels	6 ft 6 in. diameter
Heating surfaces:	
2¼ in. tubes	1,750 sq ft
5 in. flues	690 sq ft
Superheater	516 sq ft
Firebox	158 sq ft
Total	3,114 sq ft
Grate Area	37 sq ft
Boiler Pressure	180 lb p.s.i.
Nom. T.E. at 85 per cent	24,576 lb

The boiler was to have been a very large one, having a maximum diameter of 5 ft 8 in. and a length between tube plates of 22 ft. The engine weight was estimated at 90 tons, with 55 tons adhesion as with *Cardean*.

So far as tractive effort was concerned this great engine showed a surprisingly small advance over the big 4-6-os, which in their superheated state had 21,348 lb at 85 per cent boiler pressure. It can be assumed that the idea behind these engines was to provide a very high steaming capacity so that they could be worked hard, on late cut-offs, up the Beattock Bank without any risk of running short of steam. With many Pacific runs of recent date freshly in mind, however, I fear that this Caledonian Pacific might have been an easy prey to slipping in the bad weather conditions that so often occur in the Lowther Hills. I have known Pacifics with more than 10 tons greater adhesion brought almost to the point of impotence in a thick early morning mist, by repeated slipping. It is nevertheless easy to criticize a design that never reached the stage of authorization.

It would have been a superb-looking machine, and even as an unfulfilled project it forms a fitting culmination to McIntosh's work at St Rollox. He retired in 1914 in his sixty-ninth year, but in the previous autumn, on the last Royal train journey for which he was responsible, His Majesty King George V personally wished him good-bye, and a happy retirement, and created him a member of the Royal Victorian Order.

XII

The War Years and the Aftermath

THE war came at a time when Caledonian service to the public had reached a particularly high level of frequency and efficiency, and when there was every indication that the standards already attained were far from being considered static, or final. It would be wearisome to give a catalogue of even the most important departures from Glasgow Central, from Buchanan Street, and from Edinburgh Princes Street in the summer of 1914. Then, for example, there were five daily boat expresses to Ardrossan – several with names that indicated the long-disappeared services they provided: 'The Portrush & Arran Express'; 'Belfast Express'; 'Isle of Man Boat Express'; 'Belfast Night Mail' – all via Ardrossan! The lavish service to Gourock and Wemyss Bay has already been referred to, but a remarkable feature of the working from Glasgow and Edinburgh was the attention given to longer distance daily residential traffic.

The nearness of the delightful Clyde coast resorts, and the excellence of the train and steamer services provided led an unusually high proportion of Glasgow business people to live well out of the city. On the same principle the Caledonian began to develop long-distance residential traffic in other directions, and this enterprise reached its zenith in the running of the once-famous 'Tinto' express, which left Glasgow Central at 5 p.m., called at Motherwell to pick up and then ran non-stop to Thankerton. Thence it served all stations to Beattock, and terminated at Moffat. This train carried a Pullman buffet car and attached a portion from Edinburgh at Symington. The Caledonian was using slip coaches quite extensively at that time, and the up 'Tinto' slipped a coach for Lanark at Cleghorn. In 1914 the Company was operating a higher number of named trains than any other British railway. On the north main line in addition to the 'Grampian Corridor Express' there was the 5 p.m. out of Buchanan Street, named the 'Granite City'.

A very important development that took place in the summer of 1914 was the introduction of Pullman cars on a large number of express trains. On the Aberdeen service they were used as dining cars, available for meals to both first and third class passengers without the payment of any supplement. They were run on the

7.30 a.m. down as well as on the 'Grampian', and the 'Granite City'. No fewer than five buffet cars were allocated to the highly competitive Edinburgh and Glasgow service, while in addition to the 'Tinto', another car was run on the 'Strathearn' residential express between Glasgow and Crieff. Then, on to the Oban line was introduced the unique and beautiful Pullman observation car *Maid of Morven*. All the cars running on the Caledonian were given the names of ladies famous in Scottish history, such as *Flora MacDonald, Helen MacGregor, Mary Seaton, Duchess of Gordon, Fair Maid of Perth*. Mention of the 'Grampian Corridor Express' of that period also recalls that on the down journey a coach was slipped at Gleneagles, for Crieff, and that the corresponding up train leaving Aberdeen at 5.30 p.m. running non-stop from Perth, was routed via Coatbridge into Glasgow Central, instead of Buchanan Street, presumably to facilitate connections with night trains for the south.

The year 1914 also marked a most important change in the locomotive, carriage and wagon department, following the retirement of J. F. McIntosh. The outgoing chief had spent his whole life in the service of the Caledonian Railway, and its constituents, having joined the Scottish North Eastern Railway, at Arbroath in 1862, at the age of 17. Passing through the stages of Locomotive Inspector, District Foreman, he became District Superintendent at Polmadie in 1886. Five years later he was appointed Chief Inspector of the Running Department, and in 1895 he succeeded John Lambie at St Rollox. He was essentially a 'running' man, and the many beautiful locomotives for which he was responsible between the years 1896 and 1914 were designed by his drawing office staff to meet the needs of the line he knew so well.

One can imagine that the appointment of his successor caused something of a surprise. It was not the fact of his being an outsider. Some of the most famous Caledonian locomotive superintendents of the past had come new to St Rollox, such as Conner, Smellie, and Dugald Drummond. But Pickersgill had for 20 years been a 'small railway' man. A well-known Scottish *littérateur* once suggested that Pickersgill would have been the ideal man to succeed Manson on the Glasgow & South Western, but in that case Peter Drummond secured the post. Pickersgill was 53 years of age when he came to St Rollox, after 20 years service as Locomotive, Carriage and Wagon Superintendent of the Great North of Scotland Railway. For 18 years prior to that he had been on the Great Eastern Railway. He was a scholarly man, with a charming, though quiet personality very different from the breezy, jovial *bonhomie* of J. F. McIntosh.

Norman D. Macdonald tells against himself a good story of the greatest days of McIntosh at St Rollox. By sheer force of personality and white-hot enthusiasm for locomotives and trains Macdonald, professionally an advocate, came to know most of the leading railway personalities of the day. He was not content merely with their acquaintance, friendship, and learning their plans. He, like *The Times* of old, was always thundering for reform. Sir George Gibb, General Manager of the North Eastern, once exclaimed: 'When Macdonald providentially dies you will find in big red letters of blood branded deep into his back:

BIGGER BOILERS
BETTER BRAKES.'

He could well claim McIntosh of the Caledonian as one of his friends, but at one period, for some reason or another some months elapsed without their meeting. Then one day Macdonald arrived unexpectedly at St Rollox. There was never any question of an appointment where he was concerned. Whatever was going on he was shown straight into the chief's room. He burst in to find McIntosh surrounded, as he put it, 'by a galaxy from the drawing office'. The chief looked up and shouted in his usual breezy style: 'Hullo, Maister Macdonald! How have you escaped from your assielum?'

While McIntosh had some very able and strong assistants he was by far the most dominating personality, one who was completely at home in any company. He was equally popular with directors and the drivers and firemen. On the other hand, with a man of Pickersgill's retiring nature there were bound to grow up some 'powers behind the throne', and one of the strongest of these was John Barr, the Locomotive Running Superintendent. Not so many years ago I had the pleasure of meeting this great servant of the Caledonian and of the L.M.S. railways, in his home at Newlands, still hale and hearty in his retirement; and it was indeed absorbing to listen to his yarns of the old days, and see some of the old snapshots from his collection of photographs. We came to some old and faded pictures of the terrible smash at Quintinshill; Barr paused for a moment and then said quietly: 'That was the biggest job I ever had.'

It is no more than natural that the circumstances, the detail, and the aftermath of such a fearful accident should tend to overshadow everything else on the Caledonian in the early years of the war. The whole affair was all the more tragic in that no fundamental weakness in the system was involved; there were no faults or flaws in rolling stock, permanent way, or signalling. It was just the gross negligence of two men in acting first, in concert, in a most irresponsible manner, and then in neglecting to carry out certain simple, essential, and well-understood precautions. One cannot say either, that the strain of war conditions bore heavily on either of them. Traffic on the Saturday before Whitsun was certainly heavy, but nothing unusual, still less exceptional, on a line used to dealing with the pre-war rush of tourist traffic experienced just before 12th August each year. Even today, 46 years afterwards, when recalling the chain of events it seems barely credible that men charged with the responsible task of working a main line signalbox could so fail in their duties.

The circumstance that set in motion the sequence of events that ended in such catastrophe was the late running of the Euston to Glasgow sleeping car express due to leave Carlisle at 6.5 a.m. A local train publicly booked to leave Carlisle at 6.10 a.m. (working time 6.17 a.m.) had to be considered in cases when the 'sleeper' was running late, as this train provided a connection at Beattock for Moffat passengers travelling to Edinburgh and Glasgow, and it was desirable that these should not be unduly late. It was the practice therefore to dispatch the local ahead of the 'sleeper' and side-track it somewhere *en route*. Quintinshill box, 1½ miles north of Gretna Junction, was a convenient place to do this, for there were running loops on both sides of the line. One gathers that late running was not infrequent, for the day signalman at Quintinshill, James Tinsley by name, was in the habit of taking advantage of this side-tracking to travel to the box by this local train from Gretna. It saved him the walk of 1½ miles, even though it meant that he was late on duty. He had an arrangement with the signalman at Gretna to let him know when the train was going to stop at Quintinshill, and a still more reprehensible arrangement with the night man he relieved. The change-over should have taken place at 6 a.m., and so that the irregularity should remain undetected the night man kept a record of happenings after 6 a.m. on a sheet of paper, so that Tinsley could enter them into the train register book in his own hand-writing after he had taken over.

On this particular morning both the Quintinshill loops were occupied by goods trains, and the only way to side-track the local was to propel it backwards through a trailing crossover on to the up main line – a perfectly normal and safe proceeding, providing that the clearly defined routine precautions were carried out. The night man at Quintinshill carried out the signal and point movements for the shunting operation, and the local train stopped with its engine no more than 65 yards from the signalbox, and in full view

FAMOUS PERSONALITIES

Above, right: J. F. McIntosh – Locomotive, Carriage and Wagon Superintendent.
Above, left: Captain James Williamson – Marine Superintendent.
Below, right: Irvine Kempt – Superintendent of the Line.
Below, left: Sir James Thompson – General Manager.

A group of fourteen 'Dunalastairs', of the first and second series, at Kingmoor shed after working a mammoth excursion party from St Rollox works to Carlisle that required fourteen trains. The pioneer engine, No. 721, is in the centre foreground.

[*Locomotive Publishing Co*

Above: One of the twelve-wheeled non-corridor coaches built for the Edinburgh and Glasgow service.

Below: Four of the famous Grampian corridor stock. The leading coach is lettered: 'Corridor Express. Glasgow, Perth and Aberdeen.'

[*B.T.C. Historical Relics*]

Express Passenger locomotive No. 904: one of the lesser-known members of the celebrated 'Cardean' Class.

[Locomotive Publishing Co

from the window. The night man, Meakin, then made, by default, the first two steps towards the disaster. He failed to send the blocking back signal to Kirkpatrick to indicate the up line was blocked; he omitted to place the safety collars on the levers of the up line signals. Tinsley then took over, and having travelled from Gretna by the local train, and ridden on its engine one would have thought that his first concern on taking over control of the box would be to check, involuntarily, that his mate had protected the train, at least by the lever collars. Instead he handed over the morning newspaper, and immediately began to copy out the entries from Meakin's piece of paper into the train register book.

He was soon interrupted in this by calls on the block bells, not only for the down sleeping car express, but for another train. He had no sooner pulled off his signals for the former when Kirkpatrick offered an up troop special, running from Larbert to Liverpool. Unbelievable though it may seem, Tinsley accepted the troop train, and with the local on which he had himself ridden only a few minutes earlier standing on the up main line almost outside the signalbox he pulled off all his up line signals! This was a shocking error in itself, but it was made all the more easy for him to commit by the negligence of his mate in failing to warn Kirkpatrick of the obstruction, and failing to put the protecting collars on the levers. Even yet, however, disaster might have been averted but for one unlucky circumstance. This point was not mentioned in any contemporary accounts or comments on the accident, and I did not realize it until making a certain run on the footplate of the up 'Royal Scot' just over 4 years ago.

From the overbridge north of Quintinshill the line is dead straight for nearly 3 miles and from a long distance to the north the signalbox can be seen through the arch of the bridge; but from that bridge a long gradual curve to the southward begins, and while the presence on that fatal morning of a goods train in the down loop would not have obscured the roof and upper windows of the box itself, it *would* have obscured the local train. Otherwise, with such a long view ahead, the driver of the troop train must almost certainly have seen the massive obstruction that faced him, none other than the 'Cardean' Class 4-6-0 No. 907. As it was, with all signals clear and all unsuspecting he came on at 70 m.p.h., and collided with the local train in such a frightful impact that his own train, which measured 213 yd in length, was reduced to a heap of wreckage only 67 yd long. The wooden coaches of the troop train were smashed to pieces, and wreckage thrown some distance ahead of where the two engines lay smashed beyond repair. Less than a minute later the down sleeping car express, double-headed and travelling at nearly 60 m.p.h., ploughed into the wreckage. The casualty list was 227 killed and 246 injured, by far the worst in British railway history.

It was no wonder that at least one senior railway officer, on reaching the scene, was so overcome as to lose his nerve and break down. It was Barr's job to get the line clear, but for nearly a day it was virtually impossible to get near to the centre of destruction so fierce was the fire that raged among the ruins of the wooden coaches, and around the four wrecked engines. The accident happened at about 6.50 a.m. on 22nd May, 1915, and the Carlisle fire brigade did not leave until 9 a.m. next morning. The once-magnificent 4-6-0 No. 907, which took the full force of the troop train, was very severely smashed in at the front end, besides sustaining a great deal of superficial damage from both the two collisions and the fire. The troop train engine, McIntosh superheater 4-4-0 No. 121, was in such a state that she was scrapped forthwith, but in the case of No. 907 some attempt was made to repair what would have been a most valuable engine for the wartime traffic. In the end, however, reconstruction was found impossible, and the engine was scrapped in January, 1916. The two express engines of the sleeping car express, though badly knocked about, were both rebuilt and put back into traffic. These engines were a 'Dunalastair IV', No. 140, and a McIntosh superheater 4-4-0 No. 48. They had between them a very heavy train of thirteen coaches, including three twelve-wheeled sleeping cars.

Whatever losses in engine power the Caledonian Railway sustained as a result of Quintinshill, the Company had a sudden and welcome addition to the stock in the autumn of 1915 through the top-level blunder on the Highland Railway that led to the six new 4-6-0s of the 'River' Class being banned from any kind of service on that line. With all due respects to St Rollox I have always felt that full use was never made of these fine engines, though of course, they were totally unlike the twentieth-century conception of a Caledonian locomotive, with their high raised running plates, outside cylinders and Walschaerts valve gear. Their nominal tractive effort was 24,800 lb against 21,348 lb in the 'Cardeans' as superheated, and although the coupled wheels were no more than 6 ft diameter they had an excellent turn of speed. They all had their regular drivers and regular turns, and while they did do a certain amount of passenger working between Perth and Aberdeen their most profitable revenue-earning service was on the fast through goods between

Perth and Carlisle. I gathered from John Barr that after McIntosh's retirement the practice of using large 4-6-0 locomotives on specific duties gradually fell into disfavour, and instead the use of 4-4-0s, piloted where necessary, became preferred.

The first of Pickersgill's own 4-4-0s came out in 1916, and although she was every inch a Caledonian engine one noticed some difference in detail, in the shape of the chimney, in the straight line of the coupling rod splashers, in the absence of smokebox wings, and in the six-wheeled tender. Technically there were some considerable differences between the new engines and the McIntosh superheater 4-4-0s of the '139' and '117' Classes thus:

Class Designer	'139' McIntosh	'117' McIntosh	'113' Pickersgill
Cylinders, dia. × stroke, in.	20 × 26	20¼ × 26	20 × 26
Heating surface, sq ft			
Tubes	1,220	1,220	1,185
Firebox	145	145	144
Superheater	330	295	200
Total	1,695	1,660	1,529
Grate area, sq ft	21	21	20·7
Boiler pressure, p.s.i.	165	170	170
Coupled wheel dia.	6' 6"	6' 6"	6' 6"
Wt. of engine only in working order, tons	59	59	58

One is inclined to question why it was necessary to design a new locomotive at all, seeing that the '117' Class had proved very successful. The 'Pickersgills' were also very good engines, but they were on the small side. Taken by themselves they were fine, robustly built, trouble-free machines, but in the light of past Caledonian traditions it looked as though something akin to stagnation had settled over St Rollox, if not actual retrogression.

Sixteen of these new 4-4-0s were built in 1916, six at St Rollox, and ten by the North British Locomotive Company. One of the St Rollox engines took the number of the McIntosh 4-4-0 destroyed at Quintinshill, No. 121. In that year the works was surprisingly busy, for wartime, with the building of locomotives to new designs, for in November, following the new 4-4-0s, came the first of Pickersgill's outside cylinder 4-6-0s, No. 60. By now it was evident that the new chief had very definite ideas of his own on locomotive design, ideas which hitherto he had no opportunity to develop in the limited environment of the G.N.S.R. On the Caledonian new mixed-traffic 4-6-0s were needed for the heavy wartime passenger and freight trains, and while multiplying either the McIntosh '179' Class, or the Highland 'River' design would seem to have met the need, and avoided the manufacture of new patterns, jigs, flanging plates and so on, an entirely new design was worked out. In so doing the Caledonian tradition of inside cylinders was broken, after persisting from the days of Dugald Drummond.

One may question why the cylinders *were* placed outside, when the valve gear was Stephenson's and was retained inside. In this respect St Rollox were on firm ground, for while the valve gear does not need a great deal of attention it is always desirable to have the crossheads and big-ends readily accessible. It is interesting to compare the proportions of three mixed traffic 4-6-os.

Class Designer	'179' McIntosh	'River' F. G. Smith	'60' Pickersgill
Coupled wheel dia.	5' 9"	6' 0"	6' 1"
Cylinders dia. × stroke in.	19½ × 26	21 × 28	20 × 26
Heating surface sq ft			
Tubes	1,439	1,460	1,529·5
Firebox	128	139·6	146·5
Superheater	403	350	258·2
Total	1,970	1,949·6	1,934·2
Grate area sq ft	21	25·3	25·5
Boiler pressure p.s.i.	170	160	175
Wt. of engine only work- ing order tons	68·5	71·8	75
Nominal T.E. at 85 per cent B.P. lb	20,704	24,800	21,155

The Pickersgill '60' Class were massive engines for their nominal tractive effort, and because of this they were exceptionally sure-footed. A friend who for 25 years was very familiar with their comings and goings said that he had never seen or heard one of them slip on starting.

Having said that, however, one could not say that their work on the road was very inspiring. I had many runs behind them, chiefly between Glasgow and Perth and it was rare for them to touch as much as 65 m.p.h. They always seemed hamstrung at the front end, and while I have never seen the actual details of their valve events the arrangement of their eccentric rods probably gave the clue to the trouble. With the normal layout of the Stephenson's link motion the lead of the valves increases as the gear is linked up, thus giving a greater degree of pre-admission to the steam at the commencement of each stroke when the engine is running fast, and a greater freedom of entry for the steam. In the Pickersgill '60' Class the eccentric rods were crossed, thus providing just the opposite effect. It is probable that any effect to notch up resulted in severe throttling of the steam at entry to the cylinders. This would amply explain their painful sluggishness on the level, and downhill. Only six of these engines were built in Caledonian days, Nos. 60–65, in 1916–7; but a further twenty were built by the L.M.S.R. in 1925–6, and I shall have more to say about these engines and their work in a later chapter.

The '60' Class 4-6-os were followed very soon afterwards by the twelve 4-6-2 passenger tank engines of the '944' Class, also with outside cylinders. They were the first fast passenger locomotives of a new design to be built for the Caledonian by an outside contractor since the days of the Drummond 4-4-os. At that stage in the war the North British Locomotive Company was producing, at their three works, an enormous volume of war munitions, tanks, and such like, while the production of locomotives continued at high level; they built the twelve new 4-6-2 tanks during 1917, in addition to a batch of ten Pickersgill 4-4-os, in 1916. Engines Nos. 944–955 had the same nominal tractive effort as that of the '179' Class of McIntosh 4-6-os, and the dimensions that contributed to it, cylinders, coupled wheels and boiler pressure, were the same in each case. But, although the 4-6-2 tanks had smaller coupled wheels than the '60' Class they seemed livelier engines in every way. They worked on the Clyde Coast trains from Glasgow, and when travelling behind them between Central and Wemyss Bay I had a number of instances of really brisk running. At the same time they climbed well on the heavy gradients between Upper Port Glasgow and Wemyss Bay.

The Caledonian Railway retained its full pre-war engine and carriage livery throughout the war period, though the express train services were decelerated to a mere ghost of their old selves. Traffic to and from the engineering establishments on the Clyde was enormous, and in the central area passenger trains, as in the Second World War, could no longer be given priority. The deceleration of express schedules enabled economies to be effected by running very heavy loads with one engine, though one feels that this practice was carried rather to extremes. At the end of the war, and for some little time afterwards, the maximum load that had to be taken without assistance south of Carstairs by superheater engines, 4-4-0 and 4-6-0 alike, was 440 tons tare; so that one found McIntosh and Pickersgill 4-4-os staggering up the last miles from Elvanfoot to Beattock Summit with gross loads of 450 to 460 tons behind their tenders! On the Beattock Bank proper rear-end banking assistance was given freely enough, as of old, and at one time one or two of the new 4-6-2s were stationed at Beattock for the purpose.

Shortly after the outbreak of war the entire fleet of the Caledonian Steam Packet Company was commandeered for war service. Most of the steamers were used as minesweepers, though the *Duchess of Argyll* and the *Duchess of Hamilton* were used as troopships for the short runs across the English Channel. Even though the ships had been requisitioned the Company had to carry on a reduced service on the Clyde, and did so by chartering a number of vessels from the private companies. During this period some of the well-known West Highland steamers of MacBrayne's fleet, such as the *Fusilier*, *Chevalier* and *Iona* sailed on Caledonian service. In the meantime the *Duchess of Hamilton* had been lost on active service; she struck a mine off Harwich in November, 1915, and sank at once. The *Duchess of Montrose* was lost off Gravelines in March, 1917, but the rest of them returned to the Clyde after the war and took up their old duties. In those post-war years I sailed many times in the *Duchess of Rothesay* and the *Duchess of Fife* while the beautiful two-funnelled turbine *Duchess of Argyll* returned to the Arran run.

So far as outward appearances went the Caledonian returned very quickly to its pre-war smartness of turnout, and its fine stations were as spick and span as ever. Some of the pre-war schedules were fully restored, but observers could not fail to notice that the old fire and dash was rarely to be seen in the express train running. The hill-climbing was as good as ever, but drivers seemed to have acquired a new reluctance to run hard downhill, and many a good run was spoiled, and time actually lost by drifting down from Ecclefechan to Gretna, or from Elvanfoot to Lamington with speed barely reaching 60 m.p.h. Once the immediate war period was passed piloting became frequent particularly between Carlisle and Beattock Summit. The regular workings of engines and men did not re-appear, and on the heaviest trains the running department appeared to prefer using a couple of 4-4-0s, rather than any of the 4-6-0s. Just as the 'Prince of Wales' and 'George the Fifth' Classes were used indiscriminately on many North Western services, so the 'Cardeans' and the '60' Class took turns with the McIntosh and Pickersgill 4-4-0s.

Then, almost at the end of the Caledonian Railway's separate existence St Rollox works received the order to build four new 4-6-0 locomotives, larger than anything previously seen on the line. In nominal tractive power they were to be a greater advance upon *Cardean*, than that engine had been over the most powerful of the 'Dunalastairs'. With three cylinders 18½ in. diameter by 26 in. stroke,

6 ft 1 in. coupled wheels, and a boiler pressure of 180 lb per sq in. the tractive effort was 28,000 lb as compared with the 21,348 lb of No. 903 in her superheated condition. The massive construction of these engines, their great frames, their 5 ft 9 in. diameter boilers, and firebox with 28 sq ft of grate area, were all in keeping with what was expected of them, the most powerful passenger engines in the forthcoming L.M.S. group; but during their construction there was an air of scepticism among the older hands in the works. Nevertheless the interest was widespread among everyone concerned. No. 956 and her three sisters were magnificent looking engines. Despite their great size they were beautifully proportioned, but much as one regrets having to say so, rarely has there been a greater, or more complete failure.

Pickersgill used the Walschaerts gear to actuate the valves of the outside cylinders, and designed a special derived motion of his own for working the middle cylinder valves. By that time many of the troubles of the Gresley conjugated gear were known, having been discussed freely and openly at meetings, and in the published proceedings of the Institution of Locomotive Engineers. The Pickersgill derived motion was infinitely more complicated than Gresley's and the drive included no fewer than fourteen pin joints! The Gresley locomotives with the derived valve gear were fast runners from the outset, even before the troubles with the gear had been corrected; but No. 956 and her three sisters were terribly sluggish, and the curious muffled roar of their exhaust when working hard told its own tale. There were mechanical troubles with the gear too, and even before the Grouping the drastic step had been taken of removing the derived gear on Nos. 957 and 958 and fitting Stephenson's link motion to the inside cylinder. The two engines concerned originally went into service in July, 1921; they were altered in April, 1922.

It was a sad end to the long and illustrious history of Caledonian locomotive development. Whether anything could have been made of these engines by a drastic re-design of the valve gear we are not to know. The Caledonian locomotive influence in years to come was to stem from a very different direction, as the concluding chapter will show. So, on 1st January, 1923, the Caledonian was 'Grouped' with its friend and ally the Highland, and with its old enemy the Glasgow & South Western, to form the Northern Division of the London Midland & Scottish Railway, with Donald Matheson appointed Deputy General Manager for Scotland. Pickersgill, like Robert Whitelegg at Kilmarnock, became a mere Divisional Locomotive Engineer. In the civil engineering department the Engineer-in-Chief,

W. A. Paterson, retired. He had held the post since 1910, having succeeded Matheson when the latter was appointed General Manager. Paterson's chief assistant, D. McLellan, became Divisional Engineer for Scotland. Although at the time of the Grouping things were uncertain and confused, particularly in the realm of locomotive design, the final chapter will show that the contribution of the Caledonian to the L.M.S. group was massive and lasting.

XIII

Locomotive Performance

AFTER the Race to the North in 1895 the Caledonian Railway stood alone among all the protagonists in that exciting affair, in not merely maintaining, but improving upon the magnificent standards of running set up during the race itself. It was only on the very last night that the stop at Stirling was omitted, and the problem of making the water supply last out over the non-stop run of 150·8 miles influenced the work of the Drummond 4-4-0 No. 90 throughout. The feat of getting through to Perth in $149\frac{1}{2}$ minutes was a magnificent feat of enginemanship on the part of Driver Crooks, but the fastest running of the race was made on the previous night when Driver Robinson on 4-4-0 No. 78 ran from Carlisle to Stirling in 114 minutes start to stop. The load on that night was 95 tons behind the tender. A year later, when the McIntosh 'Dunalastair' 4-4-0s were making times nearly as fast, with trains of practically twice the weight, it is no wonder that the enthusiasts of the day were hard put to it in finding superlatives enough to describe Caledonian locomotive performance!

On many occasions during that brilliant summer of 1896 Charles Rous-Marten travelled through the night to Aberdeen, recording in detail the work of the 'Dunalastairs'; and while he has not left us as many detailed logs as we could perhaps desire, those that have survived amplify most vividly the briefer notes he published about many other fine runs. We cannot do better than begin with two magnificent runs on the 1.54 a.m. from Carlisle – the 8 p.m. 'Tourist Express' from Euston to Aberdeen. The logs of these two runs are set out in Table I. In the case of many of his early runs with the 'Dunalastairs' Rous-Marten does not quote the numbers of the individual engines concerned. This was perhaps an unconscious tribute to the work of the class as a whole, which in those first years was so uniformly excellent as to make references to particular engines and drivers unnecessary.

Referring now to Table I, the lightning starts out of Carlisle will at once be noted, with speeds worked up to 70 m.p.h., or so, in the first 5 or 6 miles. With locomotive running in general, when accelerating from rest it is rare to see drivers use their regulators and reversers to use the steaming rate they are going to maintain when full speed is attained. Normally they work up to it gradually. From Carlisle however these 'Dunalastair' drivers not only steamed their engines at full blast from the moment of getting the right away, but from a *cold* start. This could have been done only with the most careful preparation of the fire beforehand, and it serves to show what out-and-out enthusiasts the Caledonian enginemen of the day were. It must be added that pride in their engines and their railway gave them a tremendous superiority-complex so far as other railways and other locomotives at Carlisle were concerned. Some of them barely recognized the existence of any railway other than the Caledonian!

TABLE I

1.54 a.m.   CARLISLE–PERTH

	Engine No. Driver Load tons E/F	728 Robinson 161/170		733 Armstrong 170/180	
Dist. Miles		Actual m. s.	Av. speed m.p.h.	Actual m. s.	Av. speed m.p.h.
0·0	CARLISLE . . .	0 00	—	0 00	—
4·1	Rockcliffe . . .	5 03	48·7	4 59	49·4
6·1	Floriston . . .	6 49	68·0	6 42	70·0
8·6	Gretna Junction .	8 58	69·7	8 53	68·6
13·1	Kirkpatrick . .	13 29	59·8	13 29	58·7
16·7	Kirtlebridge . .	17 21	56·0	17 17	56·8
20·1	Ecclefechan . .	20 36	62·7	20 31	63·0
25·8	LOCKERBIE . .	25 59	63·5	25 50	64·5
28·7	Nethercleugh . .	28 20	74·0	28 15	72·1
31·7	Dinwoodie . . .	30 45	74·5	30 46	71·8
34·5	Wamphray . . .	33 12	68·6	33 19	66·0
39·7	BEATTOCK . .	37 50	67·3	38 23	61·7
49·7	*Beattock Summit* .	53 33	38·2	53 30	39·7
52·6	Elvanfoot . .	56 23	61·6	56 49	52·5
55·3	Crawford . . .	58 36	73·3	58 57	75·5
57·8	Abington . . .	60 36	75·0	60 57	75·0
63·2	Lamington . .	64 44	78·3	65 12	76·3
66·9	SYMINGTON . .	67 44	74·0	68 24	69·4
68·5	Thankerton . .	69 03	73·0	69 46	70·5
73·5	CARSTAIRS . .	72 46	80·3	73 40	76·8
80·7	Braidwood . .	81 00	52·4	81 40	54·0
84·0	Law Junction . .	83 49	70·3	84 29	70·3
89·9	Holytown . . .	89 17	64·8	89 46	67·0
94·3	COATBRIDGE .	94 13	53·5	94 29	56·0
109·7	LARBERT . . .	109 22	61·0	110 11	58·8
117·8	STIRLING . . .	116 53	—	117 40	—
2·9	Bridge of Allan .	4 53	36·6	4 10	41·8
7·6	Kinbuck . .	11 17	44·0	10 26	45·2
17·2	CRIEFF JUNCTION .	21 12	58·1	20 45	55·9
19·3	Auchterarder .	22 58	71·4	22 27	74·0
23·4	Dunning . . .	26 27	70·7	25 47	73·8
33·0	PERTH . . .	34 44	—	34 46	—

That their vigorous starts had not disturbed the firebed, and upset the steaming, is shown by the very hard work that followed, with average speeds of 64·6 and 63·3 m.p.h. over the 31·1 adverse miles from Gretna Junction to Beattock station, and by the magnificent climbs of the Beattock Bank that followed. The remarkable uniformity of the work of Drivers Robinson and Armstrong will be noted. There was never as much as a single minute's difference in their times from the start. As these performances are apt to be taken as a yardstick by which locomotive work between Carlisle and Beattock Summit can be judged, it is interesting to compare the loads that one could expect to be taken by two other famous express designs that have worked over this route, on a straight comparison of tractive effort, of grate area, and of adhesion weight.

Engine Class	Equivalent loads, ton		
	per ton of T.E.	per sq ft of grate area	per ton of adhesion wt.
'Dunalastair I' . .	170	170	170
Cardean . . .	255	215	300
'Duchess' . .	455	412	365

From this table it is clear that one could not expect the 'Cardeans' to equal the 1896 times of the 'Dunalastairs' with loads of more than about 230 or 240 tons, despite their great increase in size and weight, while adhesion weight might well cramp the style of such a fine modern design as a Stanier 'Duchess'. I have certainly clocked one of the latter to pass Beattock Summit in 49 minutes from Carlisle with a load of 405 tons, but it was a fairly exceptional performance.

The 'Dunalastairs' were free-running engines, and their drivers took them unrestrainedly down Upper Clydesdale. Had they been able to continue in the same style over the equally favourable gradient from Braidwood down to Larbert the latter junction could have been passed in 104–5 minutes and Stirling reached in 112 or 113 minutes. There are, however, numerous slacks to be observed on this downhill section, and the average speeds over the 29 miles from Braidwood to Larbert were little more than 60 m.p.h. Rous-Marten recorded an even faster run than either of the two shown in Table I, with engine No. 728 and Tom Robinson of 'Race' fame, when Beattock Summit was passed in exactly 53 minutes. The possibilities of quite a record time were cut short by a signal stop between Castlecary and Greenhill, at a point 105¼ miles from Carlisle, reached in 103 minutes 40 seconds. But for this Larbert would have been passed in about 106 minutes.

On the two runs tabulated, splendid work was done by both engines on the continuation to Perth. The average speeds of 44 and 45 m.p.h. between Bridge of Allan and Kinbuck indicate *minimum* speeds of over 40 m.p.h. on this 5½ mile bank, on gradients varying between 1 in 78 and 1 in 100, again following vigorous starts out of Stirling. On the 1 in 100 descent from Crieff Junction down to Dunning it is evident that the drivers allowed their engines to accelerate rapidly from the summit to a point near Auchterarder, and then eased them considerably. Otherwise, with 4 miles of real racing ground ahead speeds well into the 'eighties' might have been expected in the neighbourhood of Dunning. The finishing times of these runs of over the 15·8 miles from Crieff Junction into Perth are in strong contrast with the finish of the Drummond 4-4-0 No. 90 on the last night of the race, when her water supply was practically exhausted after running non-stop from Carlisle. She took 16¾ minutes, whereas the 'Dunalastairs' in Table I took 13 minutes 32 seconds, and 14 minutes 1 second respectively.

The 'Tourist Express' continued northward with the remarkable booking of 32 minutes for the 32·5 miles on to Forfar – remarkable in that the first 7¼ miles of this run are sharply adverse. Table II includes details of two runs from Perth to Aberdeen, both with 'Dunalastairs' of which Rous-Marten does not give the numbers. On the 'Tourist' one of them made short work of a load of 101 tons, though not quite attaining the brilliance of John Soutar's running with the Lambie 4-4-0 No. 17 in the race. The continuation from Forfar was easy work by comparison and Aberdeen was reached 10 minutes early. The second run in Table II was on the West Coast Postal special, on a non-stop schedule of 97 minutes from Perth to Aberdeen. How much the driver had in hand on this journey is shown by Rous-Marten's reference to another run on the same train when the 89·8 miles were completed in 88½ minutes start to stop, recovering time after a late start. On this latter run Soutar was the driver, with 'Dunalastair' Class 4-4-0 No. 724.

The second 'Dunalastairs', sometimes called the 'Breadalbanes', were put to work on the heavy West Coast corridor trains between Carlisle and Glasgow, and from their very first introduction one finds them taking loads of over 300 tons, unassisted, on the 2 p.m. non-stop from Glasgow to Carlisle. The schedule in 1898 was 2¼ hours for the run of 102·3 miles, and it remained unchanged throughout *Cardean's* long innings on the train. After the first trials with the

'Dunalastair II' 4-4-0s, however, it was evidently considered that such loads as 300 tons were too great to be taken up the long bank to Craigenhill as an all-weather standard, and Ahrons has recorded a run on which No. 767 was assisted to Carstairs with a load of 265 tons. With No. 766, brand new and just nicely run in, the up 2 p.m. 'Corridor' was worked in remarkable style with a load of 330 tons. The engine must have been worked very hard up the bank from Uddingston to Craigenhill, for speed at no time fell below 30 m.p.h. on long stretches of 1 in 100, and Carstairs was passed dead on time, in 47 minutes from Glasgow, 28·8 miles.

TABLE II
PERTH–ABERDEEN
'Dunalastair I' class 4-4-0s

Train Load tons E/F		8 p.m ex Euston 101/105		West Coast Postal 103/135	
Dist. Miles		Actual m. s.	Av. speed m.p.h.	Actual m. s.	Av. speed m.p.h.
0·0	PERTH. . . .	0 00	—	0 00	—
7·2	Stanley Junction . .	8 41	49·7	8 51	48·8
11·3	Cargill . . .	12 29	64·7	12 56	60·1
20·5	Alyth Junction . .	20 38	67·7	21 31	64·3
32·5	FORFAR . . .	30 41	69·8	32 44	64·2
39·5	Guthrie . . .	7 45	54·2	40 29	54·2
50·6	Dubton Junction .	18 47	60·4	52 40	54·7
66·5	Drumlithie . .	34 38	60·2	69 11	57·8
73·7	STONEHAVEN . .	41 49	60·1	76 48	56·8
89·5	Ticket Platform . .	58 30	56·8	93 41	56·2
89·8	ABERDEEN . .			94 56	
		Arrived 10 min. early		Sch. 97 min.	

Then came a dead stand for signals, at Symington, that caused a loss of about 5 minutes in running. Because of this Beattock Summit was passed 3 minutes late; but with 55 minutes left in which to secure a punctual arrival in Carlisle no difficulty was experienced. Without any exceptionally fast running, and no maximum speed exceeding 75 m.p.h. the 49·7 miles were covered in 50 minutes 55 seconds and Carlisle was reached 3¼ minutes early in 131 minutes 46 seconds from Glasgow. Net time was 126¾ minutes, showing an average speed of 48½ m.p.h. over this difficult road, with a train load of 330 tons behind the tender. The extent to which No. 766 was extended on this trip, particularly between Motherwell and Craigenhill Summit, can be judged from the details of a test run made in 1898 with engine No. 772 on the 2 p.m. 'Corridor', on a day when the load was 305 tons. Indicator diagrams were taken at one minute intervals on the heavily graded sections, and a careful measurement taken of the coal and water consumption. The latter figures certainly give the lie to the story that gained credence some years ago, of 'Dunalastair II' Class engines on this duty burning between 80 and 90 lb of coal per mile. Table III, herewith, gives skeleton log of the run.

TABLE III

C.R. 2 p.m. GLASGOW–CARLISLE

Load: 305 tons tare, 320 tons full
Engine: 4-4-0 No. 772, 'Dunalastair II' class

Dist. Miles		Sch. min.	Actual min.	Av. speed m.p.h.
0·0	GLASGOW CENTRAL	0	0	—
4·0	Rutherglen Junc. .	6	7¼	—
—	—	—	p.w.s.	—
8·4	Uddingston . .	13	13	—
12·9	MOTHERWELL .	18	18½	49·2
18·3	Law Junc. . .	29	29½	29·4
26·0	Cleghorn . .	44	44½	30·8
28·8	CARSTAIRS . .	47	47¼	61·2
35·4	Symington . .	56	55½	48·0
52·6	Summit . . .	77	77	48·0
62·6	Beattock . . .	89	88½	52·2
76·5	LOCKERBIE . .	105	102	61·8
—	—	—	sigs	—
85·6	Kirtlebridge . .	115	113½	47·5
93·7	Gretna Junc. . .	125	123	51·2
—	—	—	sig. stop	—
102·3	CARLISLE . . .	135	134	—

Net time 129 minutes

Between Motherwell and Craigenhill Summit (23·8 miles out) the engine was developing between 715 and 815 indicated horsepower continuously. Speed fell to a minimum of 26½ m.p.h. on the 1 in 100 approaching Law Junction. Between Lamington and Beattock Summit the power output was rather higher, ranging mostly between 800 and 900, including a very fine minimum speed of 39 m.p.h. at the summit. Except between Motherwell and Craigenhill the reverser was in the fifth notch throughout the trip, 31 per cent cut-off. On the slowest and hardest part of the climbing the lever was at 4½ notches, giving 38 per cent cut-off. Apart from this one change in cut-off all variations in power output were effected by changes in the regulator opening. Approaching Beattock Summit the regulator was practically full open, with a boiler pressure of 160 lb per sq in. and steam chest pressure 150. The water consumption worked out at 34·3 gallons per mile, and the coal consumption 49 lb per mile. The tank capacity of the tenders allowed of a maximum water consumption of 40 gallons per mile, with a coal rate of about 55 lb per mile. These figures would probably be more nearly reached on the return working with the down 'Corridor' from Carlisle to Glasgow.

When the 'Dunalastair II' Class was first introduced the load of the northbound train was lighter, and on a fine run clocked by Rous-Marten engine No. 766 had 276 tons behind the tender. The engine was evidently worked very hard from the start, for Rockcliffe, 4·1 miles, was passed in no more than 5 minutes 55 seconds and speed then averaged 56 m.p.h. over the ensuing 30·4 adverse miles to Wamphray. Rous-Marten was clearly expecting this big load to be taken up the bank without assistance, but adverse signals brought them nearly to a stand, and because of this the driver stopped for a banker. A very fast run was made downhill from Beattock Summit with a time of 20 minutes 49 seconds pass to stop for the 23·5 miles to Strawfrank Junction, and a maximum speed of 80 m.p.h. Then, with the load reduced by the detaching of the Edinburgh portion, No. 766 ran the 28·2 miles to the stop at Eglinton Street, in 31 minutes 17 seconds – very fast by later standards – and reached that station in exactly 123 minutes from Carlisle, dead on time, despite the delay south of Beattock.

The overnight expresses from Euston to Edinburgh and Glasgow were the fastest down trains out of Carlisle, and the Glasgow train in particular had the fastest overall time of any from Euston – an even 8 hours. The first of these two early morning flyers, leaving Carlisle at 5·35 a.m., served Edinburgh and the north, and had the very sharp allowance of 84 minutes for the 73·5 miles to Carstairs, in comparison with the 89 minutes booked to the famous 8.13 p.m. out of Carlisle, the afternoon 'Corridor' train from Euston. Among the records of the late R. E. Charlewood there are details of an interesting run on this train, made in July, 1907, when a heavy train of 365 tons was taken by a 'Dunalastair III', No. 889, piloted throughout by a Drummond 4-4-0 No. 83. The working times provided for a 2 minute stop at Beattock to attach a bank engine, after which no more than 16 minutes were allowed for the 10 miles up to Beattock Summit. With two engines throughout, however, the run from Carlisle to Carstairs was made non-stop.

The start, as shown in the log detailed in Table IV, was strangely slow for the Caledonian and speed did not greatly exceed 60 m.p.h. at the Solway Firth. Some reasonably good hill-climbing followed, and Beattock was passed in 43 minutes 37 seconds at full speed. One might have thought that now matters were well in hand, and that with a flying start to the bank good time would have been made over the rest of the journey. But this was in all probability a contemporary example of what I have experienced more than once on the footplate in the early morning on Beattock Bank. On the finest of mornings the mist can come rolling down from the hills and make the going exceedingly slippery. In such conditions it is useless to attempt pressing locomotives to a vigorous climb. In actual fact Nos. 83 and 889 together took as much as 20 minutes 41 seconds from Beattock station to the summit, and were $3\frac{1}{4}$ minutes *down* on passing the latter point. There was some fast running downhill to Lamington, with speed just exceeding 80 m.p.h., but nevertheless $2\frac{1}{2}$ minutes had to be booked against the engines.

TABLE IV

5.35 a.m. CARLISLE–CARSTAIRS

Load: 12 coaches. 347 tons tare, 365 tons full
Engines: Drummond 4-4-0 No. 83
'Dunalastair III' 4-4-0 No. 889

Dist. Miles		Sch. min.	Actual m. s.	Average speed m.p.h.
0·0	CARLISLE	0	0 00	—
4·1	Rockcliffe . . .		6 35	—
6·1	Floriston . . .		8 39	58·1
8·6	Gretna Junction . .	9	11 04	62·5
13·1	Kirkpatrick . . .		16 21	51·1
16·7	Kirtlebridge . . .	18	21 17	43·8
20·1	Ecclefechan . .		24 46	58·4
25·8	LOCKERBIE . . .	28	30 08	63·8
34·5	Wamphray . . .		38 38	61·4
39·7	BEATTOCK . . .	43/45	43 37	62·6
49·7	*Summit* . . .	61	64 18	29·0
52·6	Elvanfoot . . .		67 34	53·4
55·3	Crawford . . .		69 51	70·7
57·8	Abington . . .		72 07	66·8
63·2	Lamington . . .		76 16	78·0
66·9	SYMINGTON . .		79 37	66·3
68·5	Thankerton . . .		81 10	61·9
73·2	*Strawfrank Junction* .		85 21	67·2
73·5	CARSTAIRS . . .	84	86 33	—

Charlewood was travelling to Edinburgh, and the five coaches concerned, weighing 170 tons, were taken forward by a Lambie 4-4-0, No. 16. From Carstairs there are 9 miles of adverse gradients

Above: Express Goods Train leaving Carlisle hauled by superheater 4-6-0 locomotive No. 180.

[*B.T.C. Historical Relics*

Below: 10 a.m. express Glasgow to Euston in Floriston Woods. First coach is a Caledonian brake composite lettered 'Glasgow Central & Bristol via Severn Tunnel.' 'Cardean' Class 4-6-0 No. 907 destroyed after the Quintinshill disaster.

[*B.T.C. Historical Relics*

Above: McIntosh design, No. 59 at Stirling.
[*F. Moore*

4-6-0s
FOR THE
OBAN LINE

Below: A 'Pickersgill', No. 195 at Oban.
[*R. D. Stephen*

Above: McIntosh Superheater 4-4-0 No. 132 at Perth.

Below: One of the ex-Highland 'River' Class 4-6-0s, known on the Caledonian as the 'Hielan'mon'.

[*R. D. Stephen*

Above: One of the '908' Class mixed traffic 4-6-0s, No. 917 fitted with side window cab.

Below: An ex-R.O.D. 2-8-0 of the Great Central design, in Caledonian service at Aberdeen in 1920. Note 'C.R.' on the characteristic G.C.R. tender.

[*R. D. Stephen*

to Cobbinshaw Summit culminating in 4 miles of 1 in 133–138–180–155–97, and No. 16 passed Cobbinshaw in the smart time of 13 minutes 33 seconds from the start. Speed had reached 55 m.p.h. near Auchengray, and fell to nothing less than 44 m.p.h. at the summit. There was a bad signal check at Ravelrig Junction, but the sharp allowance of 33 minutes for the 27·4 miles from Carstairs to Edinburgh was practically maintained. Curiously enough one of my last trips over this route with an ex-Caledonian engine, in 1932, was behind one of the two engines concerned in the earlier part of Charlewood's journey of 1907, the 'Dunalastair III' No. 889, but in my case running as L.M.S. No. 14339. With a much heavier train of 265 tons she did well up to Cobbinshaw passing that point in 16 minutes 5 seconds, at a minimum speed of 30 m.p.h. on the bank. After that we barely exceeded 60 m.p.h. anywhere on the steep descent into Edinburgh, but reached Princes Street on time nevertheless, despite adverse signals outside, in 38 minutes from Carstairs.

By introduction of the large 4-6-0 engines it was hoped to avoid the necessity of banking at Beattock with loads of up to 300 tons, or so. But my previous analysis of the performance of the first 'Dunalastairs', in the hands of a link of exceptionally keen and expert drivers, showed that even with comparable work one could not expect to take more than about 230 to 250 tons up the Beattock Bank without assistance. The down 'Corridor' did not require anything like such fast work, in fact the allowance to passing the summit was 66 minutes. Even so, the latter timing would entail a sustained speed of 26 to 27 m.p.h. on the long 1 in 75 gradient, and with a 300-ton train this would require an output of about 1,200 indicated horsepower from a McIntosh 4-6-0. On the trial with No. 772 the indicated horsepowers recorded between Motherwell and Law Junction at speeds betwen 26½ and 28 m.p.h. varied between 753 and 807, while working in 38 per cent cut-off. If the 'Cardean' Class developed a power output in proportion to the increase in their tractive effort over the 'Dunalastair II' Class, they should provide roughly 1,000 i.h.p. – not nearly enough to work a 300-ton train up Beattock on the 'Corridor' schedule.

As far as I know *Cardean* was always banked. The minimum load of the train in her day was 305 tons gross, but in 1903 after the first introduction of Nos. 49 and 50, some successful runs were made with loads of over 300 tons, and no assistance. These two engines originally had 21 in. diameter cylinders, and a tractive effort of 24,990 lb. On the basis of the previous assessment one might expect to obtain 1,100 i.h.p. or a little over from these engines, at 26 to 27 m.p.h. and if the speed through Beattock was high, and opening out began well down the bank, a fast ascent could undoubtedly be made. But with a grate area of only 26 sq ft it would need the most expert of firing. On one occasion when No. 49 was on the down 'Corridor', and the load was no less than 390 tons, Rous-Marten records that it was fully intended to try and climb the Beattock Bank unassisted. But the train was handed over 3 minutes late by the L.N.W.R. at Carlisle, and as it was then a point of honour on the Caledonian to make up any lost time and bring the train into Glasgow 'on the tick' – as Rous-Marten put it – assistance would be taken unless they could make up that 3 minutes of arrears *before* Beattock. This was hardly likely with a 390-ton train.

Before coming to the runs with the down 'Corridor', detailed in Table V, I must mention the southbound run with No. 49 on the 2 p.m. out of Glasgow Central recorded by Rous-Marten on the same day. The load was again 390 tons, and with this they ran the 102·3 miles, non-stop to Carlisle in 134 minutes 31 seconds, arriving ½ minute early. This time included a dead stand for signals lasting 5¼ minutes at Carstairs, and two other signal checks, so that the net time was no more than 124 minutes. Speed was sustained at 27 to 30 m.p.h. on the heaviest part of the climb from Motherwell to Craigenhill and the time to the signal stop in Carstairs station was 47 minutes 38 seconds. On restarting the remaining 73·5 miles to Carlisle were covered in 81½ minutes inclusive of two bad signal checks before Symington. Beattock Summit was passed at 33 m.p.h. and the maximum speed downhill was 79 m.p.h. nearing Gretna. This was by no means the limit of capacity of these engines, and on another occasion No. 50 ran a train of 384 tons tare from Carstairs to Carlisle in 78 minutes 14 seconds inclusive of two signal checks south of Gretna.

Coming now to Table V, in which the work of No. 49 in the summer of 1903 is set against some typical work of *Cardean* in the 1910–14 period, it will be seen that the traditionally vigorous starts of the 'Dunalastairs' were persisting with No. 49, and that Gretna was passed within a few seconds of the very sharp 10 minutes allowance. Again, seeing that the section from Gretna to Lockerbie includes nearly 11 miles rising at 1 in 200, and little in the way of favourable grade to assist, the subsequent point-to-point booking leaves little to spare. No. 49 just held her own here, with a very fine minimum speed of 47 m.p.h. on the longer of the two 1 in 200 banks. On the two runs with *Cardean*, clocked by Cecil J. Allen, the starts were leisurely by Caledonian standards of earlier days, although to

TABLE V

'THE CORRIDOR'—CARLISLE-STRAWFRANK JUNCTION

Distance Miles	Engine No. Load, tons full	Sch. min.	1 — 49* — 390 Actual m. s.	Speeds m.p.h.	2 — 903* — 305 Actual m. s.	Speeds m.p.h.	3 — 903† — 360 Actual m. s.	Speeds m.p.h.	4 — 49† — 355 Actual m. s.	Speeds m.p.h.
0·0	CARLISLE	0	0 00	—	0 00	—	0 00	—	0 00	—
4·1	Rockcliffe		5 57	60	6 40	—	6 30	62½	6 54	—
8·6	Gretna Junction	10	10 17	64½	11 00	65	11 00	44	11 24	63
16·7	Kirtlebridge	20	20 22	47 (min.)	20 45	49	21 10	66	21 01	48
25·8	LOCKERBIE	30	30 10	69	30 05	69	31 05	—	30 54	70
34·5	Wamphray		38 15	65	38 20	—	39 25	—	38 59	—
39·7	BEATTOCK	44	44 28	—	44 30	—	45 35	—	45 06	—
		46	46 58‡	—	45 30‡	—	47 00‡	—	46 26‡	—
45·3	Greskine Box		—	—	56 15	37	57 40	36½	—	—
49·7	Beattock Summit	66	65 00	—	64 15	30½	65 40	32	66 32	—
55·3	Crawford		70 20	—	69 55	—	71 15	—	72 16	—
63·2	Lamington		77 05	78	76 55	68	78 20	70½	79 00	76
66·9	SYMINGTON		80 35	—	80 45	—	82 05	—	82 21	—
73·2	STRAWFRANK JUNCTION	89	86 50	—	87 20	—	88 35	—	89 10	—

* non-superheated   † superheated   ‡ Banked in rear

be sure they would have been accounted brisk enough elsewhere in the country, with such loads. On the first of the two runs the hill-climbing from Gretna was splendid, and *Cardean* had overtaken No. 49 by Lockerbie. With the heavier train on the third run in the table the going was not quite so hard up to Lockerbie, though the driver had his own methods of working. Apart from the $1\frac{3}{4}$ miles at 1 in 200 down past Castlemilk siding the favourable gradient past Lockerbie is no steeper than 1 in 528 and here speeds up to 69 m.p.h. were sustained.

The fourth run was made in September, 1913, on one of the rare occasions when *Cardean* was not available. No. 49 deputized for her, and put up a fine show with a load of 355 tons. This run was clocked by the late R. E. Charlewood, and he records that it was a very rough night, with high wind and rain. The immediate start out of Carlisle was slow, but after Gretna No. 49 gradually overhauled the times of No. 903 on run No. 3 and reached Beattock in 45 minutes 5 seconds. The bank engine was attached very smartly, but evidently the rear-end assistance left something to be desired, for the climb to summit was slow in comparison.

On the first run with No. 49, for all the insistence laid upon making up time, it is surprising that the job of getting the bank engine on in rear at Beattock took as much as $2\frac{1}{2}$ minutes. These 4-6-0s were always worked hard up the bank, however, and the trains on the first three runs were comfortably inside schedule on passing the summit. *Cardean*, on both her trips, had left Carlisle on time, and so ran easily down Upper Clydesdale; but the driver of No. 49 still had 2 minutes to make up, and in consequence allowed his engine to run more freely. On both her journeys *Cardean* was driven by David Gibson, of Polmadie, whose regular working of the up and down 'Corridors', over many years, brought a precision in timekeeping that became traditional of the train. If the sectional point-to-point times were not strictly observed it was because Gibson, from long experience, found he could run the train more easily, and therefore more economically by variations of his own. In later years the working times were adjusted to agree with those Gibson made night after night.

Mere figures cannot convey the sense of pride in the job that was so consistently manifested in all the goings and comings of *Cardean* and her driver. Whereas some drivers adorned their regular engines with engraved stars on the smokebox doors, and several of the 'Clan' Class 4-6-0s of the Highland Railway in later years had ornamental oak leaves, *Cardean* having a perfectly plain smokebox door, had a

more subtle, and personal decoration on the regulator handle. This
latter was distinguished by a beautiful piece of brass filigree work, in
which were embedded two burnished half-pennies. One wonders if
David Gibson ever had the same affection for the Pickersgill 4-6-0
No. 61 to which he was transferred in the latter part of the First
World War. In addition to *Cardean*, the sister engines 906 and 907
were regularly on the Carlisle road, and the latter engine which was
to meet such a violent end at Quintinshill in 1915, seems to have
settled into her stride very quickly. Charlewood's records include
details of two fine runs made when she was brand new, in the summer
of 1906. Table VI shows details of a trip on the 3.32 p.m. down from
Carlisle, while in Table VII is contained the log of a run on the
10.5 a.m. from Edinburgh as from Strawfrank Junction southwards.
The down journey reveals work similar to that needed on the evening
'Corridor' train to Lockerbie; but a very smart run was made on to
Beattock. Afterwards, once again, the work was just about up to
Cardean's regular standard.

TABLE VI
3.32 p.m. CARLISLE–CARSTAIRS

Load, to Lockerbie: 272 tons tare, 295 tons full
to Carstairs: 305 tons tare, 320 tons full
Engine: non-superheater 4-6-0 No. 907

Dist. Miles		Actual m. s.	Speeds m.p.h.
0·0	CARLISLE	0 00	—
4·1	Rockcliffe	6 28	58
6·1	Floriston	8 28	61
8·6	Gretna Junction . . .	10 51	64½
13·1	Kirkpatrick . . .	16 08	46¾
16·7	Kirtlebridge . . .	20 30	61
20·1	Ecclefechan . . .	24 01	50/63
25·8	LOCKERBIE . . .	30 28	
2·9	Nethercleugh . . .	4 55	59
5·9	Dinwoodie	8 03	57
8·7	Wamphray	10 55	63
13·9	BEATTOCK . . .	16 43	
5·6	*Greskine Box* . . .	11 14*	34
10·0	Summit	19 24	30½
12·9	Elvanfoot	22 49	66½
15·6	Crawford	25 15	68
18·1	Abington	27 32	66½
23·5	Lamington . . .	32 15	72
27·2	SYMINGTON . . .	35 47	57
28·8	Thankerton. . . .	37 23	68
33·5	*Strawfrank Junction* . .	41 53	62/64
33·8	CARSTAIRS . . .	42 45	

* Banked in rear

TABLE VII
STRAWFRANK JUNCTION–CARLISLE
10 a.m. ex Glasgow and 10.05 a.m. ex Edinburgh
Load: 13 coaches. 378 tons tare, 405 tons full
Engine: non-superheater 4-6-0 No. 907

Dist. Miles		Actual m. s.	Speeds m.p.h.
0·0	*Strawfrank Junction* . .	0 00	—
4·7	Thankerton	8 33	47½
6·3	SYMINGTON . . .	10 57	39
10·0	Lamington	15 16	59
15·4	Abington . . .	21 27	48½
17·9	Crawford	24 49	45½
20·6	Elvanfoot . . .	28 40	39½/45
23·5	*Summit*	33 26	31
33·5	BEATTOCK . . .	42 48	70
38·7	Wamphray	47 16	—
41·5	Dinwoodie . . .	49 52	—
44·5	Nethercleugh . . .	52 39	—
47·4	LOCKERBIE . . .	55 34	—
53·1	Ecclefechan . . .	62 04	—
		p.w.s.	
56·4	Kirtlebridge . . .	65 37	
60·1	Kirtlepatrick . . .	69 32	
64·6	Gretna Junction . .	73 27	72 max.
67·1	Floriston . . .	75 34	
		p.w.s.	
69·1	Rockcliffe . . .	77 35	
73·2	CARLISLE	82 53	

The up journey was made on the winter schedule of the 10.5 a.m. up from Edinburgh, when that train was combined with the 10 a.m. from Glasgow at Strawfrank Junction. Charlewood has recorded the actual make-up of the train, and it is interesting to study it today in the light of the present accommodation provided on the Anglo-Scottish expresses. It consisted of one coach from Glasgow to Birmingham, one from Glasgow to Bristol, six from Glasgow to Euston, including twelve-wheeled clerestory dining car, four from Edinburgh to Euston, including a similar dining car, and one from Edinburgh to Birmingham. This made up a total of 378 tons tare, no vehicle except the diners weighing more than 28 tons. With the exception of the Bristol coach, which was a Caledonian corridor composite, all the vehicles in the train were of West Coast Joint Stock. From Edinburgh the reduced load had been worked smartly by a 'Dunalastair IV', No. 146. Charlewood records that the morning was fine and frosty, with the rails slippery. This would account for the rather leisurely start out of Strawfrank, and no higher speed than 47½ m.p.h. attained in the 'dip' past Thankerton. After that No. 907

ran well with her 405-ton train. The two permanent way checks were very slight, and probably accounted for no more than the odd 53 seconds in the total time from Strawfrank to Carlisle.

The work of *Cardean* on the West Coast corridor trains was so regular and so punctual as to become almost stereotyped, and some present-day readers in studying logs like those in Table V might be misled into thinking that such work represented the limit of capacity of the class. To any such readers I would commend the details of the brief interchange trial with the L.N.W.R. that took place in July, 1909, while *Cardean* was non-superheated. Until comparatively recent times little was known of this exchange. *The Locomotive Magazine* of July, 1909, reported that *Cardean* first arrived at Crewe with the up 'Corridor' on 15th June, and that trial runs between Crewe and Carlisle continued until 10th July. It is interesting to recall that these experiments were in progress at the same time as the interchange between a Great Northern 'Atlantic' and a North Western 'Precursor', thus giving the Crewe drawing office an unusually busy time of it. Some years before the Second World War I wrote to Sir William Stanier to ask if any details of these exchanges were still extant, and he very kindly had the old records looked out for me. From these emerged brief particulars of what was probably the most astonishing climb ever made from Carlisle to Shap Summit, prior, that is, to the introduction of Sir William's own engines on the L.M.S.R.

The train concerned was the 12.58 p.m., allowed 109 minutes for the 90 miles to Preston, inclusive of a stop at Penrith. No more than 24 minutes, start to stop, was allowed for the 17·9 miles from Carlisle to Penrith, and from the re-start a modest 18 minutes was allowed to climb the 13·6 miles up to Shap Summit. The test train was made up to a tare load of 367 tons. These timings were sharper than anything worked before the Second World War (excepting the 'Coronation Scot') when the principal West Coast expresses were booked to pass the summit in 44 minutes from Carlisle, with an allowance of 19 minutes pass-to-pass up from Penrith. By dint of magnificent work on the footplate *Cardean* succeeded in keeping these fast times. To assess the power output necessary to achieve this I have made a 'reconstruction' of the run estimating the passing times and speeds. These are shown in Table VIII and it becomes reasonably clear that a sustained output of about 1,200 e.d.h.p. took place between Carlisle and Plumpton, and after Penrith the output must have been between 1,400 and 1,500 e.d.h.p. for 16 minutes on end.

TABLE VIII
CALEDONIAN AND LONDON & NORTH WESTERN RAILWAYS
12.58 p.m. CARLISLE–PRESTON
Load: 367 tons tare, 390 tons full
Engine: C.R. 4-6-0 No. 903 *Cardean*

Dist. Miles		Sch. min.	Actual m. s.		Speeds m.p.h.
0·0	CARLISLE	0	0	00	—
1·4	*No. 13 Box*		3	00	
4·9	*Wreay*		8	30	
13·1	*Plumpton*		18	30	
17·9	PENRITH	24	23	30	
1·1	*Eamont Junction* . . .		2	50	
3·3	*Milepost 48* . . .		5	40	54
4·3	,, 47 . . .		6	49	52
5·3	,, 46 . . .		7	59	50
6·3	,, 45 . . .		9	12	48½
7·3	,, 44 . . .		10	28	47
8·3	,, 43 . . .		11	45	46
9·3	,, 42 . . .		13	04	45
10·3	,, 41 . . .		14	25	44
11·6	*Shap*		16	05	53
13·6	*Summit Box* . . .	18	18	30	48
19·1	*Tebay*	24	23	45	73½ (max.)
32·1	*Oxenholme* . . .	38	37	30	—
44·9	CARNFORTH . . .	51	50	30	—
51·2	LANCASTER . . .	58	57	00	—
72·2	PRESTON	80	78	15	

In the various dynamometer car trials carried out since nationalization, with locomotives worked extremely hard under strictly controlled conditions, some power outputs have been obtained that are high in relation to the tractive power of the locomotives concerned; in some the sustained drawbar pull in heavy hill-climbing conditions has been more than 40 per cent of the nominal tractive effort of the locomotive. With the 'Britannia' Class Pacifics, indeed, in maximum conditions it rose to nearly 50 per cent. As recorded in my book on the Great Northern Railway I have personally seen even this achievement exceeded for a few thunderous minutes by a large-boilered Ivatt 'Atlantic' climbing the Ardsley Bank out of Leeds; but according to my calculations *Cardean* was exceeding it handsomely all the way from Penrith to Shap Summit, in 18½ minutes of outstanding locomotive effort, thus:

Engine Class	Rates
L.N.E.R. 'V2' 2-6-2 .	43·0
G.W.R. 'King' 4-6-0 .	42·2
B.R. 'Britannia' . .	50·0
G.N.R. 'Atlantic' . .	60·0
C.R. *Cardean* . .	61·2

Such work from *Cardean* needs no further comment from me!

Leaving the big engines for a time I come to the '140' Class, or 'Dunalastair IVs', which between them did some of the most brilliant work performed on the Caledonian in the present century. One of them, leaving Carlisle 14 minutes late with the Edinburgh portion of the 10 a.m. from Euston and a load of 170 tons ran in the style of the 'Tourist Express' of 1896, passing Beattock in 37 minutes 21 seconds, only to be stopped dead by signal right on the bank, at Auchencastle box. From this the engine recovered to a steady 36 m.p.h. on the 1 in 75. The engine in this case was No. 141. Another of the class ran the up 'Grampian Corridor Express' from Forfar to Perth, 32·5 miles, in 31 minutes 1 second start to stop with a load of 260 tons. Table IX includes details of a good run on the Edinburgh section of the up 'Corridor', leaving Princes Street at 2 p.m. The fine, uniform set train of the corresponding down express was not in evidence in Scotland, as both Glasgow and Edinburgh sections ran separately throughout to Carlisle, and conveyed through sections of other services.

TABLE IX
SYMINGTON–CARLISLE
2 p.m. Edinburgh to Euston

Load: 10 coaches, 335 tons tare, 360 tons full
Engine: 'Dunalastair IV' 4-4-0 No. 923

Dist. Miles		Sch. min.	Actual m. s.	Speeds m.p.h.
0·0	SYMINGTON . . .	0	0 00	—
3·7	Lamington		6 05	56
9·1	Abington		12 36	45½
11·6	Crawford		15 50	49½
14·3	Elvanfoot		19 28	42½/48½
17·2	Summit	22	23 36	37½
27·2	BEATTOCK	33	33 05	70
32·4	Wamphray		37 46	61
35·2	Dinwoodie		40 25	67
38·2	Nethercleugh . . .		43 12	—
41·1	LOCKERBIE	47	46 05	—
46·8	Ecclefechan		52 37	46 (min.)
50·1	Kirtlebridge	56	55 42	—
53·8	Kirkpatrick		59 08	—
58·3	Gretna Junction . .	64	62 48	—
60·8	Floriston		64 48	80
62·8	Rockcliffe		66 37	—
			sigs.	
66·9	CARLISLE	73	72 05	

On this occasion the make-up from Symington was one Caledonian Grampian twelve-wheeler, one W.C.J.S. twelve-wheeler, and one flat-roofed W.C.J.S. vehicle from Aberdeen to Euston; three W.C.J.S. 'twelves' from Edinburgh to Euston, and four older W.C.J.S. vehicles for the L. & Y. line. The engine was No. 923. Fine work was done up to Beattock Summit with this 360-ton train, while from milepost 40 successive 5-mile stretches were covered at average speeds of 68, 64, 60½, 51½, 66½ and 67½ m.p.h. It seemed traditional of those days for engines to be allowed to make their own pace south of Beattock, with no opening out to take the rising length from Lockerbie to Castlemilk siding. Consequently speed used to fall away very markedly on this slight incline, and Charlewood has annotated many of his logs 'fell badly here', and so on. No. 923 ran very fast down the final descent from Brackenhill to Gretna, and crossed the Border at a full 80 m.p.h.

The climax, so far as this class of locomotive is concerned came one day when Rous-Marten was a passenger on the 10.5 a.m. from Edinburgh to Carlisle on its summer working, then the fastest train on the Caledonian and booked to cover the 100·6 miles in the level 2 hours, non-stop. On this particular day the load was a 'modest' one of 404 tons tare, and about 435 tons full, so that the train engine, No. 140, was given a pilot, but only as far as Cobbinshaw Summit, 18·4 miles. With No. 33, one of the beautiful Conner 7-ft. 2-4-0s double-heading No. 140 the huge train must have made a wonderful picture. The two engines reached Cobbinshaw in 28 minutes 57 seconds, and then, after a brief stop to detach the pilot, No. 140 was taken smartly down the steep grades towards Carstairs, to pass Strawfrank Junction, very slowly, 9 miles from the restart in 10 minutes 32 seconds. A fine recovery followed in the gradual ascent of Upper Clydesdale, averaging 46½ m.p.h. from Strawfrank to Elvanfoot. This in itself was no mean achievement for a non-superheater 4-4-0 hauling a load of 435 tons, but for the last 2¼ miles of the ascent, on 1 in 99, Driver Stavert obviously threw in all he had.

Passing Elvanfoot at 50 m.p.h. the last 2·9 miles up to Beattock Summit took only 4 minutes 13 seconds. Rous-Marten's claim that the minimum speed of 36 m.p.h. was an *absolutely* sustained one, takes some believing as it would involve an equivalent drawbar horse-power of 1,400. The nominal tractive effort of these engines was 18,411 lb at 85 per cent boiler pressure, and the drawbar pull involved would be almost *80 per cent* of the nominal tractive effort. Nevertheless we must pay due heed to Rous-Marten's words: 'But then we got on the 1 in 100, and our speed slowly fell from 50 miles an hour to 45, 40, 38, 37 and 36. At this last point, however, it steadily kept all the rest of the way to the summit. Each quarter-mile was done regularly in exactly 25 seconds and when we passed the summit the rate was precisely the same.' Whatever the technicalities may have been it was a superb effort, and quite characteristic of the resolute way in which the Caledonian drivers were about their work. After passing the summit the rest was comparatively easy and with the 49·7 miles down to Carlisle covered in 46 minutes 7 seconds pass to stop the arrival was 2¼ minutes early in 117 minutes 50 seconds from Edinburgh. The 82·2 miles from Cobbinshaw were covered in 87 minutes 21 seconds start to stop.

TABLE X
10 a.m. GLASGOW–PERTH

Load: 9 cars, 266 tons tare, 285 tons full
Engine: 5 ft 9 in. 4-6-0 No. 913

Dist. Miles		Actual m. s.	Speeds m.p.h.
0·0	BUCHANAN STREET . .	0 00	—
1·0	St Rollox . . .	3 25	—
3·4	Robroyston. . . .	8 47	30
6·0	Garnkirk	12 20	—
9·0	Glenboig	15 55	60
13·1	Cumbernauld . . .	20 43	48
18·5	Greenhill	26 17	61 (max.)
22·1	LARBERT	30 13	57
26·1	Plean	34 29	46
27·8	Bannockburn . . .	36 29	—
		p.w.s.	20
30·2	STIRLING	39 20	—
33·1	Bridge of Allan . . .	42 41	52 (max.)
35·1	Dunblane	45 52	30½
37·8	Kinbuck	51 12	28 (min.)
41·0	Greenloaning . . .	55 41	easy
45·2	Blackford	60 49	—
47·4	GLENEAGLES . . .	63 48	52
49·5	Auchterarder . . .	65 45	65
		p.w.s.	15
53·6	Dunning	70 24	—
56·4	Forteviot	74 02	52
59·3	Forgandenny . . .	77 06	57
61·2	*Hilton Junction* . . .	79 09	
		sigs.	
63·2	PERTH	83 25*	

Schedule 82 min: Net time 78½ min.
* Stop at extreme north end, with Inverness portion off the platform

Another interesting run from R. E. Charlewood's records was made on the 10 a.m. down 'Grampian' from Glasgow Buchanan Street to Perth, in the autumn of 1913 and set out in Table X. The train was then a combined one for Inverness and Aberdeen, and only the last four vehicles were of the famous twelve-wheeled Grampian stock.

The first four coaches were for Inverness, two via Carr Bridge and two via Forres. The engine was one of the 5 ft 9 in. '908' Class 4-6-0s, non-superheated. The start up through the tunnels from Buchanan Street is on a gradient of 1 in 79 for 1½ miles, easing then to 1 in 98 for one mile, and finally to 1 in 125 till the level is reached near Robroyston. With no rear-end banking assistance the engine made a very good start, but as usual no appreciable speed was made along the level to Glenboig, and the steep though broken descent to Larbert was taken with speed barely exceeding 60 m.p.h. Good work was done up the 2 miles at 1 in 126 up to Plean, and following this came a bad permanent way check approaching Stirling. The recovery on the level to the foot of the Dunblane Bank was brisk, from 20 to 52 m.p.h. in 2 miles, and on the bank itself, 5½ miles at 1 in 100–88–134, the minimum speed was 28 m.p.h. Time was now well in hand, and although there was a second, and more severe permanent way check to come the driver continued very easily to Gleneagles. Speed had not exceeded 65 m.p.h. down the Auchterarder Bank when the slowing came for the Dunning check. Not exceeding 57 m.p.h. afterwards the train passed Hilton Junction in time for a punctual arrival in 82 minutes from Glasgow; but signals compelled a slack to walking pace at the entrance to Perth station, and the driver was then waved to a dead stop three coach lengths *beyond* the north end of the platform, presumably to facilitate remarshalling of the train.

In post-war years I had many good runs behind Caledonian engines, though naturally none to equal the finest efforts of the 'Dunalastairs' and of the big McIntosh 4-6-0s. These engines were unfortunately long past their prime by the time of my stopwatching days. One of my best runs (Table XI) was on the 5 p.m. from Glasgow Buchanan Street when it was still unofficially known as the Granite City Express', before the transference of that title to the 10 a.m. train. After a characteristically sluggish run to Perth with one of the '60' Class 4-6-0s, a Pickersgill 4-4-0, No. 84, came on and gave a thoroughly lively performance. Up the stiff initial section to Stanley, including more than 3 miles at 1 in 125, the engine was vigorously driven, and the minimum speed was 38 m.p.h. Good speed followed on the level and slightly rising length to Forfar, after which the heavier grades from Bridge of Dun northwards were excellently tackled. The Marykirk Bank is 3 miles long, inclined at 1 in 98–138, while the 4½-mile bank from Fordoun to Drumlithie is continuously at 1 in 170–191–141. With a load of 335 tons the minimum speeds of 35½ and 37 m.p.h. on these two inclines were very good.

TABLE XI

PERTH–STONEHAVEN

Load: 315 tons tare, 335 tons full
Engine: Pickersgill 4-4-0 No. 84

Dist. Miles		Actual m. s.	Speeds m.p.h.
0·0	PERTH	0 00	—
1·6	*Almond Valley Junction* . .	4 05	44½
4·2	Luncarty	7 45	40/45
7·2	Stanley Junction . .	12 15	38
11·3	Cargill	17 05	61½/55
15·8	COUPAR ANGUS . .	21 45	65
20·5	*Alyth Junction* .	26 15	62/63
26·8	Glamis . . .	32 25	58
31·8	*Forfar South Junction* . .	36 25	61
32·5	FORFAR	38 40	—
2·4	Clocksbridge . . .	4 55	55 (max.)
7·0	GUTHRIE . . .	10 30	
5·3	*Farnell Road* . . .	7 30	69 (max.)
8·4	BRIDGE OF DUN . .	10 50	
2·7	Dubton Junction . .	5 30	39
3·9	*Kinnaber Junction* . . .	7 35	33½
6·0	Craigo	10 35	56
8·1	Marykirk . . .	13 05	45
10·2	*Milepost 209¼* .	16 05	35½
11·3	LAURENCEKIRK . .	18 10	
3·3	Fordoun	5 25	53
7·3	Drumlithie	10 45	37
11·9	*Dunnottar Box* . .	16 20	68
14·5	STONEHAVEN . .	19 10	

My records with the '60' Class, mostly with the batch built by the L.M.S.R. in 1925–6, do not make very inspiring reading, and there seem to be inconsistencies in the way in which they were assisted. Rear-end banking assistance was freely taken out of Buchanan Street, but more surprisingly from Stirling up the Dunblane Bank. On the other hand I have known equal and greater loads taken southbound from Perth up to Gleneagles without help, and quite satisfactorily. Some of the best work ever done by a '60' took place during the dynamometer car trials on the L.N.W.R. main line in 1926, and I am therefore leaving final comments on these engines until the succeeding chapter of this book. After the war, the great days of Caledonian express running never returned, and it was with alien engines – Midland compounds, 'Royal Scots', and Stanier Pacifics – that the one-time glories of the Caledonian, as a line of really fast running, were eventually revived.

XIV

The Caledonian, the L.M.S. and the Future

FROM the time of the Grouping, except in the realm of mechanical and electrical engineering, ex-Caledonian officers virtually took charge of the Northern Division of the L.M.S.R. The appointments of Matheson, and McLellan were mentioned in the last chapter; in addition to these J. Ballantyne became General Superintendent, under the new traffic organization set up by the L.M.S.R. This was based wholly upon the Midland model developed in pre-war days under Sir Cecil Paget, and brought to full maturity by the time of Grouping by J. H. Follows. The Midland principle was at once applied to the whole L.M.S. system, and in the new organization it is remarkable that Caledonian officers were selected not merely for one, but for two divisions. While Ballantyne took the Northern Division, R. Killin was appointed to the Midland Division. The operating methods of Derby were gradually brought to bear upon Scotland, and gradually the old Caledonian train services, particularly in respect of the Anglo-Scottish expresses, began to take a new form.

On the Clyde the Caledonian Steam Packet Company remained, but became a subsidiary of the L.M.S.R. There must have been some hard feelings when the magnificent fleet of the age-old enemy, the Glasgow & South Western, was gathered into the Caledonian fold. The once distinctive house colours of the rivals were combined in a hybrid style that looked something quite new on the Clyde. Previously the Caledonian steamers had yellow funnels without any black band at the top; those of the G. & S.W.R. had red funnels with black tops. The new style combined the two, with a broad black band at the top, then a narrow red one, and with the lower part of the funnel buff. Among Glaswegians, of course, the names of the one-time rivals' steamers were household words, but to those who did not know them the previous ownership could be seen from the colour of the hulls. Those of the Caledonian were black, while those of the G. & S.W.R. were grey.

With locomotives the subsequent history of the Caledonian stock provided an interesting study. At the time of the Grouping the Caledonian possessed 1,077 locomotives; 10 years later, despite the intense drive towards standardization, only 137 of them had been scrapped. In this respect the Caledonian figures make impressive and almost startling reading compared with those of the other major constituent companies of the L.M.S.R., thus:

Railway	Number of locos at Grouping	Number scrapped 1923–32	Percentage reduction of stock in 10 years
L.N.W.R.	3,360	1,339	39·8
Midland	2,925	1,173	40·5
L.Y.R.	1,654	430	26·0
North Staffs	192	104	54·5
Furness	136	105	80·1
G.& S.W.R.	528	419	79·4
Highland	173	63	36·4
Caledonian	1,077	137	12·7

It is interesting to inquire into the reasons for Caledonian immunity from the general slaughter. It is to be found mainly in their robustness of design. Cracked frames were practically unheard of, and the absence of racking stresses made the locomotives relatively light on repair costs. In his paper 'A Modern Locomotive History', read before the Institution of Locomotive Engineers in 1946, E. S. Cox quoted the repair costs for certain L.M.S.R. locomotives of pre-Grouping types, and in this the Caledonian engines showed up very well. The design showing the lowest repair cost was the Midland Class '2' Superheater 4-4-0. This result may have been due to the lightness of the work on which they were usually employed, and the

Power Class	Railway	Type	Class	Coal lb. per mile	Comparative repair cost index
4	L.N.W.R.	4-6-0	Prince of Wales	51·1	157
4	Caledonian	4-6-0	'60'	66·3	117
4	G.& S.W.R.	4-6-0	Manson	59·0	190
4	Midland	4-4-0	3-cyl. compound	46·5	136
3	L.N.W.R.	4-4-0	'George the Fifth'	56·4	149
3	Caledonian	4-4-0	Pickersgill	59·1	110
3	G.& S.W.R.	4-4-0	P. Drummond	63·4	147
2	Midland	4-4-0	'483'	45·9	100

average coal consumption of the whole class in each case might be some indication of the severity of their duties. Nevertheless the results are of much interest, for whatever may have been the duties of some designs, no Caledonian engine of that time had an easy time of it. From the above it will be seen that the Pickersgill 4-4-os and 4-6-os were the lightest on repair of all engines tabulated, after the Midland '2P' 4-4-0. At the same time the figures for the Manson 4-6-os of the G. & S.W.R. are revealing.

A new Caledonian 4-6-0 design made its first appearance just at the time of the Grouping, the feeble little non-superheater Oban 4-6-os. They were quite pretty little engines to look at, and they were unquestionably the most comfortable small engine I have ever ridden on; but so far as my own experience goes the less said about their performance the better! Another new Caledonian design that was ready to go into production in 1923 would have been a very different proposition so far as hard pulling was concerned. This was the Pickersgill 2-6-0, which would have been a very handsome, large boilered, two-cylinder machine. Hughes, as Chief Mechanical Engineer of the L.M.S.R., was very interested in this design, and it was examined carefully with a view to adoption as one of the new standard types. Unfortunately the large 21 by 28 in. cylinders, mounted with their centre lines horizontal, fouled the loading gauge of every English constituent of the L.M.S.R. Hughes accordingly had it redesigned in the Horwich drawing office, and the result was that familiar, ugly, honest-to-goodness hardworker, the Horwich 'Crab'. The close correspondence in basic dimensions between the Caledonian proposal and the engine actually built will be apparent from the accompanying table.

L.M.S.R. 2-6-0 designs

	Caledonian	Horwich
Cylinders, dia. × stroke, in. .	21 × 28	21 × 26
Coupled wheel dia. .	5' 6"	5' 6"
Heating surfaces sq in.		
Tubes . . .	1,564	1,345
Firebox . . .	168	160
Superheater . .	178	307
Total . . .	1,732	1,817
Grate area, sq ft . .	27	27·5
Boiler pressure, p.s.i. . .	180	175
Nom. T.E. at 85 per cent b.p. lb	28,624	26,580

With characteristic robustness of design the Caledonian engine would have been considerably the heavier. The estimated weight

Above: 4-4-0 No. 81 built by Armstrong Whitworth.

PICKERSGILL
EXPRESS TYPES

Below: Two-cylinder 4-6-0 No. 65.

Three-cylinder 4-6-0 No. 959.
[*all R. D. Stephen*

Above: Euston – Perth Express leaving Carlisle. 4-4-0 engines,
No. 928 (Pickersgill) and 890, ('Dunalastair III' Class).

[*B.T.C. Historical Relics*

Below: The first Pickersgill three-cylinder 4-6-0 No. 956 on
test at Perth in 1921, fitted with indicator shelters. The
engine on the right is the Highland 4-6-0 *Brodie Castle*.

[*R. D. Stephen*

was 72 tons, with 60 tons adhesion, as compared with the actual weight of 66 tons in the 'Crab'. John Barr's stout advocacy of Caledonian designs, and the strong case he made for their retention and multiplication in the future, led to the inclusion of Pickersgill 4-4-0s and 4-6-0s in the interesting comparative trials with the dynamometer car that were conducted between Leeds and Carlisle in 1923–4, and between Preston and Carlisle in 1925–6. By the courtesy of Mr E. Robson, the present Chief Mechanical & Electrical Engineer of the London Midland Region, British Railways, I have had the opportunity of studying the reports of these trials, and it is clear that the 4-4-0s had a very tough task with the Midland Scotch expresses over Ais Gill Summit, specially augmented in load for the trials. On the other hand the Pickersgill '60' Class 4-6-0 did well against the L.N.W.R. and L.Y.R. 4-6-0s over Shap. The Caledonian engine tested was the first of the new batch of twenty built in 1925–6, and had run little more than 7,000 miles at the time of the trials.

Taking the trials of November, 1924 first, the test trains were the 12.10 p.m. nonstop from Carlisle to Leeds, returning with the 4.3 p.m., which included a stop at Hellifield. During some of the preliminary running I believe engine No. 96 was used, but the official report concerned only one engine, No. 124, and a single round trip made on 26th November. The run of 113 miles made non-stop on the southbound journey was longer than anything being regularly performed on the Caledonian at the time; and the climb to Ais Gill was a formidable test of engine capacity and the stamina of the fireman. But where Caledonian locomotive performance is concerned one is always inclined to look back to the summer of 1896 and the work of the 'Dunalastairs' on the 1.54 a.m. 'Tourist Express' from Carlisle. The run to Leeds by the Midland route has some features of similarity, so far as physical characteristics of the road are concerned:

Railway	Caledonian	Midland
Section	Carlisle–Stirling	Carlisle–Leeds
Distance (miles)	117·8	113
Summit point	Beattock	Ais Gill
Summit level above datum ft . .	1,015	1,151
Distance of summit from Carlisle (miles)	49·7	48·3
Average gradient	1 in 270	1 in 232
Speed m.p.h. to summit . . .	56·3*	42·5†
Booked time for whole run (min.) .	125	143
Average speed m.p.h. . . .	56·5	47·4

* Time made on usual fast runs
† Scheduled speed

The 'Dunalastairs' took loads of 170–200 tons on the 1.54 a.m.; on the Midland test trains the Pickersgill 4-4-0 was required to haul 300 tons tare, about 320 tons full. The average drawbar horsepower, uncorrected for gradient, required by the above two trains, to Beattock Summit in the first case and to Ais Gill in the other, are 520 and 630 respectively or 680 and 770 corrected for gradient. Seeing that the Pickersgill engine has a nominal tractive effort of 31 per cent greater than the 'Dunalastairs', with the advantage of superheating, and 20 years advancement in design one might have thought that the Midland test trains would have been taken in their stride. It is true that I am drawing comparison with some of the very finest work of the 'Dunalastairs'; equally, the tests of 1924 were taken as a challenge to the Caledonian, and engineers who rode in the dynamometer car have told me of the deadly earnest with which everybody concerned regarded the test. The honour of the Caledonian was at stake, and the driver and fireman apparently gave of their utmost.

It can only be said that the result was very disappointing. No. 124 had the very life flogged out of her, and yet she took 69 minutes 52 seconds to pass Ais Gill, and with the hindrance later of a signal stop reached Leeds in 148 minutes. Like her competitors she lost time on the fast initial timing of 21 minutes to Lazonby, but whereas an L.N.W.R. 'Claughton' on one occasion, and one of the Midland compounds cut the subsequent allowance of 46 minutes to Ais Gill by 6 and 5 minutes respectively the Caledonian 4-4-0 only just held her own. On the return trip she went down heavily between Settle Junction and Blea Moor. If her actual work on the road fell considerably below expectations the technical results did so to an even greater extent. Details are given in the accompanying table. It was reported that the engine steamed well, but it was evident, and most surprisingly, that the engine was not up to the job. On the non-stop run southbound from Carlisle the driver may have been a little apprehensive of his water supply lasting out. The Pickersgill engines had six-wheeled tenders, with a total capacity of 4,200 gallons. With a consumption of 33·9 to the mile they were getting a little 'near to the bone', using over 3,800 gallons on a single trip. From whatever reason, however, the engine was completely outclassed by the Midlands compounds, and the popularity of the latter engines when batches of them were sent new to Kingmoor and Polmadie was a measure of their superiority over the indigenous Scottish product – alas!

Caledonian Railway: Engine No. 124
Load: 301 tons tare, 320 tons full

	Direction	
	Up	Down
Average speed m.p.h.	46·6	46·3
Min. speed on bank m.p.h.	27·5	27·8
Average d.h.p.	487	462
Maximum d.h.p.	675	680
Coal per mile (lb) on round trip	54·7	
Coal per d.h.p. hr. lb	6·53	
Coal per sq ft of grate area per hr. lb	120	
Water gall. per mile	33·9	
Water lb. per lb. of coal	6·21	

In the spring of 1925 a further series of trials was conducted, between Preston and Carlisle, this time between Midland, Lancashire & Yorkshire and London & North Western locomotives. In the autumn of that same year St Rollox works was busy with the construction of another twenty Pickersgill 4-6-os of the '60' Class, and again at Barr's instigation, the first of these new engines was put through a series of trials corresponding exactly with what the English engines had been required to do a year earlier. And so No. 14630, resplendent in Midland red, with her five-figure number blazoned in huge figures on the tender sides, ran dynamometer car trials first with a 300-ton and then with 350-ton trains. She did splendidly uphill, as comparison with the other four engines will show:

L.M.S.R. Dynamometer Car Tests
CARLISLE–SHAP SUMMIT

Railway	Midland	L.N.W.R.	L.N.W.R.	L.Y.R.	C.R.	C.R.
Engine No.	1065	90	30	10460	14630	14630
Engine Class	4-4-0	4-6-0*	4-6-0†	4-6-0‡	4-6-0	4-6-0
Load tons tare	347·9	345·9	347·9	342·6	350·6	350·6

Dist. Miles		m. s.	m. s.	m. s.	m. s.	m. s.	m. s.
0·0	Carlisle . .	0 00	0 00	0 00	0 00	0 00	0 00
17·9	Penrith . .	27 55	27 31	27 10	27 39	27 32	28 00
		—	—	p.w.s.	p.w.s.	—	—
31·4	Shap Summit .	45 55	47 33	48 40	48 28	47 19	48 00
	Reduced speed at at Penrith p.w.s. .	—	—	17	28	—	—

* 'Prince of Wales' Class   ‡ Hughes rebuilt superheated type
† 'Claughton' Class   . Schedule time to pass summit 50 min.

On the return runs there were quite a number of checks from both adverse signals and permanent way causes. On the best run No. 14630 just kept the 28 minutes point-to-point booking between Oxenholme and Shap Summit with the 350-ton train, whereas in the earlier trials, all the competing engines had bettered that time – indeed both the Horwich 4-6-0 and the 'Claughton' substantially bettered it with 400-ton trains. The overall results with the Caledonian engine No. 14630 were far better than from the 4-4-0 on the Midland line. Coal consumption was fairly constant between 48·69 and 52·63 lb per mile, while related to the power output the consumption worked out at between 4·73 and 5·18 lb per d.h.p. hour. The engine steamed well, but the traditional sluggishness was apparent in the downhill and level running. On every northbound journey Shap Summit was passed behind time, due to the various checks, but nothing was regained on the easy allowance of 32 minutes for the 31·4 miles down to Carlisle, with maximum speeds up to 73 m.p.h. Taken all round the engine put up a good show, and gained qualified praise in the official report.

The logs of the four down journeys are shown in the accompanying table. It was unfortunate that so many checks were experienced, though from runs 1 and 3 it is clear that time could have been kept uphill had the road been clear. The boiler pressure was well-maintained on all trips, with a fairly constant water level. The working recorded by the observer on the footplate indicates that the engine was being well extended on Shap. On the first and second runs the regulator was full open and cut-off 48 per cent for the last 2 miles, while on the third and fourth runs the cut-off was 60 per cent, with full regulator. On the faster stretches the engine was worked in 30 to 35 per cent with regulator from one-third to two-thirds open. Although point-to-point times were kept there was literally no margin with the 350-ton trains, and no time was recovered in running down the bank from Shap Summit to Carlisle.

This was the last occasion that any Caledonian locomotives figured in official tests. The report showed clearly that a Midland compound could do superior work with train loads up to 350 tons, on a considerably lighter coal consumption, and from that time the drafting of standard types of Derby origin to Scotland proceeded on an increasing scale. The ex-Caledonian engines continued to do good work on secondary duties, though on the Aberdeen line pre-Grouping types were handling all the principal expresses, except the through workings to Carlisle, as late as 1932. It was in 1930 that I enjoyed my last ride behind a McIntosh 4-6-0, a short one it is true, only from Aberdeen to Stonehaven behind No. 49 – then No. 14750 and painted black. We had not a heavy load, only 225 tons, but she climbed the heavy bank up past Cove Bay in almost complete silence, and then ran like a stag for Stonehaven.

L.M.S.R. PRESTON–CARLISLE
Tests of 4-6-0 locomotive No. 14630

Run No. Date Load tons tare		1 1/6/26 301·6	2 2/6/26 301·6	3 3/6/26 350·6	4 4/6/26 350·6
Distance Miles	Sch. min.	Actual m. s.	Actual m. s.	Actual m. s.	Actual m. s.
0·0 PRESTON	0	0 00	0 00	0 00	0 00
1·3 Oxheys Box	3	3 58	3 41	3 57	3 53
		p.w.s.	p.w.s.	p.w.s.	p.w.s.
21·0 LANCASTER	23	24 50	23 37	25 06	24 40
—		—	p.w.s.	p.w.s.	—
27·2 CARNFORTH	29	32 54	31 32	33 08	33 04
—		p.w.s.	p.w.s.		
41·1 Oxenholme	44	49 22	49 00	48 53	48 03
47·2 Grayrigg	55	59 55	61 35	60 23	59 26
—					sigs.
53·2 Tebay	61	66 30	68 10	67 08	68 58
—			sigs.	—	
58·7 Shap Summit	72	76 25	80 31	76 50	79 48
90·1 CARLISLE	104	107 51	113 50	108 58	111 33
Oxenholme–Summit	28	27 03	31 31	27 57	31 45
Speed reductions:		m.p.h.	m.p.h.	m.p.h.	m.p.h.
p.w.s. Lancaster		21	23	22	19
p.w.s. Carnforth		—	26	30	37
p.w.s. Burton		23	—	—	—
sigs. Oxenholme		—	11	—	—
sigs. Low Gill		—	—	—	16
sigs. Scout Green (Shap Incline)		—	4	—	—
Max. drawbar h.p. uncorrected		812	787	837	802
Min. speed on Shap m.p.h.		24	24	25	23
Max. speed on trip m.p.h.		72	71	73	73

By that time Caledonian engines were beginning to penetrate far beyond their own native system. I found 'Dunalastair IV' Class 4-4-0s working on the Portpatrick and Wigtownshire line; on the first stage of a journey from St Enoch to St Pancras a Pickersgill 4-4-0 acted as pilot to Kilmarnock, and by the Second World War Caledonian 4-4-0s were doing various jobs on the Highland line. One Sunday afternoon in the summer of 1932 I paid a visit to Friarton shed, Perth, and found any number of interesting Caledonian engines in residence, as it were; they ranged from the big McIntosh superheater 4-6-0 goods of the '179' Class, to the one and only 4-2-2 single, then still in traffic, grubby in unlined black and numbered 14010. She was not swooped upon as a photographic collector's piece that afternoon, for by that time the word had gone forth that she was not to be scrapped, and one felt almost impatient for her to be restored in the blue livery.

Despite Grouping, despite the strong influences of standardization old Caledonian practices survived, and none more picturesquely than the semaphore headcodes of old. The full collection of codes is shown on page 184/5, and the indicators came to be carried by Midland Compounds, 'Royal Scots', 'Baby Scots' and other strangers from south of the border which came to work in Scotland. Some of my readers may seize pens in wrath at my suggestion that the 'Royal Scots' were strangers. True, they were built in Scotland, and many of them bore honoured Scots names; but their origin was entirely English. It was, however, when Sir William Stanier's 'Pacifics' first began to work through from Glasgow to Euston that the semaphore headcode travelled its farthest afield. The second engine of the class, the record-breaking No. 6201 *Princess Elizabeth*, was stationed at Polmadie and when working the up 'Royal Scot' the shed staff sent her out adorned with the old 'Glasgow–Carlisle' indicator – the bow-tie, as I have heard it called – borne for so many years by *Cardean*, and generations of St Rollox engines. On the 'Royal Scot' the Polmadie men worked only as far as Carlisle, and one might have thought they would have removed the indicator when they were relieved. Not a bit of it! Many a time in the summer of 1934 I saw No. 6201 arrive in Euston with the Caledonian headcode on her uppermost lamp iron.

On the L.M.S.R., officially at any rate, there was a determined effort in the 'thirties' to build a new tradition. Memories of the Caledonian, the Highland, the North Western – even of the Midland – were pushed aside, and the staff were exhorted 'to think L.M.S.' It was a wise counsel, and with the introduction of Stanier locomotives in their hundreds it did much to integrate the diverse, and sometimes warring elements of that great, far-flung railway system. But in many odd corners one found much evidence that the old allegiances survived. A running superintendent transferred far from his old territory would have photographs of his former charges on his office walls; in the running inspector's room on Carlisle station only a year ago, I found a beautifully preserved copy of a *Locomotive Magazine* coloured plate of the 'Dunalastair II', No. 769, and it was therefore with special interest that I paid a visit to Polmadie, a few years ago. But there all traces of the Caledonian had gone and photographs of none but modern L.M.S. engines decorated the office walls.

Memories of the old 'Caley' remained in a more subtle way. The modern version of the whistle, penetrating hooter though it is, is no more than an imitation of the real thing. The wheezing, asthmatic cough of many a Stanier engine cannot be compared with the deep, full-throated siren blast of the true product of St Rollox, and *Cardean*, for so long queen of them all, had a siren fit for a Cunarder. The Caledonian was a line men were proud to work for, and it was a pride that lasted through the Grouping era to nationalization. In 1948, with the Scottish constituents of both the L.M.S.R. and the L.N.E.R. merged into a single entity of Scottish Region, I shall always remember some contacts I had with Scots railwaymen, and the replies one and all gave when I casually asked which company they had previously served. It was the reply of the first that prompted me to ask several more: 'Glasgow & South Western' – not L.M.S. mark you, but the far older allegiance. A day or so later I asked another, and this time came the reply: 'O ay, the Caley.' So it was, with appropriate variations each time.

More recently the Scottish Region has been pleased to perpetuate the old name on the third day Anglo-Scottish service by the West Coast Route, in times that have indeed changed. Recalling the old days of cat-and-dog relations between the two old rivals I must say I was amused to see a poster on Dumfries station exhorting the public to travel to London by 'The Caledonian' and advertising the diesel service to Carlisle that connects with the new 'flyer'. Admirable advice today. But when rivalry was running at fever heat, and the fires of loyalty and enthusiasm for their company burned white hot in the breasts of many on both sides, a rhymster on the 'Sou' West' side extolled No. 259, in verses that ended:

'and we beat the Caledonian with the 259.'

'Beat the Caley'; that was then the aim of every good 'Sou' West' man. Could one then have imagined a time when Dumfries would advise its passengers to travel by anything with the name of Caledonian!

Since Grouping the Caledonian Steam Packet Company has greatly expanded its activities. The steamers plying on Loch Awe and Loch Tay were acquired in 1922, and the company now owns all the railway steamers in Scotland including the Kyle of Lochalsh ferries and the Loch Lomond steamers. The Williamson–Buchanan steamer business was acquired in 1935, and a still more striking

TRAINS ORIGINATING OR TERMINATING IN GLASGOW

1

MAIN LINE VIA MOTHERWELL

2

*MAIN LINE VIA HOLYTOWN

3

TO BOTHWELL

4

TOLLCROSS AND BURNSIDE

5

TO AND FROM HAMILTON, STRATHAVEN AND LESMAHAGOW AND TO DAWSHOLM

6

TO AND FROM EDINBURGH DIRECT

7

HIGH LEVEL TO AND FROM, AND LOW LEVEL TO NEWTON

8

TO TOLLCROSS

9

TO AND FROM EAST KILBRIDE AND HAMILTON, LOW LEVEL, TERMINATING AT RUTHERGLEN

10

TO AND FROM GOUROCK, ALSO TO DUMBARTON OR BALLOCH

11

TRAINS OF EMPTY CARRIAGES

12

TO AND FROM RENFREW

13

TO AND FROM PAISLEY, KILBOWEY OR CLYDEBANK

14

TO AND FROM ARDROSSAN OR KILMARNOCK VIA CATHCART

15

TO AND FROM ARDROSSAN, OR KILMARNOCK VIA BARRHEAD

16

FOR TRIAL RUNNING OF CARRIAGES

17

TO AND FROM COATBRIDGE

18

TO AND FROM AIRDRIE

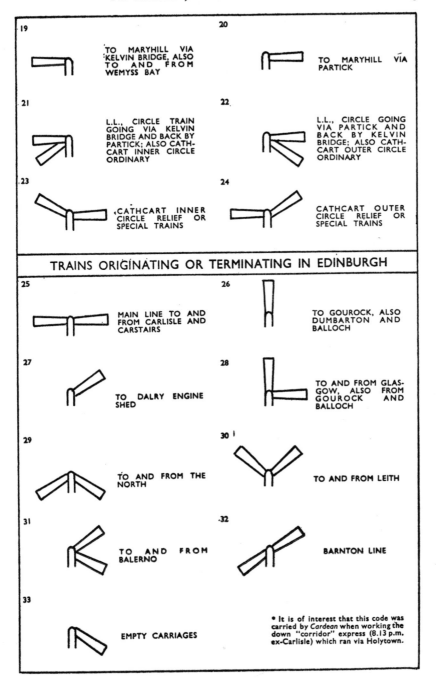

19   20

TO MARYHILL VIA KELVIN BRIDGE, ALSO TO AND FROM WEMYSS BAY

TO MARYHILL VIA PARTICK

21   22

L.L., CIRCLE TRAIN GOING VIA KELVIN BRIDGE AND BACK BY PARTICK; ALSO CATH-CART INNER CIRCLE ORDINARY

L.L., CIRCLE GOING VIA PARTICK AND BACK BY KELVIN BRIDGE; ALSO CATH-CART OUTER CIRCLE ORDINARY

23   24

CATHCART INNER CIRCLE RELIEF OR SPECIAL TRAINS

CATHCART OUTER CIRCLE RELIEF OR SPECIAL TRAINS

TRAINS ORIGINATING OR TERMINATING IN EDINBURGH

25   26

MAIN LINE TO AND FROM CARLISLE AND CARSTAIRS

TO GOUROCK, ALSO DUMBARTON AND BALLOCH

27   28

TO DALRY ENGINE SHED

TO AND FROM GLAS-GOW, ALSO FROM GOUROCK AND BALLOCH

29   30

TO AND FROM THE NORTH

TO AND FROM LEITH

31   32

TO AND FROM BALERNO

BARNTON LINE

33

EMPTY CARRIAGES

* It is of interest that this code was carried by *Cardean* when working the down "corridor" express (8.13 p.m. ex-Carlisle) which ran via Holytown.

development followed the acquisition by the British Transport Commission of the Clyde Campbeltown Shipping Co Ltd in October, 1949. As a subsidiary of the B.T.C. this concern naturally became a close associate of the Caledonian Steam Packet Company, though even then one could hardly have expected the change that took place in 1961. At this recent date the Clyde & Campbeltown had its name changed to the Caledonian Steam Packet Company (Irish Services) Ltd, and now operates the Stranraer–Larne packet service. On the narrow seas around Scotland, indeed, the name Caledonian is more familiar than ever.

'Caley blue has been adopted as the distinctive colour of the Scottish Region, used on timetable covers, station nameboards and more recently as the coach livery of the new Clydeside electric trains. As an engine colour, used for a time on British Railways Class '8' express passenger classes it was not a great success. The effectiveness of the original St Rollox colour scheme lay not only in the wonderfully fresh and pure shade of the blue itself, but in its harmonizing so well with the purple lake of the running plate valances and of the tender underframes. The British Railways livery put these parts in black, and the blue alone did not ring true to anyone who knew the Caledonian. I always felt it looked its worst on the ex-Great Western 'Kings'; which retained all their native Wiltshire brass and copperwork, and looked its best on the ex-L.N.E.R. 'A4s' largely because it was the nearest B.R. style to the original Garter blue of these latter engines.

But engine colours and siren whistles are passing, ephemeral things – fragments that the cynics might say are fit for nothing, save to delight some doting sentimentalist. Climb rather, into the cab of one of the new diesels, as I did one September evening and ride through from Carlisle to Glasgow at the head end of the 'Midday Scot'. Call it L.M.S., Scottish Region, or what you like, the 'Caley' is still there. As one gets away, past Etterby, past Kingmoor, past the great new marshalling yards now taking shape, the whole intensely colourful pageant of railway evolution hereabouts comes vividly to mind: Baldie Crooks, Armstrong, Tom Robinson, tearing away from Carlisle on those early morning dashes to Stirling; *Cardean*'s nightly work with the 'Corridor', the brilliant running of Sir William Stanier's Pacifics. But neither time, nor political events, nor modernization plans have flattened out the Beattock Bank, and there was a familiar ring of the old days when the diesel driver announced that he would 'whistle' for the banker. A load of 418 tons was too much, on the 'Midday Scot' timing.

The weather was stormy. Clouds were touching down on the high hills to the north-east, and nightfall was going to be early that day. Driving in to our 'loco stop' at Beattock one could no more than glimpse something of the little upland town of Moffat, some 3 miles away under the lee of those hills. There the great engineer that built the Caledonian made his last home. There, living in semi-retirement, Joseph Locke seemed as tireless as ever, walking game-keepers off their feet, just as he had exhausted railway contractors in earlier days. But he died relatively early in life, worn out by the prodigious scale of his work in the very beginnings of railways. Joseph Locke, a romantic if ever there was one, country-lover, eloquent Parliamentary speaker, as well as being one of the greatest of the early railway engineers, has words that could well sum up this appraisal and appreciation of the Caledonian Railway, and of those who served it. In 1859 the death of Robert Stephenson followed less than a month after that of Brunel, and to Locke, as President of the Institution of Civil Engineers, and as a long-standing personal friend of both, fell the task of delivering a funeral oration. Never before had Locke spoken more eloquently or with more emotion. He concluded thus:

'We, at least, who are benefited by their successes, who feel that our Institution has reason to be proud of its association with such names as Brunel and Stephenson, have a duty to perform; and that duty is, to honour their memory and emulate their example.'

Those who listened were not to know that Locke himself would be dead within a year, but recalling his final words, in the majestic setting of Annandale, the Beattock Bank, and the wild, storm-swept reaches of Upper Clydesdale, one is indeed moved to honour the memory, and to try and emulate the example of those who built and ran the Caledonian Railway.

Index